TWENTIETH-CENTURY CRIME FICTION

For my father
Arthur Morgan Plain
November 25th 1913 – November 25th 2000

TWENTIETH-CENTURY CRIME FICTION

Gender, Sexuality and the Body

Gill Plain

FITZROY DEARBORN PUBLISHERS
CHICAGO • LONDON

Published in the United Kingdom by
Edinburgh University Press Ltd
22 George Square, Edinburgh

Published in the United States of America by
Fitzroy Dearborn Publishers
919 North Michigan Avenue
Chicago, Illinois 60611

Typeset in 11 on 13pt Monotype Bembo
by Hewer Text Ltd, Edinburgh, and
printed and bound in Great Britain by
MPG Books Ltd, Bodmin

A Cataloging-in-Publication record for this book
is available from the Library of Congress

ISBN 1-57958-340-7 Fitzroy Dearborn

Cover photograph: Hulton Deutsch Collection
Cover design: River Design, Edinburgh

Contents

Part III – Shifting Paradigms

Acknowledgements

Popular fiction is a popular subject, and over the past five years I have benefited enormously from the thoughts, suggestions and enthusiasm of a vast number of people. Among these, special mention should undoubtedly be made of those who attended the Association for Research in Popular Fictions conferences in 1997 and 1998. At these events I found a body of generous and informed critics who gave me invaluable advice and criticism in the early stages of this project. The work has also been aired in seminars and talks at the Universities of Reading, Stirling, Dundee, Glamorgan and St Andrews, and parts of Chapters 1 and 6 have appeared, respectively, in *Medical Fictions*, edited by Julia Hallam and Nickianne Moody, and in *Women, a Cultural Review* (vol. 9, no. 3, autumn 1998).

The early ideas for this project were formulated at the University of Glamorgan and the later ones took shape at the University of St Andrews. Many thanks are consequently due to the students on my crime fiction courses at both institutions, who brought fresh perspectives and very different attitudes to bear on the connections between gender and genre. Although it is difficult to isolate the exact source of some of the excellent insights that emerged from these classes, particular mention must be made of Kim Lakin, to whom I owe much of my knowledge of sadomasochism, and Joe Crighton, who put me straight on pulp fiction! Friends and colleagues have also been a valuable source of inspiration. Andy Smith started me thinking about Christie's destructive mothers and generously shared his thoughts on Thomas Harris, while James McKinna introduced me to Kuhn and his scientific revolutions. Others who pointed me in useful directions include Ian Blyth, Alison Chapman, Kate Chedgzoy, Nick Lawson, Nickianne Moody, Susan Rowland, Pauline Young and Harry Ziegler.

Once again I have benefited enormously from the gentle editorial hand of Jackie Jones, who has kept me focused with her incisive criticism and sceptical eye: a truly noble effort on the part of a woman who is no lover of the gory and gruesome. Helen Boden stepped in at the last moment providing fresh insight and clarity just when I thought this book would never be finished. Two others have acted as long-term readers on this project, and I really cannot thank them enough. Susan Sellers has been a wonderful source of inspiration and support since I moved to St Andrews, and her comments throughout have been invaluable. Berthold Schoene has kept me going since the University of Glamorgan with his enthusiasm for and belief in this book. I am deeply grateful for his pleasure in the text, his detailed criticisms and his countless invaluable suggestions.

Finally, there are those whose provision of moral support has been every bit as crucial. My mother, Prim Plain, communicated to me her love of a 'damn good story', and so is largely to blame for this book. She would, I know, prefer me to write a detective story than to write about them, but I hope, in the interim, this will provide narrative enough. My friends have put up with a lot over the past five years, but they have also enabled me to finish what at times seemed an impossible project. Kaite O'Reilly always has the capacity to make me believe in what I'm doing, while Ben Winsworth, from a distance, has kept the 'Dunkirk spirit' alive. The two people, however, who have had most to endure are Helen Boden and James McKinna. They have kept me afloat throughout, and this book is for them, with love. It is also, however, in memory of Clare Tarplee, who would have loved this excuse for a celebration.

Gill Plain
University of St Andrews, 2000

Introduction: Criminal Desires

> Murder makes a mess in a clean place. Stories about murder are therefore stories as much about dealing with mess as about deciphering clues. (Trotter, 1991: 70)

> The social intervention of a text (not necessarily achieved at the time the text appears) is measured not by the popularity of its audience or the fidelity of the socioeconomic reflection it contains or projects to a few eager sociologists, but rather by the violence that enables it to *exceed* the laws that a society, an ideology, a philosophy establish for themselves in order to agree among themselves in a fine surge of historical intelligibility. This excess is called: writing. (Barthes, 1971/1989: 10)

In March 2000, while taking a brief holiday in Madrid, I stumbled by accident into the most vivid and disturbing of exhibitions. *Monstruos y Seres Imaginarios* (Monsters and Imaginary Creatures) at the *Biblioteca Nacional* was an exhibition exploring conceptions of the monstrous from medieval manuscripts to nineteenth-century fairy tales. Although the books in the exhibition stopped at the end of the nineteenth century, the display began with contemporary horror. Two distorting mirrors confronted the voyeuristic visitor, destabilising the self-image of the complacent spectator before he or she moved to pass judgement on the monsters of earlier times. The books themselves were a breathtaking confirmation of the extent to which our sense of the monstrous negotiates the species barrier:

image after image transgressed the boundary between mankind and animal, creating hybrid creatures that embodied the cultural terror of miscegenation and the fear of absorption by an 'other'. But the depiction of such monsters is also an act of reassurance. The pristine human body is contaminated by a clearly definable alien other, and in this hybrid construction comes absolution from the guilt of our own inherent monstrosity. The monstrous is no longer something without form or reason, category or explanation. It is a terrifying, but nonetheless accountable, instance of an other's invasion of our corporeal integrity.[1]

In this gruesome yet compelling exhibition I found myself confronting my own abject fascination with the repulsive contortions of the human body. I was also, however, confronted by an absolute absence of explanation. Having presumably imagined that foreign tourists would be quite busy enough visiting the Prado, the curators had offered their explanatory notices in Spanish alone and, speaking no Spanish, I found myself in the unusual position of being displaced from the comforts of language. Hundreds of years of bogeymen passed before my eyes and, due to my linguistic ignorance, I could only guess at their meaning – until, with relief, my eyes alighted upon an English-language text. Suddenly I had words again. The comprehensible was back within my grasp and I hungrily consumed the two open pages of Alfred Swinbourne's *Picture Logic or the Grave Made Gay* (1875), where I was amazed to discover both an image of detection and an account of its appeal:

> That night, my nerves being, I suppose, in an excited state from my attempts to follow my tutor's arguments . . . I dreamed a strange dream about the form and matter of thought. In the midst of a plain I beheld a huge machine. At first sight it resembled a coffee grinder, but on closer inspection it proved to be more like a monster sausage-machine. A college friend of mine was working it by a small handle, the perspiration pouring from his forehead.
>
> On the left of the machine sat an old Professor, and on the right of the machine there was an indescribable confusion of all kinds of things; there were birds, balloons, pyramids . . . a lion was just entering the machine, followed by a lady, a frog, a tortoise, and a clergyman. I should never have had my curiosity satisfied, had not the lion roared terribly in his reluctance to enter, thereby eliciting the following remarks from my friend at

> the wheel. 'Now then, in with you, you needn't make all that fuss; you're not in the least formidable to us; why we had a whole menagerie through the other day, and trains, elephants, whales, worlds – all have to pass through this machine and become terms for the inspection of the great Professor Logic.'
>
> For the first time I then noticed some things that looked like sausages issuing from the left side of the machine, only from having such big things inside them they were swollen to the shape of eggs. In one I observed a fish, in another a house, in a third a bird, and in a fourth a man – all were painfully cramped for want of room.
>
> 'Ah! yes,' he went on, 'it's with our machine here as it is with the common ordinary sausage machine, never mind what the material is – so long as the shape is right. Large or small, young or old, flesh or stone, you must all pass through, for Professor Logic isn't particular about the matter, all he concerns himself with is the form.' (Swinbourne, 1875: 34–6)

Crime fiction in general, and detective fiction in particular, is about confronting and taming the monstrous. It is a literature of containment, a narrative that 'makes safe'. Swinbourne's image epitomises the 'process' of detection: the inexplicable, the unspeakable and the excessive are fed into the sausage-machine of genre, worked upon by remorseless professors of logic, and spat out in conclusion as nuggets of certainty, closure and explicability.

I began with monsters, and in the consideration of Hannibal Lecter that concludes this book, I will end with them too. In between there is the detective – a figure bracketed by the tide of unreason that twentieth-century crime fiction seeks to contain. Although the detective has appeared to be the lynchpin of the formula, providing certainty and stability at the centre of the narrative, closer inspection reveals an ambiguous and uncertain figure. Over the course of the century, the detective's centrality has been eroded, and ultimately it is only the presence of a crime that gives coherence to the genre. Hence my title: 'crime fiction' becomes the most suitable 'catch-all' for a formula that continues to proliferate in ways undreamt of by Sherlock Holmes, and it is also sufficiently broad a term to encompass the neighbouring territory of the thriller.[2] In some shape or form all the fictions I examine negotiate a criminal act – whether it be the archetypal body in the library, or the systematic violence of an unjust social order. How each fiction defines this criminality will be subject to differences both subtle and radical. Some of the writers considered here can undoubtedly be seen to conform to the patterns of the traditional detective story. Others destabilise the notions of individual agency associated with the figure of the detective, making their hero a reactive rather than a pro-active figure. Others move still further from the authority of the individual towards fictions of co-operative discovery, fictions that pose a challenge to both social and formulaic structures, and in so doing displace the archetypal detective story's structural foundation: the restoration of the law. Ironically, it is the rupture of crime rather than its safe resolution that provides the genre's common denominator.

However, although banished from my title, the detective remains fundamental to conceptions of the genre, and the forms taken by this figure over the course of the century are crucial to any consideration of the character's later fragmentation and dissolution. Broadly speaking, the detective assumed two significant manifestations during the first half of the twentieth century. The 'classical' detective is a seemingly omniscient investigator who enters an enclosed environment that has been invaded by the 'cancer' of crime. With surgical precision the detective identifies the criminal and exonerates the community from any imputation of responsibility or guilt. Order is restored and stability returns to what is depicted as an homogenous society. Irrespective of either writer or detective's actual national identity, fictions such as those of Agatha Christie, Dorothy L. Sayers, Margery Allingham and Ngaio Marsh have been regarded as archetypally British, and are generally assumed to have enjoyed a 'golden age' between 1920 and 1940.[3] However, a second tradition was evolving almost simultaneously with the development of the classical model. The 'hard-boiled' detective emerged from the pulp magazines popular in early twentieth-century America and seemingly represented a completely different conception of the investigator's relationship to law, order and society. These fictions, exemplified by the work of Dashiell Hammett and Raymond Chandler, presented a radical challenge to the notion of a stable society, situating the detective in a hostile urban environment. The detective also underwent a transition. No longer omniscient, he tended to detect through provocation rather than deduction, identifying the criminals through the mark of their violence – which was frequently left on his no longer inviolable body. However, although this detective had neither class nor money behind him and was displaced from the social and epistemological authority enjoyed by many of his predecessors, he undoubtedly remained an aloof and morally superior figure.[4]

While these snapshot typologies of classical and hard-boiled detectives oversimplify the complexity of popular fictional representations, this duality is still to be found in most analysis of the detective genre. My concern with the instability of this duality will be the subject of Part I, which analyses Agatha Christie and Raymond Chandler as respective 'exemplars' of the classical and hard-boiled modes. Part II is concerned with the reappropriation and revision of the genre by writers of the 1970s and 1980s, a period in which crime fiction was recognised as a uniquely adaptable formula, capable of carrying a complex social and political agenda while still attracting a mass audience. Predominantly that agenda was gender, and the chapters of this section consider four attempts to re-create the sexual politics of detection. Part III, in contrast, considers not the reappropriation, but the breakdown of the genre, focusing on the inexplicable and monstrous, and the collapse of detective agency.

This is not, then, a history of the genre. Indeed, it wants, if anything, to move away from the developmental model established by genre historians. The gospel of crime history is paradoxically both definitive and nebulous: in the beginning there was Poe. Or should that be the Newgate Calendar? Or *Caleb Williams*, or Aesop's fables, or the Bible, or even the Jewish Apocrypha?[5] Detection is a genre of dubious origin – but irrespective of its exact date of birth, the murky past of the formula has been very well documented – and ultimately all roads lead to Edgar Allan Poe. Useful accounts of this history have been formulated by many, and range from pocket-sized surveys to detailed analyses. The writings of T. J. Binyon, John G. Cawelti, Stephen Knight, Martin Priestman and Julian Symons together comprise an excellent introduction to the history and development of the form. This book, however, has a different purpose: namely, the re-reading of twentieth-century crime fiction through the critical lense of gender. Rather than considering the evolution of the genre in terms of detective methodologies, I have focused my attention on socio-cultural constructions of gender, sexuality and the body – or the 'corporeal landscape' of the genre. Such a focus has had unexpected repercussions. The re-examination of the 'body' has led to the uncovering of evidence that if not actually previously overlooked, could certainly be said to have been misinterpreted.

What has emerged, then, is a series of textual readings centred around crime fiction's deployment of gendered and sexualised bodies, both living and dead, that at the same time reflect the adaptability of form that has made detective fiction one of the century's most influential modes of popular fiction. Gender transgression and the disruption of 'normative' sexuality have always been an integral part of crime narrative. Although superficially conservative in its reliance upon resolution and the restoration of the status quo, implicit within the genre is a considerable degree of resistance to reductive gender categories. Even in its earliest days crime fiction could not be reduced to a binary opposition between female pathology and masculine self-reliance.[6] However, the genre's transgressive 'potential' is not to be found in its conclusions: rather, it finds expression in the writing *before* the ending – in the body of the text – which demands that we return anew to these deceptively familiar fictions. Crime fiction has been fixed in a rigid set of critical and historical paradigms that define it as a narrative of the always already known. Yet these texts cannot be reduced to the sum of their resolutions; they must also be considered in the light of the conflicts and tensions that they mobilise en route, and, in exploring these tensions, the possibility must be considered that crime, like its counterpart respectability, is seldom quite what it seems.

I suggested above that it is the repeated production of textual closure that gives the crime genre its conservative appearance. John G. Cawelti supports this interpretation, arguing that the classical detective story operated both as individual escapism and a cultural safety valve (1976: 104):

> [B]y reducing crime to a puzzle, a game, and a highly formalized set of literary conventions, it transformed an increasingly serious moral and social problem into an entertaining pastime . . . something potentially dangerous and disturbing was transformed into something completely under control. (Cawelti, 1976: 104–5)

But is this process *necessarily* conservative? It is important to recognise that even a 'highly formalized set of literary conventions' can admit a considerable degree of flux and uncertainty, and it is this potential that has been in part responsible for the renaissance experienced by crime fiction over the last thirty years. Although the genre has mutated almost beyond recognition, crime fictions remain as culturally potent at the beginning of the twenty-first century as they were in the early decades of the twentieth. Perhaps the genre's concern with the transgression of boundaries makes it a particularly appropriate mode for the *fin de siècle*? The optimism that greets the new world of a new century inevitably carries with it a commensurate fear of the unknown – a fear that would also make the genre an ideal arena for the construction and development of modern bogeymen. In a world that, paradoxically, is both increasingly explained and increasingly mystified by science, new forms of the inexplicable are required to fill the void left by evil spirits, and in the 1990s this vacuum was filled by the ubiquitous figure of the serial killer. Equally ubiquitous in the brave new world of crime is the pathologist – a new 'hybrid' detective formed by crossing two key symbols of reassurance: the doctor and the private investigator. The pathologist has come to prominence in response to developments in medical science that have complicated bodies beyond all amateur comprehension. The professional detective is no longer sufficiently specialised to cope with a modern world of on-line identities and DNA coding, and is in danger of being usurped by the scientist – a figure who, thanks to the remarkable metamorphoses of Hollywood, has already become a stalwart of popular cinema thrillers.[7] In such a context, though, the detective's continued appeal might actually lie in a refusal of evolution. The technologically unsophisticated detective struggles to 'make sense' of an increasingly alien world, and becomes a figure who reassures not through authority, but through his or her proximity to the reader's own disenfranchisement.

INSTITUTIONALISING CRIME: THE ANALYSIS OF DETECTION

> [T]he terms 'art' and 'literature' are neither spontaneous nor innocent. They are bestowed by the gatekeepers of the cultural apparatus, and should be understood as tactics for conferring authority upon certain works. (Sinfield, 1998: 146)

Much of the substantial critical work undertaken within genre studies has been historical or sociological, producing either an uncritical celebration of the history of detection, or an analysis of readership patterns more concerned with *why* people read genre fiction than with the fiction itself. Students approaching a crime novel will thus undoubtedly consider its form, readership and relation to a specific socio-historical moment, but they are rather less likely to explore its textuality. Dennis Porter offers a possible explanation:

> [T]he popular literature of a consumer society in an age of mass literacy has long been regarded by critics of a broadly Marxian tradition as a reflector and valuable barometer of the society's ideological norms. The importance of popular works resides in their status as meaning-systems that embody implicit world views. (Porter, 1981: 1)

Due to the work of such cultural theorists as Janice Radway, Porter's depiction of genre as an inert reflector of external socio-political change has largely been superseded; but his observation nonetheless succinctly encapsulates the dominant critical framework within which genre studies has operated.[8] Criminal fictions have predominantly been regarded as historical documents and cultural artefacts, the substance of their textuality overlooked in favour of the conditions of their production.[9]

To complain of these textual absences is not, however, to depreciate recent work on popular fiction. The historical surveys, the readership studies and the deconstructive performances have all been of enormous benefit to the fundamental project of opening up the canon of English studies to the diversity of the popular. All these approaches are necessary: the problem is not their presence, but rather the absence of substantial text-based analyses that would supplement their debates.[10]

However, although it has weighed against serious attempts to study crime fiction as 'literature', the perceived status of detective fiction as a gauge of cultural norms has had its advantages. It has, for example, provided a prime site for the development of feminist readings. The pronounced gender-blindness of many of the subject's founding critical interventions has been counter-balanced by a number of recent enquiries emerging from the diverse landscape of gender studies. The sexual politics of criminal fictions have been put under the microscope by critics such as Maureen Reddy (1988), Sally Munt (1994) and, most recently, Priscilla Walton and Manina Jones (1999). The increasing centrality of gender to studies of crime fiction is the inevitable outcome of a belated critical acknowledgement that the genre's profound investment in dynamics of power inevitably incorporates discourses of gender and sexuality. The *femme fatale*, probably the genre's most famous stereotype, is merely the tip of a huge gender iceberg, and recent critical studies have identified much more complex patterns of gendered authority within detective fiction.[11]

Detective fictions, then, are multifaceted. They are historical artefacts, sites of gendered negotiation, but they are also literary texts. Despite the still prevalent division between high art and popular culture, genre fictions are as available for close reading and as open to literary theoretical interrogation as their more 'respectable' counterparts.[12] Ironically, however, the comparison with the 'literary' has a further dimension. Within the genre of crime fiction there rages a struggle for canonical legitimacy every bit as fierce as those conducted in the academic mainstream, and inevitably the question is asked: how can a study of crime fiction possibly ignore Edgar Allan Poe, Arthur Conan Doyle, Dorothy L. Sayers, P. D. James, Dashiell Hammett, Ellmore Leonard, James Ellroy? The list of possibilities is endless, but with every inclusion comes the necessity of saying less about those writers included, and it is on these grounds that I have restricted the numbers in this book. The exact criteria for inclusion has varied in response to the different demands of the book's three parts, but in the study as a whole I have been concerned to select writers who, irrespective of their reputation or status, have made a significant engagement with the body. This has resulted in a curious, and I hope fruitful, juxtaposition of writers from both the apparent mass-market 'mainstream' and from the cutting edge of revisionist reappropriations of the genre.

WHODUNNIT? SOME THEORETICAL SUSPECTS

My critical approach can broadly be categorised as feminist in its focus upon gender and sexuality, and materialist in its concern with the contexts and conditions within which twentieth-century genre fiction is situated. However, in the critical dialogues that form the basis of my chapters, I have also responded to the often noted 'sympathy' that exists between the processes of detection and psychoanalysis (Lacan, 1973/1983; Žižek, 1991/1994).[13] Sigmund Freud's 'Beyond the Pleasure Principle' (1920) has been central to much of my thinking, particularly in its fascinating insights into modes of repetition. Freud's observations have informed my speculations as to why the body should be the site to which popular fiction endlessly returns, and why readers should be attracted to a genre premised on loss, which endlessly repeats the painful experience of death. The other critic who has perhaps most influenced my thinking on crime and its bodies is Julia Kristeva. Her theorisation of the abject is almost painfully appropriate to the dialectic of fascination and repulsion that motivates the production and consumption of criminal fictions. According to Kristeva, the abject is an intangible yet pervasive boundary, 'a border that has encroached upon everything' (Kristeva, 1982: 3). It is neither self nor other, but a residue of both. It is that which 'is thrust aside in order to live' (1982: 3), and there can be no more powerful site of the abject than the corpse:

> The corpse, seen without God and outside of science, is the utmost of abjection. It is death infecting life. Abject. It is something rejected from which one does not part, from which one does not protect oneself as from an object. Imaginary uncanniness and real threat, it beckons to us and ends up engulfing us.
>
> It is thus not lack of cleanliness or health that causes abjection but what disturbs identity, system, order. What does not respect borders, positions, rules. The in-between, the ambiguous, the composite. The traitor, the liar, the criminal with a good conscience, the shameless rapist, the killer who claims he is a saviour . . . Any crime, because it draws attention to the fragility of the law, is abject, but premeditated crime, cunning murder, hypocritical revenge are even more so because they heighten the display of such fragility. (Kristeva, 1982: 4)

In *Powers of Horror* Kristeva articulates the dynamics of abjection through the tropes of psychoanalysis and religion, although the concept has far wider potential signification:

> [A]bjection, when all is said and done, is the other facet of religious, moral, and ideological codes on which rest the sleep of individuals and the breathing spells of societies. Such codes are abjection's purification and repression. (Kristeva, 1982: 209)

The abject is fundamental, but like Medusa, it cannot be directly confronted. Kristeva suggests that the analyst might perhaps construct a discourse 'around the braided horror and fascination that bespeaks the incompleteness of the speaking being' (209), but beyond the ranks of this contemporary priesthood, it is perhaps the popular fictions of horror that come closest to negotiating society's abject fascination with its most destructive and repulsive drives. Crime fiction's vicarious confrontation of death thus simultaneously exposes and disguises the abject. The narrative catharsis of fiction eases the pressure of repression, and through displacement on to the repetitious pleasures of genre, the subject's fascination with dissolution and death can be both contained and indulged.

This book has also been shaped by Roland Barthes's conception of pleasure, and by recent work on gender and sexuality – in particular that of Jonathan Dollimore, Eve Kosofsky Sedgwick, Terry Castle, Judith Butler and Angela Carter. I have also been fortunate in writing this book at the same time as a series of stimulating analyses of masculinity have appeared to complement the now extensive literature on representations of femininity. Thinking about masculinity has been an integral component of the project. Whether the detective is male or female, straight or gay, she or he always exists in negotiation with a series of long-established masculine codes. The extent to which a detective conforms to or challenges these models is thus essential to an understanding of crime fiction and the changing role of the investigator within the genre. Given that, in its hard-boiled form at least, crime fiction is seen to be almost synonymous with conventional discourses of masculinity, it is perhaps only through reconceptualising the masculine that the genre and its paradigms can be successfully recuperated. I have chosen in the main to explain theoretical positions and ideas when they first become relevant to my analyses, and these explanations have been cross-referenced in order to ensure that chapters can stand in isolation. Nonetheless, the argument of the book is a cumulative one. The three parts can be seen to represent three distinct stages of development, analogous to what Thomas S. Kuhn has termed a 'scientific revolution': first, there is the early establishment of a crime-fiction paradigm; second, there follows the 'normal' practice of genre; and third, the genre arrives at a point of fundamental change.

GENDER, SEXUALITY AND THE BODY: PUTTING THE CORPUS BACK INTO CRIME

Detecting issues of gender and sexuality in twentieth-century formula fiction all too often results in the uncovering of a 'crime'. These fictions are permeated with the marks of misogyny, homophobia and racism; they are embedded in contemporary attitudes that often seem themselves to border on the criminal. Yet this 'ideological criminality' is no reason to avoid the popular, for these are also fictions of pleasure and desire, and beneath their surface conformity they frequently reveal unexpected pockets of resistance. Crime fiction thrives on the unexpected and as a result creates a world in which the usual suspects must for once be exonerated. Irrespective of the contempt which the butler may face as one of the lower classes, the fact remains that within the conventions of the genre he cannot be the criminal. The illegitimacy of his class position ironically guarantees his unimpeachability in the bourgeois world of classical crime fiction, and the same curious inversion applies to a whole range of social and sexual transgressions. This is not to say that the genre does not have its stereotypes, nor that it hesitates to deploy them at every available opportunity; rather, it is important to recognise that the genre is not limited to a certain set of formulaic patterns. Throughout its history, its survival has depended upon its capacity to surprise, and this in turn has had the result of creating a popular genre which constantly poses at least the possibility of subverting cultural 'norms' and expectations. More recent manifestations of the genre, however, have made subversion central. Increasingly criminal fictions present a world in which the 'criminal' dissent found on the margins has been legitimised by the decay of centralised authority. Counter-culture is validated, while the dominant culture is revealed as tarnished and fraudulent. These, then, are paradoxical fictions, and not the least of the pleasure they offer lies in the exploration of the tensions generated by these contradictions.

Gender and sexuality, then, are key discourses within the genre – but what about the body? At the root of nearly all twentieth-century criminal fictions lies the literal body of the corpse. The corpse is a contradictory site within criminal fictions: the end point of a life that simultaneously signifies the beginning of a narrative. It is a deep structural irony of the detective genre that the 'body' is both crucial to and yet often overlooked by the fictional process.[14] In the terms of Margery Garber, it could be argued that the corpse is looked *through* rather than *at* (1992/1993: 187). Like the cross-dresser, the original subject of Garber's distinction, the corpse embodies a culturally unassimilable ambiguity and a problematic excess that challenges codes of linguistic and textual representation; and in consequence it is consigned to the margins – carried off in the opening pages and safely translated into symbol. Detectives, police and pathologists scrutinise the corpse-as-text, seeking clues to facilitate a reading of the crime, while the material reality of the corpse decomposes beneath their narrative indifference. Does it matter *who* dies in detective fiction? By keeping a critical eye on the body within these fictions, I hope to indicate that it too remains an active signifier, subject to constructive re-readings and capable, through the residual traces of the act of murder, of identifying its assailant. Murder literally is 'written on the body' and bodies are never neutral. They inevitably bear the inscriptions of their cultural production – socially determined markers of gender, race, sexuality and class that profoundly influence the ways in which they are read by witnesses, police, detectives and readers. We can also not afford to forget that the detective has a body. From this perspective, the concept of the 'pure puzzle' mystery is immediately put into question. Any intellectual 'purity' is always already compromised by the figure of the detective, who must be embodied, and with embodiment comes implication within the social. In short, the detective has a body, and with a body comes baggage.

Crime fiction is thus never in danger of being conflated with the superheroic tradition of comic-book fantasy.[15] Although it mobilises the dream of a man above men (sic), capable of solving the crime and restoring social cohesion, or even just of standing firm against the rising tide of urban corruption, it never suggests that the detective is a man above the body. Crime fiction's conception of a saviour is distinguished from the ethos of the comic book by its insistence upon corporeality. While superheroes can effortlessly transcend their bodily limitations, crime fiction by contrast seems remorselessly to have insisted upon the extreme corporeal constraints of its heroes. Conan Doyle can arguably be seen to stand outside this paradigm, along with such stalwarts of masculine indestructability as Bulldog Drummond, but in a lineage that owes more to Wilkie Collins than to Edgar Allan Poe, the mobility of the detective's mind stands in marked contrast to an often paralysing embodiment. Ernest Bramah created a blind detective, Rex Stout produced a corpulent one, and Agatha Christie gifted her detectives with possibly the most intense form of embodiment conceivable: old age.[16] Sayers's Lord Peter Wimsey exhibits another type of embodiment. His appearance of upper class idiocy disguises a state of incipient hysteria – an emotional frailty that consistently cuts the hero down to size just at the point of his detective 'triumph'.[17] The centrality of the body to the hard-boiled tradition scarcely needs to be reiterated. The constant battering of Philip Marlowe defies medical science, but there is a curious Calvinist dimension to the bodily suffering of the detective. The mortification of the flesh seems to promote clarity of vision. Time and time again, violence is figured as the prelude to knowledge. Only after the 'puzzle' has literally been written on the body can it ultimately be comprehended and resolved.

I began this introduction with two epigraphs: David Trotter's succinct suggestion that crime fiction 'mops up' the excess created by the disruption of the symbolic order, and Roland Barthes's conception of writing as a 'violence' that exceeds symbolic constraint. Barthes's comment, from *Sade, Fourier, Loyola,* is prefaced by an assertion of his structuralist credentials: 'I listen to the message's transport, not the message' (1971/1989: 10). But in the context of genre fiction, Barthes's statement begs a crucial question: what distinguishes the transport from the message? Is the formula the message or the vehicle? Do we pay attention to what we expect of crime fiction (repetition, resolution, containment), or to what we actually find: namely, the individual piece of writing, representing variation and resistance to the containment encoded in the formulaic message? Does crime fiction become transgressive through its radical content, or in its resistance to form? Like the conundrum of the chicken and the egg, it is an impossible question.

However, Barthes's methodology in *Sade, Fourier, Loyola* offers a route out of this dilemma. In this work he focuses on the fragments of three lives, the points that remain in the memory, that connect outside the familiar frameworks of historical or biographical understanding, and this provides a potential model for the research that is yet to be done on crime fiction. Barthes's reading of his three lives is an 'attempt to dissipate or elude the moral discourse that has been held on each of them . . . [to] unglue the text from its purpose as a guarantee: socialism, faith, evil' (1971/1989: 9). Until critics begin to pay attention to the fragments of crime fiction – the individual transports that supposedly comprise the 'message' of the genre – our understanding of the pleasure of these texts will remain fundamentally limited: not least because these transports are all in excess of the message they supposedly bear. Crime fiction is not what it seems and my aim in this book has been not to totalise or write the biography of the genre, but rather to explore the 'biographemes' of the form – the fragments that lodge in the memory, their cultural imprint, their transgressions. For me, the key biographemes of the genre are gender, sexuality and the body, and it seems vital that crime fictions be 'unglued' from the moral discourses that would contain them, in order that we might consider their significance as texts which exceed and transgress the dimensions of their form.

NOTES

1. It is worth noting that a special section was devoted to women's bodies, and the images gathered here seemed to confirm that woman is monstrous not in hybridity, but of herself.

The womb stands as a central symbol of the fear of the unknown, its inexplicable generative capacities a source of profound cultural terror.

2. Generic definition is notoriously difficult (Symons, 1992/1994; Winks, 1980), and the exact boundary between the thriller and the detective story is almost impossible to define. Much of what is categorised as one form or the other will contain characteristic elements of both. Nonetheless, a substantial account of the thriller formula is provided by Jerry Palmer (1978).
3. These writers are cited as probably the most famous exemplars of the 'golden age' classical mode. However, they represent merely the tip of a very large iceberg, the body of which includes such writers as Gladys Mitchell, Nicolas Blake and John Dickson Carr. It is also important to note that although regarded as British, the formula was far from confined to Britain, and was practised, with variations, by Americans such as S. S. Van Dine.
4. In 'The Simple Art of Murder' Raymond Chandler famously commented that Dashiell Hammett had 'given murder back to the kind of people that commit it for reasons, not just to provide a corpse' (Chandler, 1950/1964: 194). In terms of its early readership, the hard-boiled formula undoubtedly enjoyed a wider class appeal than its classical contemporary, not least because it acknowledged the corruption of the status quo and questioned whether it was worth either restoring or preserving.
5. All possibilities cited by Dorothy L. Sayers as foundational texts of detection in her introduction to *Great Short Stories of Detection, Mystery and Horror* (1928).
6. The work of Wilkie Collins provides an early example of the transgressive potential of the genre. Collins is often cited as a key figure in the genre's development, but his fiction is diametrically opposed to the model established by Poe and Conan Doyle. Edgar Allan Poe's Chevalier Auguste Dupin appeared most famously in two short stories of the 1840s, 'The Murders in the Rue Morgue' and 'The Purloined Letter'. His adventures were narrated by an anonymous friend in a model of homosociality most famously adopted and developed by Sir Arthur Conan Doyle in the creation of Dr Watson, narrator of the adventures of Sherlock Holmes. Holmes first appeared in *A Study in Scarlet* (1887) and both detectives embody a detached, ratiocinative approach to the problem of crime. They investigate to prove their skills, test their intellects and to ward off the ever-present threat of boredom. Detection for Collins, by contrast, is not an exercise in logic but a pressure on the boundaries of the comprehensible. He does not conceive of the detective as a figure invested with power who brings the authority of knowledge to bear on a problem, but rather as a powerless figure seeking empowerment through confronting and attempting to make sense of the unknown.
7. Recent years have seen a breathtaking collection of scientists emerge from Hollywood. The venerable old men in white coats have been banished, to be replaced by sexy and improbably young experts in all manner of obscure disciplines. Jeff Goldblum's leather-clad chaos theorist in *Jurassic Park* (1993) set a new standard in mathematical chic, but it is predominantly women who are being cast in the role of decorative genius (the 'brainbo'?). From Mira Sorvino's entymologist in *Mimic* (1995), to Liv Tyler in *Armageddon* (1996), it seems that cinema's latest fantasy claims that you can become a world authority by the age of thirty – and without losing your looks.
8. Radway's seminal *Reading the Romance* (1984) was one of the first studies to argue that readers of popular culture, in this case romance fiction, could be active critics rather than simply uncritical consumers of ideologically conservative narratives.
9. Conversely, David Trotter argues that the critical picture has also been distorted by the a-historicism of post-structuralist approaches which displace popular culture from its context and ignore the significance of its readership (1991: 74).
10. There are some notable exceptions to this rule. Detailed textual analysis accompanies the arguments of Cawelti (1976), Knight (1980) and Priestman (1990).
11. Alison Light's contention that the classical detective of the 1920s and 1930s is a 'feminised' figure provides a good example of the extent to which the matrix of gender and crime fiction is being rethought (1991: 8). Light's work is supplemented by studies such as Shaw and Vanacker (1991), who contend that Miss Marple resists conventional representations of both age and femininity, and by the recent development of masculinity as a critical focus, which has put the hard-boiled detective himself under the spotlight (Nyman, 1997).
12. Martin Priestman (1990) engages directly with the construction of this boundary and the problems of defining literary quality, and although his work has a very different focus to that proposed here, he makes the welcome assumption that 'all texts *can* be discussed in equivalent detail' (1990: xi). Priestman calls this assumption 'routine', but I am not convinced

that all critics of the genre, and certainly not those in the wider world of literary studies, would agree.

13. The detective as analyst works backwards from a given point (the symptom or crime) in an attempt to uncover the repressed or hidden desires at its root. But critics have also suggested that the genre itself serves a crude analytic function, absolving the reader from responsibility, and laying the blame for crime or unhappiness firmly at the feet of someone else (Cawelti, 1976: 104).
14. Arguably the current trend for pathology fictions challenges the invisibility and intangibility of the corpse. Patricia Cornwell's Kay Scarpetta mysteries and television series such as *Silent Witness* certainly bring the body centre stage, often focusing in gruesome detail upon the process of post-mortem examination. However, although these fictions facilitate an understanding of the textuality of the corpse – these bodies are 'read' by the detective's medical expertise – they do little to challenge the invisibility of the body. Rather, their impact is one of fragmentation. The corpse is reduced to a series of component parts, its bodily integrity more radically violated by the detective than by the criminal. The pathologist's proximity to the body does not in itself challenge the genre's traditional distance from the corpse. However, as David Trotter has convincingly argued, there is a context in which the corpse has an opportunity to reassert its substantiality. Ironically, the longer the corpse is left, the more powerful its presence becomes. Through the peculiar sensitivity of smell, the dead attain the capacity to violate and disrupt the bodily boundaries of the living. (David Trotter, 'The View From the Slab' conference paper, *Murder in Bloomsbury* symposium, University of London, June 1996.)
15. I argue what might seem to be precisely the opposite of this position in Chapter 4, where I suggest that Dick Francis *is* rewriting the comic-book tradition of the indestructible superhero. However, Francis's heroes have no power of *effortless* transformation. Rather, their power is rooted in the body and its pain, and they achieve their heroic effects through an extreme experience, rather than a transcendence, of corporeality.
16. Bramah's Max Carrados was the eponymous hero of a collection of stories that first appeared in 1914, while Stout's Nero Wolfe became a stalwart of library shelves in the interwar years. The immense Wolfe sits at the centre of an information web, content to let others do the legwork while he contemplates his orchids.
17. Wimsey's problem is a crisis of responsibility, rooted in the shellshock he suffered during the First World War, and emerging with the realisation that every murderer he identifies will in turn be killed by the machinery of the state. When a death penalty is in operation, the detective becomes a legally sanctioned killer, emphasising once again the moral complexity and ambiguity of the genre.

Part I

Establishing Paradigms

Establishing Paradigms: Introduction

[Paradigm] stands for the entire constellation of beliefs, values, techniques, and so on shared by members of a given community. (Kuhn, 1962/1970: 175)

[O]ne of the things a scientific community acquires with a paradigm is a criterion for choosing problems that, while the paradigm is taken for granted, can be assumed to have solutions. To a great extent these are the only problems that the community will admit as scientific or encourage its members to undertake. Other problems . . . are rejected as metaphysical, as the concern of another discipline, or sometimes as just too problematic to be worth the time. A paradigm can, for that matter, even insulate the community from those socially important problems that are not reducible to the puzzle form, because they cannot be stated in terms of the conceptual and instrumental tools the paradigm supplies. (Kuhn, 1962/1970: 37)

In the midst of death we are in life, Hastings . . . Murder, I have often noticed, is a great matchmaker. (Christie, 1936/1993: 125)

I was a blank man. I had no face, no meaning, no personality, hardly a name. I didn't want to eat. I didn't even want a drink. I was the page from yesterday's calendar crumpled at the bottom of the waste basket. (Chandler, 1949/1955: 177)

The last two epigraphs suggest something of the vast philosophical gulf assumed to divide the work of Agatha Christie from that of Raymond Chandler. The quotations evoke diametrically opposed worlds. Christie, writing shortly before the outbreak of the Second World War, suggests the possibility of social cohesion and repair, the prospect of healing and reunion. Chandler, writing shortly after the war, heads remorselessly for the abyss, focusing upon fragmentation, loss of identity and the threat of extinction. Philip Marlowe's glass is half-empty; he oozes weary cynicism and knows that things fall apart. Hercule Poirot's glass is half-full; he provides reassurance and believes that broken lives can be made whole again. These differences emerge from a considerable cultural divide: Christie and Chandler are separated by class, gender and the Atlantic Ocean. Their fictions are set in different worlds – the one close-knit and rural, the other disaffected and urban – and from these divisions spring countless further contrasts in attitude, assumptions and style. Nonetheless, although Marlowe's glass is half-empty, and Poirot's half-full, they are both drinking from the same glass, and that glass is crime fiction. Surface differences, no matter how substantial, should not obscure a fundamental shared concern with the disruption of order, the violence of shattered community and the search for some form of viable resolution that will set the world back within its familiar, if tarnished, parameters.

I suggested in the introduction that crime fiction has become trapped within an interpretative framework incapable of adequately answering the questions raised not just by but *within* the form. The body of crime fiction is comprised of a surprisingly diverse range of texts, and the frequently unexpected and anomalous material that emerges within these narratives gives rise to fundamental questions regarding the stability of the genre. To what extent can the formula of crime, or any other generic paradigm, contain and accommodate change? Some answers are offered by what might seem at first to be an incongruous critical tool: Thomas S. Kuhn's *The Structure of Scientific Revolutions*.[1] In his influential study Kuhn argues that historians of science have been asking the wrong questions. In their desire to produce a viable linear model of 'development-by-accumulation', they have constructed a narrative of scientific progression that fundamentally misrepresents the relationship between the 'event' of scientific discovery and the ongoing processes of scientific practice (1962/1970: 2). Much the same could be said of crime fiction's historiography. Critics have argued that hard-boiled crime fiction superseded the classical mode and in so doing rendered it redundant: the clue-puzzle mysteries of the interwar years are thus translated in history into a normative, conservative, 'feminine' centre against which the revolutionary edge of hard-boiled masculinity can be both honed and measured.[2] But just as science cannot adequately be contained within a model of incremental progression, so crime fiction demands a more multidimensional reading. Kuhn's alternative historiographical model asks that:

> Rather than seeking the permanent contributions of an older science to our present vantage, [scientists should] attempt to display the historical integrity of that science in its own time. (Kuhn, 1962/1970: 3)

It is in this spirit of re-reading and re-contextualisation that the following chapters consider the works of Agatha Christie and Raymond Chandler, which represent two distinct formulations of what Kuhn describes as a 'universally received paradigm'.

The paradigm of twentieth-century crime is itself the product of a 'scientific revolution'. While much nineteenth-century fiction exhibits a fascination with the 'event' of crime, its approach to this event is characterised by diversity, making the formulation of a paradigm impossible. Crime appears rather as a component of other literary paradigms, manifesting itself as an integral part of such disparate modes as gothic fiction and the social problem novel. Although there were undoubtedly popular fictions concerned with crime – from the Newgate Calendar, to the tales of Edgar Allan Poe, to the novels of Wilkie Collins – it is not until the phenomenal success of Sir Arthur Conan Doyle's Sherlock Holmes stories that the basis of a revolution can be detected. This revolutionary beginning was consolidated by the explosive emergence of the classical crime novel in the years immediately after the First World War, and the concept of detection as a narrative *raison d'être* was augmented rather than undermined by the parallel growth of the American hard-boiled tradition. From these roots a paradigm of twentieth-century crime was established, mobilising the epistemological and formulaic basis that would underpin experimentation during the second half of the century.[3]

My focus in Part I is, then, a fresh examination of the founding fictions of twentieth-century crime, and my departure from traditional critical approaches has been greatly assisted by the useful new work that has recently emerged on the contexts of both classical and hard-boiled narrative. While Raymond Chandler has long been recognised as a significant writer of American vernacular literature, it is only more recently that critics such as Scott R. Christianson have begun to analyse his fiction as a fundamental expression of late modernism. The linguistic parallels that might be drawn between the pared-down prose of Hemingway and Chandler's tough-guy narratives are not difficult to detect, but Christianson has also emphasised the shared thematic concerns that bind Chandler to foundational texts of 'high' modernism such as T. S. Eliot's *The Waste Land*:

> The Tiresian posture of the poet/hero of *The Waste Land* – the isolated modern hero sitting before a spectacle of modern chaos and trying to make sense of it all – is the posture of the autonomous and lonely hardboiled detective. The attempt of the poet/hero to order that experience, at the same time that he remains true to its futility, describes the linguistic efforts of the hardboiled narrator . . . In general, both *The Waste Land* and the works of hardboiled novelists project an attitude of disgruntled alienation toward a distinctively *modern* civilization. (Christianson, 1990: 142)

Christianson's analysis is enlightening, suggesting both the instability of the modernist canon and the artificiality of the still powerful distinction between the 'high' art of the cultural elite and the 'low' art of the popular. Unfortunately, such potentially liberatory parallels can also backfire. Rather than prompting a wider rethinking of critical categories and the assumptions of cultural value, comparisons with modernism see Chandler elevated and 'canonised' as the one good writer to emerge from an otherwise debased literary form.[4]

Closer to my project than attempts to 'elevate' Chandler is Jopi Nyman's recent study, *Men Alone: Masculinity, Individualism, and Hard-Boiled Fiction* (1997). Although not primarily focused on Chandler, Nyman's account of the genesis and development of the hard-boiled formula pays welcome attention to the gendered dimensions of the genre. 'Hard-boiled fiction', she argues, 'can be regarded as a symbolic representation of anxieties over gender which stem from its historical and cultural context' (1997: 3). The formula functions as a specific reworking of the American Dream and constitutes a 'cry for help uttered by the insecure and alienated men of the period' (1997: 361). Nyman also suggests that hard-boiled fiction is characterised by a romantic yearning for a lost ideal, and argues that the object of that yearning 'is not a relationship or human being, but a different social order' (1997: 360). In Chandler's fiction, however, this is not entirely the case, and critics have suggested that his novels incorporate a more individualist ideology. Stephen Knight, for example, argues that Chandler was 'writing personalised emotional adventures for a hero, not plots which created a sharply focused problem or pattern of social reality' (1980: 149). Urban disaffection and social discontent thus form a backdrop to the existential anxieties of the individual questing detective and, in Chapter 2, I will argue that Chandler undertakes a very specific embodiment of this quest in the form of his hero's obsessional search for an impossible masculine ideal.

Yet irrespective of whether Chandler is regarded as an influential modernist or a reactionary romanticist, he has been, unusually for a 'popular' writer, granted a place within the arena of cultural debate. Until recently, the same could not be said for Agatha Christie. However, some of the most remarkable work of recent years has related to her reconceptualisation. Stephen Knight draws attention to Christie's methodology, observing that she 'alters Doyle's pattern towards a passive problem-solving that rejects romantic male heroism as a protecting force' (1980: 108). She is, he notes, 'essentially less authoritarian' than Doyle in her avoidance of 'individualistic heroics' and in her creation of an 'imitable method, not a comforting élite personality' (Knight, 1980: 109).[5] Alison Light concurs and, in her groundbreaking study *Forever England*, argues that Christie might be read as a 'popular modernist', whose fictions present a radical embracing of the modern at the same time as they recuperate and reinforce certain conservative notions of value (1991: 64). According to Light, Christie undermines traditional gendered assumptions of the heroic, a strategy that can be read as part of a wider change in discourses of national identity between the wars:

> [T]he 1920s and '30s saw a move away from formerly heroic and officially masculine public rhetorics of national destiny and from a dynamic and missionary view of the Victorian and Edwardian middle classes in 'Great Britain' to an Englishness at once less imperial and more inward-looking, more domestic and more private – and, in terms of pre-war standards, more 'feminine'. (Light, 1991: 8)

With the First World War still painfully immediate in the mind of the nation, the genre became a 'literature of convalescence' (1991: 69), reassuring its readers, both male and female, that the bloodshed was behind them.

Critics have thus begun to reconsider the work of both Christie and Chandler, identifying in particular the complex gender discourses that circulate within their texts. However, it remains the case that the two writers are largely considered not only as different, but actually in opposition. In his consideration of the 'story' of science, Kuhn warns of the danger of rewriting the past in the light of present utility. All too often it is assumed that what contemporary science considers of value in a theory must also have been considered of value at the time of the theory's inception. This pattern translates easily into the realm of fiction. Hard-boiled narrative has become one of the most influential discursive modes of twentieth-century fiction, reappropriated and revised by countless practitioners in the years since the Second World War. But does this necessarily mean that the first consumers of Chandler's fiction understood or acknowledged that in Philip Marlowe they were witnessing the birth of a modern icon?

The early sales of Chandler's fiction were notoriously slow. On its first publication in 1939 *The Big Sleep* failed to make an impact in either America or Britain, and languished in critical and popular obscurity until 1943, when Chandler's publisher, Alfred Knopf, authorised the publication of a cheap 'pulp' edition. This revolutionised Chandler's sales, and brought him widespread and favourable reviews for the new Marlowe novel, *The Lady in the Lake*. Ironically, critical acclaim arrived on the back of mass consumption (Hiney, 1997: 107–8, 131–2). These fluctuating critical and popular fortunes remind us that the first readers of Chandler's fiction consumed his narratives in a profoundly different literary and cultural context. They were unprepared for the remarkable metaphoricity of his prose, and were as yet unaware of the archetypal properties of his hero. My point here is simply that, in reading Chandler, we must be wary of viewing him only through the lense of late twentieth-century approbation of the hard-boiled mode. There are other narrative possibilities in the fictions of Raymond Chandler, stories and inscriptions that have been overlooked because we read him as 'familiar' and consider his fictions to be already known. Much the same could be said of Agatha Christie. She is part of a British cultural consciousness: everybody 'knows' something called an 'Agatha Christie', but to what extent do her texts actually bear out the presumptions under which they have been categorised and contained (Light, 1991: 62–5)?

A concern of the following chapters is consequently to revisit the texts that underpin the definitive paradigms of twentieth-century crime writing, and to ask whether we are not misguided in our assumption that we know the 'significant' features of these fictions. In an eloquent plea for the rediscovery of crime fiction's sexual politics, David Glover argues that 'the myth of the Golden Age and Chandler's potent counter-aesthetic of the hard-boiled private dick still delimit the terms in which we write the history and theory of the detective story, disguising some of its most important features' (1989: 67). Hard-boiled and classical detective fiction must be seen, then, not as binary opposites, but as competing discourses emerging from a complex cultural milieu. The mode of detection is different, but not the underlying structure of puzzle and conspiracy. Both types of fiction provide an isolated community of suspects, and although Christie's characters might be more polite, underneath they too are driven by greed, jealousy and illicit desires. It is, then, an issue of focus. The same premise underpins both forms, but while Chandler focuses on the detective's physical, intellectual and emotional response to the events in which he is embroiled, Christie is careful to keep the detective in the background while she maps out the evidence for her readership. Philip Marlowe is compromised by association, and the reader cannot see beyond his perceptions. Hercule Poirot retains his distance, but the reader cannot penetrate his inscrutability. The end result in both cases is a form of mystification that has proved peculiarly satisfactory to the demands of an ever-changing body of twentieth-century readers.

If the story of twentieth-century crime is thus not quite what we think, what other narratives might be encoded within these popular fictions? David Glover, quoted above, has demanded a reconceptualisation of the sexual politics of crime, and in so doing has drawn attention to one of the genre's most complex discourses. On the surface, however, crime fiction presents an effective façade of gender conformity. Women writers dominated the culturally 'feminised' classical tradition with its elision of masculine modes of heroism and its emphasis on domesticity and detail, while male writers made their mark in the hard-boiled mode. It is probably no coincidence that hard-boiled fiction has come to carry more cultural cachet than its golden age sister! Gender conservatism also seems to be evident in the absence of the female detective. In both the classical and the hard-boiled form, detectives remained predominantly male throughout the interwar period.[6] Constraints upon women-as-agents, even within a supposedly 'feminine' form were still largely insurmountable.[7] Yet there is an overlooked irony in the fact that the discourse of rationality and logic, so beloved of both Virginia Woolf's archetypally masculine Mr Ramsay and Christie's infinitely less masculine Hercule Poirot, when displaced into a despised genre form, undergoes a change of gender, and becomes a 'feminine' form.

That 'logic' can be culturally coded as both masculine and feminine is revealing. It suggests that the signifiers operating within crime fiction cannot be taken at face value, nor necessarily assumed to share meanings fixed by other contemporary discourses such as modernism. It is also significant that the much vaunted masculinity of the tough-guy detective emerges not from rationality and logic, but rather from what might otherwise be seen as a feminine corporeality. These detectives detect with their bodies in a combination of radically destabilising modes. They are driven either by the concept of the 'gut reaction', an instinctive corporeal knowledge that represents the supremacy of body over mind and overturns the fundamental binary oppositions structuring western patriarchal society; or they detect through the experience of pain, the assault on the body, the literal imprinting of knowledge on the body of the detective through proximity rather than distance.

The role of the body in detective fiction is complex and diverse, and in Part I the bodies of both the living and the dead play a central role in the process of decoding the illicit desires of crime fiction. In the work of Christie and Chandler, the body is at the centre of a fundamental trope of boundary crossing, foregrounding the uncertain division between law and disorder, desire and repulsion, attraction and aggression. These tensions are themselves indicators of a more substantial border: that which divides the articulable from the unspeakable, and in so doing constitutes the narrow line between the stability of social organisation (the symbolic), and the chaotic rupture of corporeal desire (the semiotic).

In Chapter 1, 'Sacrificial Bodies', I use Julia Kristeva's concept of 'underlying causality' to examine the ways in which Agatha Christie's fiction presents the body as the site of a particularly intense negotiation of the boundary between symbolic structures and semiotic drives. Christie's key bodies are the corpse, which may be either 'grievable' or 'semiotic', and the monstrous body of the mother – both of which are, for Julia Kristeva, sites of abjection. The corpse and the mother inhabit borderline states between life and death, being and annihilation, but Christie's deployment of these bodies attempts to challenge such uncertainties, and to 'make safe' or defuse a range of cultural anxieties emerging in the aftermath of the First World War. Christie's 'therapeutic' fictions are followed in Chapter 2 by a consideration of Raymond Chandler's 'love stories'. While Christie largely succeeded in containing or evading the unruly body of desire, Chandler's fictions mobilise a series of uncontainable and excessive bodies, raising a question that will be fundamental to the later development of the genre: what difference is made by a desiring detective? Yet although the hard-boiled detective is motivated by bodily desires, the world of the tough guy is categorically not about women. The *femme fatale* is less an object of desire than an excuse. In a world in which women are permitted but repulsive, and men are desirable but taboo, her waywardness legitimises the detective's uncertain relationship to the heterosexual matrix. Chandler's novels thus become models of erotic displacement, focusing on an unobtainable homosocial ideal embodied by the concept of 'semiotic masculinity'.

In their encounters with the body both Christie and Chandler reveal themselves as writers of abjection. Their fictions are dependent upon the return of the repressed and focus remorselessly upon the forces of the ego's dissolution that must be thrust away in order to survive. They repeatedly confront the subject's terror of annihilation: the collapse of corporeal integrity through death or desire, through decay or absorption by another. Kristeva argues that the abject 'is the violence of mourning for an "object" that has always already been lost' (1982: 15), and crime fiction is premised upon this loss. However, as a literary mode that attempts the symbolic articulation of this impossible semiotic yearning, crime fiction also becomes a mode of resurrection and reconfiguration. What Kristeva says of abjection holds equally true for crime fiction's attempt to assert authority over the abyss: '[i]t is an alchemy that transforms death drive into a start of life, of new signifiance' (1982: 15).

NOTES

1. Kuhn comments explicitly upon the widespread appropriation of his theories, agreeing that 'to the extent that the book portrays scientific development as a succession of tradition-bound periods punctuated by non-cumulative breaks, its theses are undoubtedly of wide applicability' (1962/1970: 208). However, he expresses himself puzzled by this popularity, claiming that his conceptions are themselves drawn from the construct of periodisation in fields such as literature, music and politics. Nonetheless, I have found Kuhn's particular articulation of 'revolution' particularly helpful in considering the patterns of change within genre fiction.
2. This simplified critical dichotomy is not universally acknowledged. David Glover, for example, observes that 'the rise of the hard-boiled detective was a refurbishing of already existing masculine forms, drawing imperialist credentials from the North American prairies

rather than from Africa' (Glover, 1989: 74). However, the predominant critical orthodoxy continues to operate around the notion of a fundamental binary divide between the 'British' and 'American' forms.

3. Kuhn observes that a single paradigm can 'simultaneously determine several traditions of normal science that overlap without being co-extensive' (1962/1970: 50).
4. Some notable examples of this mode of thinking can be found selling Penguin editions of Chandler's work. The reprint of *The Little Sister* quotes Anthony Burgess's claim that Chandler is a 'serious writer', and Frank MacShane's assertion that 'it was a triumph of style that he was able to transform a limited type of fiction into something having universal appeal . . . *The Little Sister* and *The Long Goodbye* established him not simply as an American crime writer of the first rank, but as a novelist who rendered the actualities of American life as vividly and independently as any "straight" novelist' (Chandler, 1949/1955: back cover). Tom Hiney's biography of Chandler provides many further examples of the cultural anxieties surrounding popular fiction, which was still, in the late 1940s, perceived by some critics as a 'disease' (Hiney, 1997: 172).
5. Poirot's 'domestic' methodology is, arguably, only the first step along the road to revolution. Shaw and Vanacker suggest that it is the invention of Miss Jane Marple in 1930 that truly breaks new ground, as it is here, for the first time, that the detective becomes a member of the community under investigation (Shaw and Vanacker, 1991: 2–3).
6. The spinster detective is an obvious exception to this rule. Christie's Miss Marple and Patricia Wentworth's Miss Silver achieved a degree of authority by virtue of their age, while Sayers's Miss Climpson evolved into a remarkably active investigator. However, her agency remained subject to the whim of her employer, Lord Peter Wimsey – and throughout the period it seemed that writers found it difficult to construct a fictional space in which to deploy an active, desiring, female investigator. This observation is doubly applicable to the hard-boiled genre, where the woman detective, although not absent, was a rare commodity. Kathleen Gregory Klein (1988) provides an overview of the emergence of female detectives in the American tradition, while a thoroughly enjoyable example is provided by Rex Stout's 1937 novel *The Hand in the Glove*, featuring the tough-talking 'she-dick' Theodolinda 'Dol' Bonner.
7. Although perceptions of women had been altered by the events of the First World War, the cultural expectation that middle-class women would return to domesticity and motherhood in peacetime remained strong. The vote was won, but traditional discourses of femininity had undergone little change, and it was assumed that women would put domestic duty above personal satisfaction (Rowbotham, 1997/1999; Ingman, 1998: 1–21).

1

Sacrificial Bodies:
The Corporeal Anxieties of Agatha Christie

> The corpse (or cadaver: *cadere*, to fall), that which has irremediably come a cropper, is cesspool, and death . . . without makeup or masks, refuse and corpses *show me* what I permanently thrust aside in order to live . . . The corpse, seen without God and outside of science, is the utmost of abjection. It is death infecting life. (Kristeva, 1982: 3–4)

> As a matter of fact I don't care two pins about accuracy. Who is accurate? Nobody nowadays . . . What really matters is plenty of *bodies*! If the thing's getting a little dull, some more blood cheers it up. (Christie, 1935: 71)

Agatha Christie's texts are riven with unstable and insufficiently examined bodies, both dead and alive. Yet perhaps because her fiction is so ubiquitous and familiar, the actual constitution of these texts passes without comment. Some of the responsibility for this oversight must lie with Raymond Chandler, who pulled no punches in his attack on the conventional pieties of 'golden age' detective fiction. Wittily venting his spleen in 'The Simple Art of Murder', he claimed that:

> The only reality the English detection writers knew was the conversational accent of Surbiton and Bognor Regis . . . [the product of] . . . flustered old ladies – of both sexes (or no sex)

> and almost all ages – who like their murders scented with magnolia blossoms and do not care to be reminded that murder is an act of infinite cruelty, even if the perpetrators sometimes look like playboys or college professors or nice motherly women with softly greying hair. (1950/1964: 196–7)

Agatha Christie has long had a reputation for superficiality – but can we really recognise her fiction in Chandler's description? Chandler had a vested interest in convincing his audience of the impermeability of the great divide separating the hard-boiled from the classical tradition, but nonetheless criticism has largely followed his lead and accepted the genre as emerging from this foundational binarism. But closer examination suggests that we might learn as much from comparing as contrasting the works of Christie and Chandler. Neither writer is wholly as their reputation suggests. Legend has metamorphosed Miss Marple from an acidic spinster into a kindly old lady, while the hard-boiled exterior of Chandler's Philip Marlowe frequently cracks to reveal a distinctly soft centre.[1] It seems crucial, then, that we consider the extent to which the wider assumptions that shape our knowledge and understanding of the genre are based not on textual observation, but on a series of distorted generalisations. The familiar landscape of genre fiction needs to be remapped, and one of the many possible routes to this remapping is through an analysis of the body.

Two paradigms of detection were established in the interwar period. The first was the domain of the 'soft-boiled' British – quietly committed to a peaceful regime of poison and pokers, expertly wielded in the peaceful environs of their country vicarages. The second witnessed 'hard-boiled' Americans clubbing each other to death with empty bourbon bottles amid grim scenarios of urban decay. As I suggested above, there are several good reasons to dispute the clear-cut boundaries of this division – and the body is one of them. The troublesome body of the woman is a generic constant of the interwar period that effortlessly crosses the binary divide. The *femme fatale* of tough-guy legend is equally a stock character in the more sedate classical mode – the only difference being that she is harder for the unwary male to spot when dressed in a twinset and pearls. Raymond Chandler has become renowned for his misogynistic deployment of female stereotypes, but a number of Christie novels are dependent upon almost identical typologies of female behaviour. Indeed, in terms of detection, of decoding the mystery, these supposed polar opposites are not so far apart. The resolution of the mystery in Christie frequently depends, as it does in Chandler, on an accurate reading of the female body. If you cannot tell your *femme fatale* from your virginal innocent, you're likely to be in serious trouble.[2] Repeatedly, Poirot's skill as a detective is revealed by his ability to accurately decode the female – unlike his stolid sidekick Hastings, who, like his contemporary the hard-boiled detective, inevitably falls for the bad girl.[3]

However, although his detection relies heavily upon the psychology of motive, Poirot's detective skills are equally manifest in his ability to read the other fundamental body of crime fiction – the corpse. And it is by looking at the dead that we might begin to recognise the cultural complexity that underpins Christie's seemingly innocuous texts.

THE DEAD

Christie's bodies have long been regarded as empty signifiers. Intensely underwritten, they appear at the beginning of the novel as a 'tabula rasa' upon which the script of detection will be written, and any degree of corporeal complexity they might possess seems secondary to their function as instigators of narrative causality. But how appropriate are these generalisations? Are Christie's corpses as bloodless as their reputation suggests? It would take a strong stomach to sift through the entire seventy-nine novels that comprise Christie's detective oeuvre, and the difficulty of drawing fresh conclusions would in any case be compounded by her longevity. Christie's writing career extended from 1920 to 1976, a 56-year period over which attitudes to death, violence and bodies underwent something of a transformation. However, by focusing upon a smaller sample, drawn from a coherent historical period, it becomes possible to establish not only a clearer picture of the corpse and its function within Christie's texts, but also to reconsider the wider cultural significance of Christie's writing.[4] The interwar years, from 1918 to 1939, are generally considered to represent the apotheosis of 'golden age' crime fiction. This is also the period in which Christie first rose to prominence, and in order to consider her relationship to Britain between the two world wars, I intend to examine two Poirot novels: *Murder on the Links* (1923) and *Murder in Mesopotamia* (1936).

The bodies that litter the pages of these two texts are typical of the corporeal diversity that confounds critical generalisation, and force the conclusion that it is impossible to homogenise Christie's corpses.

But perhaps by looking at this diversity, at the various individual manifestations of death, we might be able to draw some conclusions about both the status of the body within these fictions and the relationship of the fictions to their wider socio-political contexts. The acknowledgement of context seems crucial. As readers we bring to these texts a cultural awareness of the corpse-as-signifier that has been finely honed by our consumption of Patricia Cornwell's carefully anatomised bodies and our national viewing of *ER* and *Casualty*. The reader's ability to read the corpse has advanced far beyond that envisaged by Christie in *Murder on the Links*, a novel in which the police are found unable to tell the difference between a fresh corpse and one that has been dead for two days. Only Poirot and the doctor are aware of the fact, now painfully familiar to all consumers of criminal fictions, that post-mortem wounds do not bleed. As we have become ourselves more corporeally sophisticated, are we in danger of subjecting Christie to inappropriate bodily expectations? George Orwell, writing in 1944, puts the matter into a very different contextual framework:

> Some of the early detective stories do not even contain a murder. The Sherlock Holmes stories, for instance, are not all murders, and some of them do not even deal with an indictable crime . . . Since 1918, however, a detective story not containing a murder has been a great rarity, and the most disgusting details of dismemberment and exhumation are commonly exploited. (Orwell, 1965: 68)

There is, as every good detective knows, more than one way to read a body, and the conventions that govern the narrative mapping of bodies have undergone such a revolution that our twenty-first-century perspective misreads the Christie corpse, seeing blandness and bloodlessness where her contemporaries witnessed the full significance of ritual death.[5]

Critics sensitive to historical change have argued that the absence of violence within Christie's interwar oeuvre is symptomatic of a state of national post-traumatic stress. Probably the fullest account of this national malaise is provided by Alison Light, who analyses Christie in terms of 'conservative modernity'. Arguing firmly against Chandler's condemnation of the classical detective tradition, she observes that:

> It might seem more than churlish, then, to complain, as many have done, of the 'gutting' of characters, their insulation from life and the bloodlessness of crime between the wars, when that anaemia can be seen as a revolt against the sanguinary rhetoric of 1914, and as part of the haemorrhaging of national languages of romantic self-esteem. The idea [proposed by Julian Symons] that murder 'has to do with human emotion and deserves serious treatment' was hardly the angle on slaughter which post-war readers would find revelatory. Nor were they likely to confuse literary fantasy with the real thing. It is in this light that we might assess those who preferred acrostics to aggression. (Light, 1991: 74–5)

In the aftermath of the First World War, British society was unable or unwilling to engage with the all too familiar realities of death and destruction. This explanation, however, cannot quite contain a full account of Christie's corpses. Although the emotional response evoked by most of these bodies is deserving of the epithet bloodless, the same cannot be said for the actual corpses.[6] While the majority may rest in tidy repose, sanitised parcels for the detective to unwrap, the novels are also characterised by bizarre eruptions of truly violent death: by fire, by acid, by convulsive poisons and multiple stabbings.[7] These deaths are not always central to the narrative, but their textual presence remains as a gruesome reminder of memories not easily repressed.

There are, then, two types of body that characterise Christie's fictions. The ritual corpse, or 'sacrificial' body, and the rather more sordid, disruptive and uncontainable 'semiotic' body. The first of these, the 'sacrificial' body, must be presented whole, and death should leave only the minimum of marks upon what is in effect an offering to the gods, or ghosts, of war. The significance of corporeal integrity cannot be underestimated in this context.[8] Contrary to appearances, then, detective fiction is an arena that displays the body made safe. The dismembered bodies of the battlefield become the tidily reassembled corpses of Christie's fiction. There is a transition from fragmentation to wholeness that replicates a wider social need for the reinstatement of the rituals of death. Describing the changing meanings of mourning in modern Britain, David Cannadine argues that in the aftermath of the First World War 'bereavement had become a more universal experience than ever before' (1981: 217). He goes on to consider some of the implications embodied in this new mass culture of grief:

> Those six millions who had served at the front had seen more death in their relatively brief spell of armed service than they might reasonably have expected to encounter in a lifetime. And the deaths which they saw were violent, horrible, bloody, degrading and brutal, when, if they had been civilians all their lives, they would probably have limited their repertoire of death to old age and natural causes. At the same time, the soldiers themselves had been the agents of death . . . Shock, guilt, anguish, grief, remorse: these were only some of the emotions which such an experience left behind: above all, a desire to forget, and yet also a recognition that such experiences could not be, must not be, forgotten. (Cannadine, 1981: 217)

In the postwar popularity of detective fiction, a trend can be discerned towards the validation and restoration of the individual. In the excesses of death that characterise a world at war, the individual corpse is obliterated; it becomes impossible to mourn for each and every loss. But in detective fiction the reader enters a fantastical world in which the meticulous investigation of a single death is not only possible, but central to the narrative. Both exact cause and ultimate responsibility can be attributed for each single newly significant death. *Someone* is to blame, and the wartime absence of explanation is superseded by detective fiction's excess of possible solutions. Thus the fragmented, inexplicable and even unattributable corpses of war are replaced by the whole, over-explained, completely known bodies of detection. The detective *reassembles* that which war had exploded, and the over-invested signifier of the corpse becomes a ritual, 'grievable' body reassuring society with both its integrity and its explicability. There is even comfort in the certainty of death offered by detective fictions. This is a world in which no one is maimed, blinded or left hovering in the limbo of intensive care. The value of the sacrificial body lies also in its clear-cut avoidance of the unstable boundary between life and death.

The concept of the 'grievable' body may begin to account for the corporeal fascination that characterised the interwar period, and it also provides a context for Christie's second novel, *Murder on the Links*. This is a novel in which Christie wastes no time in getting to the body. In a little over ten pages a man has been murdered, and shortly afterwards we encounter the first inscription of his body:

> 'Going to call her mistress as usual, a young maid, Léonie, was horrified to discover her gagged and bound, and almost at the same moment news was brought that Monsieur Renauld's body had been discovered, stone dead, stabbed in the back.'
>
> 'Where?'
>
> 'That is one of the most extraordinary features of the case. Monsieur Poirot, the body was lying face downwards, *in an open grave.*' (Christie, 1923/1988: 19)

Not only is the corpse wholesomely complete, it is laid out with ritual precision in an already prepared grave; while the knife in the back turns the victim's corpse into a postwar sacrificial atonement for the thousands of unburied and unnecessary dead. That the corpse's grave should turn out to be a golf bunker is perhaps only appropriate in a world so frequently associated with the superficial. Alison Light has described Christie's tendency to debunk the heroic, and her movement away from romantic rhetorics of sincerity (Light, 1991: 65–75), and this tendency is equally in evidence in her attitude towards the body. After Poirot has viewed the corpse of M. Renauld, the chapter concludes with a parody of religious observance that clearly indicates the distance between Christie's contemporary rituals and pre-war rites of death:

> Poirot lingered for a moment, looking back towards the body. I thought for a moment that he was going to apostrophize it, to declare aloud his determination never to rest till he had discovered the murderer. But when he spoke, it was tamely and awkwardly, and his comment was ludicrously inappropriate to the solemnity of the moment.
>
> 'He wore his overcoat very long,' he said constrainedly. (Christie, 1923/1988: 34)

Yet, perhaps the most fascinating aspect of the body within *Murder on the Links* is that everyone wants to *see* it. Characters are practically lining up to view the corpse. Hastings, the narrator, cannot wait to get a look at the spectacle of unnatural death, and when he wants to impress his new girlfriend, what better entertainment than a trip to view the sacrifice?

> 'Perhaps you've heard about this crime – at the Villa Geneviève – ?'

> She stared at me. Her breast heaved, and her eyes grew wide and round.
> 'You don't mean – that you're in on *that*?'
> I nodded. There was no doubt that I had scored heavily . . .
> 'Well, if that doesn't beat the band! Tote me round. I want to see all the horrors' . . .
> I turned away, sickened. What were women coming to nowadays? The girl's ghoulish excitement nauseated me.
> 'Come off your high horse,' said the lady suddenly. 'And don't give yourself airs. When you got called to this job, did you put your nose in the air and say it was a nasty business, and you wouldn't be mixed up in it?' . . .
> I capitulated. Secretly, I knew that I should rather enjoy the part of showman. (Christie, 1923/1988: 63–4)

And so Hastings and 'Cinderella' proceed to face the thrill of 'something nasty in the woodshed', where much to Hastings's gratification, the lady's 'debonair high spirits' are 'quenched utterly' upon sighting the corpse. As Cinderella promptly crumples into unconsciousness, Hastings comments:

> I felt this to be so feminine that I could not forebear a smile. Secretly I was not dissatisfied with her collapse. It proved that she was not quite so callous as I had thought her. After all she was little more than a child, and her curiosity had probably been of the unthinking order. (1923/1988: 66)

The collapse of the female spectator adds another dimension to the role of the corpse in this novel. The body in the shed (whence Renauld has been unceremoniously removed) festers on for pages, acting as a handy gauge of female somatic reactions, and illustrating the extent to which guilt is written on the body of the criminal as well as that of the victim. This book gives full reign to what can best be described as the phenomenon of the fainting woman, and it is here that we can detect the specifically gendered nature of the need for postwar reassurance.[9] As Hastings's comments on the collapse of his beloved suggest, there is a powerful postwar urge to see women restored to their proper place in the order of society. They should be caring, not callous, they should not think, and, unlike the nurses of the First World War, they should very properly fall down at the sight of the prostrate male. What Sandra Gilbert has described as the 'revolutionary socioeconomic transformations wrought by the war's "topsy turvey" role reversals' (1987: 212) provoked a backlash, a momentum towards a postwar reconstruction of pre-war gender ideologies that rendered the working woman both unwelcome and superfluous.

Yet although Christie seems to endorse this gendered conformity, her female bodies are not quite as pliant as they may seem. *Murder on the Links* is heavily dependent upon the capacity to decode signifiers of femininity, and it will perhaps come as no surprise to learn that not only was Cinderella's faint a fake, but also that at the novel's dénouement it is she rather than the blundering Hastings who saves the day. Cinderella is both saviour and symptom of an emasculated postwar world. At the climax of the novel Hastings and Poirot are found battering helplessly on the locked door of a bedroom, within which the classic stereotypes of femininity are fighting for supremacy. The matriarch, Mrs Renauld, is struggling with the deadly seductress, Marthe Daubreuil, and in this brave new world where old-fashioned men fear the ascendency of the new woman, there is nothing that Hastings and Poirot can do. It is down to Cinderella (herself a third stereotype – the asexual, boyish flapper) to climb a tree, leap through a window and break up the fight.[10]

This messy scrabble among the living stands in marked contrast to the composure of the dead. Both corpses within *Murder on the Links* are characterised by this sacrificial tidiness (the second being a tramp scrubbed ritually clean to act as a scapegoat for the escaping Renauld). They fit neatly into the contemporary desire to deny the messy realities of death and are gloriously overladen with narrative explication. But the same cannot be said for the corpses that populate the later *Murder in Mesopotamia*, where Christie manifests what might best be described as 'Second Body Syndrome', that is, the production of a second, gratuitous and frequently gruesome death that serves little obvious narrative purpose. Morally, the reader is reminded that murder is a dangerous game. Practically, the detective may pick up another clue. But does this really account for the agonies of Miss Johnson, *Murder in Mesopotamia*'s second unfortunate corpse? Christie writes:

> Miss Johnson was lying in bed, her whole body contorted in agony. As I set down the candle and bent over her, her lips moved and she tried to speak – but only an awful hoarse

> whisper came. I saw that the corners of her mouth and the skin of her chin were burnt a kind of greyish white . . .
>
> Somehow or other, intentionally or otherwise, she'd swallowed a quantity of corrosive acid – oxalic or hydrochloric, I suspected . . .
>
> I won't dwell on the details. Poisoning by a strong solution of hydrochloric acid (which is what it proved to be) is one of the most painful deaths possible. (Christie, 1936/1962: 169)

Although there remains a degree of evasion, a qualitative difference can be discerned between this and the tidily completed murders characteristic of Christie's sacrificial bodies – and not the least of this difference lies in the immediacy of the death. Miss Johnson's demise erupts into the here and now of the narrative: it takes place centre stage rather than off stage, it is incomplete, messy and relatively gruesome. This is the uncontainable excess of the 'semiotic' body. An uncomfortable trace of authentically shocking violence that disrupts the symbolic order (in both senses) of Poirot's investigation.

Julia Kristeva's concept of the semiotic as a textual inscription that exceeds and evades narrative order has been concisely explained by Elizabeth Grosz. Defining the semiotic as an 'interruption, a dissonance, a rhythm unsubsumable in the text's rational logic', she contends that the semiotic is 'both the precondition of symbolic functioning and its uncontrollable excess' (1990b: 152). This paradoxical state of centrality and surplus forms an admirable parallel for the role of the corpse within classical detective narratives. The necessity of a body, while underpinning the whole textual project, is nonetheless unwelcome, bringing with it, as it does, uncomfortable resonances of wider social signification. In the words of Elizabeth Grosz:

> These semiotic eruptions represent transgressive breaches of symbolic coherence or, put in other terms, the symbolization or representation of hitherto unspeakable or unintelligible phenomena, instances on the borders of the meaningful which reveal the coercive forces vested in the domination of the symbolic over the semiotic. (Grosz, 1990b: 153)

In their reliable production of narrative closure, detective fictions are undoubtedly coercive fictions that restore order where none existed. The impossibility of this project is evident within the problematic traces of the bodies they deploy, and within *Murder in Mesopotamia*, the semiotic dimension of 'Second Body Syndrome' is evident at several narrative levels.

In the first place the detective narrative itself presents such a murder as committed out of unthinking, irrational urges. *Murder in Mesopotamia* tells us repeatedly that 'murder is a habit' (1936/1962: 112, 168). Once Pandora's box has been opened, the forces of destruction cannot easily be recontained. Kristeva's conception of social organisation offers a framework for the interpretation of this dynamic. Following Freud and Lacan, Kristeva argues that the destructive impulses that society demand we repress in order to enter the adult world never go away, but remain omnipresent as a substratum of the individual and collective psyche. These drives can be theorised as an 'underlying causality', succinctly defined by Kristeva as 'the social contradictions that a given society can provisionally subdue in order to constitute itself as such' (Kristeva, 1976/1986: 153). Christie's world suggests that the fissure opened by the transgression of murder effectively weakens the bond that ties the criminal to the regulatory processes of society. The pressure of the investigation then gives rise to another semiotic irruption – the second body. However, rather than allowing this to threaten a resurgence of primitive drives, the superficially conservative logic of the detective story meets transgression with repression. From the killer's now uncontrollable urge to destroy derives in turn the killer's own downfall. The later crime committed to eradicate 'loose ends' becomes itself a loose end that bears all too plainly the imprint of the killer.

Yet *Murder in Mesopotamia* bears a further imprint of the semiotic that problematises this strategy of containment. Throughout the novel characters bear witness to the collapse of the group dynamic that precedes the murder of Louise Leidner. The community is destabilised and undermined by the resurgence of its underlying causality, that is, the immense destructive potential of the urge to possess, the desire to kill, and the close proximity of love and hate. However, in this novel, the return of the repressed assumes the additional horrific dimension of a bodily form, and in the historically resonant context of 1936, it is the dead of the First World War who figure as the underlying causality that pressures, and threatens to invade, the security of the contemporary moment. Louise Leidner's fear of her long-dead husband – supposedly shot as a German spy during the First World War – crystallises both the classical anxieties of the detective novel and the specific historical concerns of 1936. Would the defeated Germany, arguably the 'underlying causality' of interwar social organisation, come back to haunt and destroy Britain as Frederick Bosner appears to have done to Louise Leidner? In a device later used by Elizabeth Bowen in her eerily distressing short story 'The Demon Lover', the husband assumed dead reasserts his primitive rights of possession: '*You thought you could escape. You were wrong. You shall not be false to me and live. I have always told you so. Death is coming very soon.*' (Christie, 1936/1962: 59).

The process of coming to terms with the past is never straightforward, and it is in the problem of resolving the traumas of recent history that some answer may be found to the question of why, given the supposed national aversion to blood, these sordid semiotic bodies continue to appear in Christie's interwar fictions? The compulsion to repeat suggested by this endless return to the corpse might be seen to have a therapeutic function. As Freud observes in 'Beyond the Pleasure Principle', the staging and restaging of loss can facilitate the restoration of agency to the passive and dependent subject. Describing the '*fort/da* game' he comments:

> [T]he child turned his experience into a game from another motive. At the outset he was in a *passive* situation – he was overpowered by the experience; but, by repeating it, unpleasurable though it was, as a game, he took on an *active* part. (Freud, 1920/1955: 16)

Significantly, however, Freud's further analysis of the *fort/da* game uncovers the extent to which the child's repeated re-enactments of loss outnumber his reworkings of the satisfaction of recovery – a discovery that leads him to the conclusion that the death drive is fundamental to the organisation of the human psyche. And as child's play reveals the infant's obsession with the trauma of loss, so detective fiction bears the traces of society's obsession with its own annihilation. This compulsion takes us beyond Kristeva's earlier concept of underlying causality and into the realm of the abject. Elizabeth Grosz defines Kristeva's conception of this paradoxical space as follows:

> Like the broader category of the semiotic itself, the abject is both a necessary condition of the subject, and what must be expelled or repressed by the subject in order to attain identity and a place

> within the symbolic. Even at times of its strongest cohesion and integration, the subject teeters on the brink of this gaping abyss, which attracts (and also repulses) it. (Grosz, 1990a: 88–9)

This dynamic is evident in Christie's fictions. Her texts respond to both the human obsession with mortality and the specific interwar desire to evade this imperative. In the case of *Murder in Mesopotamia*, the compulsion to revisit a deadly past is all too evident. Louise Leidner is so physically attracted to her politically repulsive husband that she inadvertently marries him twice. On the first occasion, the pressures of responsible citizenship demand that she expel him from the conjugal body, and indeed from life, as her denunciation will see him shot as a traitor. Yet the attraction nonetheless remains and will draw her to repeat the trauma of her marriage, but this time the death will be her own.

There is, then, a curious dynamic of corporeal repulsion and fascination evidenced by detective fiction in general and Christie's corpses in particular. At the same time that Christie's society rejected and turned away from the senseless bloodletting of the First World War, it remained fascinated by the discourses of death, drawn back to the unbearable by what Clare Whatling terms a 'nostalgia for abjection' (1997: 81). Pertinently, David Cannadine observes that:

> As far as pre-occupation with death and bereavement as the result of war is concerned, it seems likely that inter-war Britain was more obsessed with death than any other period in history. The 'lost generation' may in some ways have been an elite myth. But the widespread bereavement which prevailed in inter-war England allied with the rituals of remembrance and the success of spiritualism, leave no doubt that it was also a mass reality. (Cannadine, 1981: 232)

Popular fiction and, in particular, detective fiction thus become, paradoxically, an integral part of both those rituals of remembrance and the self-preserving necessity of forgetting. Adapting Julia Kristeva to an end she is unlikely ever to have imagined, and in contradistinction to Alison Light's claim that 'in Christie's world nothing is sacred' (1991: 67), I would suggest that detective fiction ironically becomes an embodiment of the sacred that is both uncomfortable and transgressive in its 'cosiness'. Kristeva argues that:

> [C]ontemporary literature, in its multiple variants . . . propounds, as a matter of fact, a sublimation of abjection. Thus it becomes a substitute for the role formerly played by the sacred, at the limits of social and subjective identity. (Kristeva, 1982: 26)

The sacred requires a sacrifice, and postwar society needed a body in order to grieve. Detective fiction provided this 'grievable' body, and perhaps Christie's massive success can in part be attributed to the extent to which her fictions exactly replicated the contemporary desire both to see and evade the body. It is by now well documented that it took postwar society around ten years to face up, in literary terms, to the memory of war; but nonetheless, in order to make sense of the carnage of conflict, the horror of war had to be revisited and reworked, it could not simply be evaded. Detective fiction, then, represented a safe arena of fantasy within which at least an echo of this impulse to review could be satisfied – perhaps in the hope suggested by Clare Whatling that '[t]he terrible past, when viewed through the rose-tinted perspective of recollection in repose, offers up a different story' (1997: 81). It is only the horror of the corpse that can give substance and validity to the agency and resolution of the detective's work, or to use a medical metaphor, it is only the intimate knowledge of illness that can make the patient conscious of the cure.

Yet perhaps the most wonderful thing about the painkilling qualities of detective fiction's fantasy is that for all its obsession with death, the narrative remains one of resurrection.[11] The reader, facing the abyss of chaotic meaningless death, is restored to the security of a fully explained body. Writing reassembles the fragmented corpses of war, forming a bandage over the open wound of the abject, and interfacing the uncertain boundaries between inside and out, past and future. 'The abject', writes Kristeva, 'is the equivalent of death. And writing, which allows one to recover, is equal to resurrection' (1982: 26). Popular fiction offers this dynamic at its most fantastical, and the bodies that it mobilises, both sacrificial and semiotic, form an integral part of a specifically interwar narrative of reassurance. Agatha Christie does not need to litter her pages with the manifold corpses of Chandlerian 'realism', for those few bodies that she does deploy are freighted with the abject terrors of historical reality. Palliative medicine it may be, but in its deployment of the corpse, detective fiction transforms the inarticulable griefs of mortality into an all-in package tour through the process of bereavement.

A journey which insulates its travellers from any contact with the reality of their environment, and deflects the fear of the unknown. Christie's corpses, then, are both bloody and bloodless, and to the shellshocked society of interwar Britain this duality precisely constituted their appeal. The hysteric, says Freud in a comment equally applicable to the postwar state, suffers 'mainly from reminiscences' (1920/1955: 13), and in the 'hysterical' aftermath of the First World War, society's deadly compulsion to repeat found a safe and controlled micro-environment in the seemingly 'superficial' textual play of detective fiction.

THE LIVING

That Christie's living bodies are as complexly coded as her dead ones is evident from the bizarre encounter between Cinderella and her adversaries that closes *Murder on the Links*. Three contrasting modes of femininity come literally to blows over the body of the father. These are familiar types: first there is the *grande dame* or 'dignified' woman – sometimes, but not always, a mother – but inevitably capable of great restraint and even greater self-sacrifice. Second comes the deadly seductress, the sexual 'bad' woman. She may also sometimes be a mother, but will generally be proven to be an inadequate or 'inauthentic' respository of maternal values. Finally, there is the boy-girl, the antithesis of traditional female sexuality. Typified by 'Cinderella', this plucky girl-assistant conforms to the thoroughly modern template of the flapper, and would much rather climb a tree than entice a man to murder.

Yet irrespective of their stereotypical construction, the living bodies of Christie's fictions are freighted with complex cultural baggage. The sacrificial corpse was integral to a post-First-World-War narrative of regeneration, but, as the 1930s progressed, the increasing threat of a second war effected considerable change upon the landscapes of popular fiction.[12] By the time the war begins, the living have begun to assume a number of the symbolic functions previously contained by the corpse; a dynamic that is particularly well illustrated by the 1941 novel *N or M?*. This hybrid thriller resuscitates Christie's ageing 'partners in crime', Tommy and Tuppence Beresford, and its combination of espionage and detection offers a direct engagement with the cultural and political anxieties emerging from the Second World War. As usual in Christie's fictions, the detective duo are presented within an isolated community of suspects, but here their task is to identify not a murderer, but a spy.

The novel forms an excellent illustration of the wartime adaptability of the detective formula. As far as the security and the homogeneity of the community are concerned, the ideological compatibility between espionage and detection is obvious: the detective must identify the 'enemy within', and it matters little whether this enemy takes the form of a murderer or a traitor. However, the pressures of war do effect one significant change upon the formula: the detective as outsider is replaced by the detective as 'one of us'. It is no longer the case that the detective must come from elsewhere, uncontaminated by the taint of crime, to repair the rupture of the social fabric; rather it is crucial that he or she be an insider, someone whose loyalty and commitment to the values of the symbolic order cannot be questioned. Such an imperative is particularly problematic for women. Gender stereotypes of the 1930s and 1940s clearly established woman as a creature ruled by her heart, not her head. She could not be trusted to get her priorities right, and was liable at any moment to transgress the rules preserving patriarchal society. Paradoxically the Second World War saw women culturally positioned as 'disloyal' to the nation they were simultaneously obliged to symbolise (Plain, 1996: 20–5). Yet within such constraints, the amateur familiarity and cosy coupledom of Tommy and Tuppence represent an ideal vehicle for the production of wartime reassurance. They ooze a low-key, middle-brow typicality from every middle-class pore, and they epitomise the wartime spirit of co-operation. As British films exhorted the nation to do its bit and throw all hands to the pump, so Tommy and Tuppence can be seen to embody this willingness, while at the same time reinforcing one of the vital propaganda myths of the war. *N or M?* is a classic example of the wartime fantasy of agency. Its central conceit is that every little really does count and the individual does signify in spite of the overwhelming nature of mechanised mass warfare.

N or M? is thus both familiar and different. Once again the crux of the narrative hangs on the reading of bodies. However, the locus of meaning has shifted from the inert form of the corpse to the potential agency of the living, and the narrative seeks not to uncover the past, but rather to 'rewrite' the future. The detective evolves into a fortune-teller, no longer piecing together events that have already happened, but instead attempting to assert control over those that are yet to take place. Within this framework, then, we need to consider the body that replaces the corpse as a repository of the sacred and transgressive – namely, the mother. In *Powers of Horror* Kristeva describes what she designates as the 'two-sided sacred':

> Could the sacred be, whatever its variants, a two-sided formation? One aspect founded by murder and the social bond made up of murder's guilt-ridden atonement, with all the projective mechanisms and obsessive rituals that accompany it; and another aspect, like a lining, more secret still and invisible, non-representable, oriented toward those uncertain spaces of unstable identity, toward the fragility – both threatening and fusional – of the archaic dyad, toward the non-separation of subject/object, on which the language has no hold but one woven of fright and repulsion? One aspect is defensive and socializing, the other shows fear and indifferentiation. (Kristeva, 1982: 57–8)

What Kristeva describes here are two foundational aspects of the subject's negotiation with the abject – that which is 'permanently thrust aside in order to live' (1982: 3). She argues that an 'unshakable adherence to Prohibition and Law is necessary if that perverse interspace of abjection is to be hemmed in and thrust aside' (1982: 14), and the construction of the sacred is one of the ways in which societies negotiate the abject disruptions that would otherwise threaten to dissolve both individual and community. In her definition of the two-sided sacred, Kristeva sees murder and maternity, the corpse and the mother, as related through their transgression of bodily integrity. The corpse, she reminds us, is 'death infecting life' (1982: 4), while the archaic figure of the mother undermines the symbolic demand for the rigorous demarcation of boundaries between the 'I' and its 'Others'. Social rituals are thus constructed to 'ward off the subject's fear of his very own identity sinking irretrievably into the mother' (1982: 64), and to conceptualise both corpse and mother as sacred is to attempt a social policing of this inarticulable terror. The sacred renders 'safe' the realm of dread and horror, and regulates the subject's yearning for the impossible security of the pre-symbolic dyad. The taking of life and the giving of life can thus be seen to comprise the boundary states of patriarchal society. They are the sites at which the regulatory processes of the symbolic are stretched to breaking point, and just as the murderer must be expelled from the body politic, so the mother must be contained through her elevation to the role and status of figurehead. She becomes both symbol and vessel, worthy of tribute and essential to the furtherance of society, but wholly devoid of subjectivity.

In patriarchal societies, the mother is thus contained within rigidly defined boundaries. Her procreative role is overseen, if scarcely understood, by the father's authority, and transgression – failure to be a 'good-enough' mother – is liable to punishment. In *N or M?* the security of the nation rests upon the detective's ability to recognise the body of the 'authentic' mother. Authenticity, as I use it here, should not be confused with any conceptions of the 'natural'; rather, it can be seen to operate as a synonym for fixity, stability and, by extension, loyalty. The authentic is *known*. It is what it says it is, free of the taint of indeterminacy, and, unlike the abject, does not disturb 'identity, system, order' (Kristeva, 1982: 4). Authenticity might therefore be seen as a force against the abject, as a defence mechanism. It is aligned with the symbolic, attempting to recuperate the potentially transgressive figure of the mother and bring her safely within the patriarchal fold. Rather in the tradition of 'set a thief to catch a thief', the events of the narrative suggest that the identification of the authentic mother is a task best performed by a woman – in this case, Tuppence, who is herself an 'authentic' mother:

> '[S]top looking upon me as that sacred object, Deborah's mother, and just tell me what dangerous and unpleasant job there is for me to do.' (Christie, 1941/1962: 189)

I will return to the implications of the complex and contradictory concern with authenticity which dominates *N or M?* – a deep-rooted anxiety that manifests itself not only through the trope of motherhood, but also through ideas of national and racial identity. However, first it seems necessary to consider the cultural and political specificities defining not only the mother, but women in general, within the interwar period.

Many writers have analysed the complex catalogue of stereotypes defining acceptable and unacceptable modes of femininity in the aftermath of the First World War.[13] These stereotypes ranged from the frivolity of the flapper, through a familiar phalanx of virgins, whores and respectable mothers to the particularly potent stigma of the 'superfluous' woman. In a recent study of women's writing between the wars, Heather Ingman points out that the 'surplus' woman was 'believed to constitute a serious threat to the social fabric' (1998: 9), but it is interesting to note how seldom Christie deploys this threat either as red herring or reality. The spinster is seldom psychotic in Christie's interwar fictions; indeed, the woman most likely to exhibit socially disruptive, or even destructive, tendencies is not the childless spinster, but that supposedly positive archetype of femininity, the mother. This distrust of the mother is remarkable, but Christie is not alone in demonstrating hostility towards the overbearing atavistic figure of the pre-symbolic or 'phallic' mother. Surveying the depiction of the mother by Christie's contemporaries, Ingman concludes that:

> Those mothers who did try to preserve 'the old order' by, for example, keeping their daughters at home, began to be criticised after the war . . . Novel after novel written by women in the inter-war period demonstrates sympathy for the dutiful daughter trapped at home and castigates the selfishness of parents who keep her there. (Ingman, 1998: 8)

In terms of interwar sexual politics, Christie can be read as part of a wider group of women writers concerned with redefining the domestic and remapping the relationship between public and private spheres. The extent to which the term feminist can be applied to Christie is uncertain – the epithet is an unstable one, and its categories are constantly evolving – but irrespective of Christie's opinions on the public forms of women's activism, the assumption underlying her interwar fiction is one of female agency.[14] Women can, and they do. Young and old, married, single or widowed, mothers or career girls – in Christie's novels women have their own agendas, and are assumed to be responsible for their own actions.

A typical example both of Christie's construction of female agency and of her distrust of the mother is provided by *Dumb Witness* (1937). The novel is peopled by such an utterly unpleasant assortment of selfish, greedy and narrow-minded characters that the reader is hard pressed to care which one of them will eventually hang for the murder of Emily Arundell. However, in the midst of this misanthropic depiction of human nature there resides an extremely revealing portrait of a marriage. In a classical deployment of the red herring, Christie plays on the likely xenophobia of her readership to throw suspicion on to the Greek doctor Jacob Tanios. Throughout the novel characters give voice to the assumption that a marriage between a foolish Englishwoman and a clever Greek will inevitably be marked by violence and disharmony – and, indeed, the browbeaten Bella Tanios seems terrified of her powerful, ebullient husband.

Typically, however, all is not as it seems, and only Poirot has the capacity to identify the agency that underpins Bella's performance of fear. While Hastings believes they are fighting to save Bella from the murderous attentions of her husband, Poirot sees it differently:

> 'I realized at once, not that she feared her husband, but that she disliked him . . .'
>
> 'As time went on she could no longer conceal her dislike for her husband. In fact, she did not try to. He, poor man, was seriously upset and distressed. Her actions must have seemed quite incomprehensible to him. Really, they were logical enough. She was playing the part of the terrorized woman . . . she wished me to believe that her husband had committed the murder. And at any moment that second murder which I am convinced she had already planned in her mind might occur.' (Christie, 1937/1994: 244, 247)

However, it is not only the fact of Bella's agency that is significant, but also the motivation for her actions. The amorality of Bella Tanios is seen to be if not actually excused, then at least rendered comprehensible, by the condition of maternity. Christie suggests that motherhood sets women outside the symbolic order. The very fact of having children gives rise to the belief that the mother is free to circumvent the rules of patriarchy. In *Dumb Witness* Bella believes murder to be entirely justified if it will provide for her children's education.[15] Society, in defining the mother as the servant of her child, has in effect created a monster, a criminal or traitor within its midst, whose primary loyalties lie not with law and nation, but with the atavism of the pre-symbolic. Licence has been given to the irrational and the selfish, creating a state within a state, an autonomous region founded upon radically different priorities. As one traitorous mother observes to another in the later *N or M?*, ''Tis a mother's privilege' to circumvent the rules of wartime censorship when writing to her children (Christie, 1941/1962: 50). Shortly before this, in 1938, Virginia Woolf would write in *Three Guineas* of the 'freedom from unreal loyalties' characteristic not just of mothers, but of all women (1938/1986: 90). Christie's monstrous mothers suggest that she too recognised the disjuncture between women and patriarchy, but her recognition of the unassimilable excess of maternal signification was accompanied not by hope but by fear.[16]

Describing the widespread popularisation of Freudian ideas in the interwar period, Heather Ingman offers a cultural diagnosis that closely approximates the condition of Christie's fiction:

> As long as the classic Freudian paradigm dominates, the mother will continue to be seen as an obstacle to individual growth, the point of danger, whilst the father will be the place of rescue, of separation and rationality. (Ingman, 1998: 23)

When 'Papa Poirot' is available to identify the transgressive body, he undoubtedly figures as a place of rescue and rationality – but what will happen in his absence? Without Poirot's capacity to cut through the sentimental gendered assumptions of interwar Britain, what hope has patriarchal society of identifying and containing this maternal monster of its own making?[17]

Some answers to these questions might be found in *N or M?*, a novel which raises the spectre of the phallic mother to new heights at the same time that it offers new hope of protection against this uncontainable phenomenon. That hope is Tuppence Beresford, but the task in front of her is far from easy, as she must battle not only against the force of the 'fifth column', but also against the prejudices of a patriarchy that believes that women belong at home, not at war. The novel first appeared in 1941, the third year of the Second World War. The underlying causality or return of the repressed that threatened the social bond in *Murder in Mesopotamia* had indeed become a reality, and the emphasis in the opening chapter falls upon the powerlessness experienced by Tommy and Tuppence Beresford – a powerlessness that would have been common to much of the nation and Christie's readership. The Beresfords have been deprived of agency by age and they crave activity as a distraction from the pain of wartime consciousness: 'I wish we could find a job of some kind,' sighs Tuppence. 'It's so rotten when one has time to think' (Christie, 1941/1962: 8).[18]

Fortunately help is at hand in the shape of spymaster Mr Grant, who employs Tommy, as a trustworthy former employee, to uncover a network of fifth column activity, improbably emanating from a boarding house on the south coast of England. Tuppence, as a middle-aged woman, is surplus to requirements, and is left to go it alone – an act that paradoxically manages to simultaneously assert both her loyalty and disloyalty to the patriarchy! Significantly, Mr Grant must turn to these insiders-cum-outsiders because of corruption at the heart of Britain's own secret services. In a landscape of paranoia, no one can be trusted – not even the harmless looking residents of 'Sans Souci'; all of whom, in true genre style, are offered as suitable subjects of suspicion. No one is quite who they seem, and from the outset the emphasis falls on the process of reading bodily signifiers. Race and national identity, it is suggested, are written on the body: hence the ease with which landlady Mrs Perenna's closet-Irishness is unveiled. Although she pretends her name is Spanish, her Irishness is there to be read in her face. This is another mother who refuses the 'unreal loyalties' of patriarchy, as is revealed in an impassioned speech to Tuppence:

> 'I'm sick of the cruelty – the unfairness of this world. I'd like to smash it and break it – and let us all start again near to the earth and without these rules and laws and the tyranny of nation over nation.' (Christie, 1941/1962: 185)

But even as the corporeal inscription of Mrs Perenna's dubious national identity reassures the anxious wartime reader of the ease with which the 'Other' might be detected in their midst, the novel moves to undermine this reassurance with a reminder of the specifically heinous nature of 'fifth column' activity. The fifth columnist is precisely not a German-in-disguise, but is instead 'one of us', and thus seemingly undetectable.[19]

However, even the problem of detecting the common-or-garden spy in disguise proves rather too taxing for the devastatingly ordinary Tommy. His problems stem from the uncertainty of racial boundaries – the terrifying fact that German and Briton are marked more by proximity than by difference. In an absurd mid-story climax, Tommy succeeds in identifying a German waiter, only to find a rather more serious threat waiting in the wings:

> The fellow spoke perfect English, true, but then many Germans did. They had perfected their English by years in English restaurants. And the racial type was not unlike. Fair-haired, blue-eyed – often betrayed by the shape of the head – yes, the head – where had he seen a head lately . . .
>
> Had he been blind up to now? That jovial florid face – the face of a 'hearty Englishman' – was only a mask. Why had he not seen it all along for what it was – the face of a bad-tempered overbearing Prussian officer. (Christie, 1941/1962: 142–4)

Although the stakes could not be higher, Christie cannot resist 'making fun of heroes' (Light, 1991: 70). The scene of discovery is played for laughs and edged with slapstick – as is Tommy's eventual rescue. Gagged and bound in his adversary's cellar, he attracts help by snoring in morse code (1941/1962: 181). This refusal of seriousness was integral to British society's attempts to assimilate and cope with the overwhelming reality of the Second World War. Writing in 1943 of her experiences as a fire watcher, Inez Holden describes popular attitudes to the war as 'a kind of gigantic debunk of the whole Nazi melodrama' (Holden, 1943: 7), and in *N or M?* a significant part of Christie's narrative of reassurance emerges from exactly the same deflationary impulse. After all, if Tommy Beresford can defeat the Nazis through snoring, there is surely some hope for the marginally better equipped soldiers, sailors and pilots of the British armed forces.

However, simply to focus on the element of farce is to do an injustice to the intrepid Tuppence Beresford, who, fortunately for the nation, is a rather more serious character than her husband. She is also a more effective reader of bodies. In an appropriately gendered division of labour, Tommy struggles to decode the markers of national identity, while Tuppence is confronted by the enigma of the maternal:

> 'Would you really shoot me?' said Tuppence.
>
> Anna answered quietly:
>
> 'You need not try to get round me. In the last war my son was killed, my Otto. I was thirty-eight, then – I am sixty-two now – but I have not forgotten.'
>
> Tuppence looked at the broad, impassive face. It reminded her of the Polish woman, Vanda Polonska. That same frightening ferocity and singleness of purpose. Motherhood – unrelenting! So, no doubt, felt many quiet Mrs Joneses and Mrs Smiths all over England. There was no arguing with the female of the species – the mother deprived of her young. (Christie, 1941/1962: 200–1)

From these observations comes Tuppence's long-awaited revelation regarding the identity of the super-spy. Held at gunpoint by one psychotic mother, Tuppence is reminded of another woman driven mad by maternity, and is thus alerted to the signifiers that will enable her to correctly read the body of the spy. And who *is* the fiendish double agent, N or M? None other than the insipid young mother Mrs Sprot. This is the paradox that makes the mother such a threat to patriarchal society. Although defined in terms of her corporeality, the mother is more precisely a spectral presence, and it is this invisibility that makes motherhood the ideal cloak with which to disguise the agency of the spy. Puzzling over the reasons for everyone's failure to suspect Mrs Sprot, Tuppence makes an observation that succinctly answers her own question: 'And all the time . . . it was that milk and water creature we just thought of as – Betty's mother' (1941/1962: 209).

Thus the novel concludes with the authentic mother's successful decoding of the signifiers of disloyal maternity. Tuppence's ability to identify, to 'name' authenticity, plays a vital role in holding at bay the threat of dissolution represented by both the spy and the mother. The literal body of the mother can be seen to merge with the symbolic or national body, the land over whose inert body the war is being fought. In one sense we might read this as an Oedipal struggle for access to the mother's body, but, ironically, given the threat of invasion by a stronger power, it is a battle which must be won by the son rather than the father. Mrs Sprot is thus not simply an inauthentic mother, she is also, as a spy, the agent of a 'false' or inauthentic national body, that is, Germany. Nazi Germany thus becomes a national body that would invade the borders of the 'true' nation (Britain) and fatally dissolve the difference between the two. 'The abject', argues Elizabeth Grosz, 'demonstrates the impossibility of clear-cut borders, lines of demarcation, divisions between . . . order and disorder' (1990a: 89), and to be invaded, to lose the integrity of national boundaries, is precisely that which threatens and most terrifies the patriarchal nation state. Invasion's abject dissolution of the clear-cut distinction between the national 'I' and its 'Others' is microcosmically enacted in the spy story. Within this narrative, the mother must metonymically function as a tangible terror in place of a wider, scarcely articulable fear. Succinctly paraphrasing Kristeva, Grosz suggests that:

> By naming or speaking [the abject], [writers] can maintain an imperilled hold on the symbolic and a stable speaking position. Naming it established a distance or space which may keep its dangers at bay. To speak of the object is to protect oneself against it while at the same time relying on its energetic resources. (Grosz, 1990a: 93)

Just as the presentation of the corpse can act as such a naming for the imperilled cultural consciousness of post-First-World-War Britain, so the identification of the authentic mother (and by extension the national body) acts as a reassertion of stability within the new dislocations of the Second World War. And just as the substantial body of the corpse was essential in order to give validity to the therapeutic function of *Murder on the Links*, so the threat of the fifth column can only be made 'real' through its manifestation in the sacred heart of the nation: the mother.

Christie's interwar fiction thus both reveals and attempts to heal the ruptures of social organisation. In her construction of the grievable body she offers a talisman against death's fragmentation and dissolution, a sacrifice to ameliorate the wounds of war, and in Tuppence Beresford she offers reassurance, in the face of a second war, that women/mothers are loyal to the patriarchal nation state. Yet Christie's smooth surfaces and romantic resolutions cannot ultimately disguise the dislocations of the 'underlying causality' upon which society is founded, and it is these contradictions that make themselves felt throughout her narratives of reassurance in the figures of the semiotic body and the Frankensteinian monster of destructive maternity. However, although these abject bodies remind us of what interwar society would both depend upon and deny, Christie's narrative does not seek to explore these contradictions. Rather, in her hands, the detective novel becomes a secular, and very modern, manifestation of the sacred.

Grosz concludes that 'where the poetic anticipates a language to come, the sacred attempts to stabilize a situation of decay or breakdown' (1990a: 99), thus evoking the traditional understanding of detective fiction as a conservative form, which seeks to contain the disruptive elements of society. But what exactly is the relationship between transgression and punishment in Christie's fiction? It would be difficult to argue that Christie has any interest in the law that must intervene after the criminal has been identified, and her fictions famously depend upon the premise that every character is guilty in thought if not in deed. There is no scent of 'magnolia blossoms' about Christie's willingness to sacrifice any 'body' in order to activate the tension between the semiotic and the symbolic that underpins her criminal fictions. It is also difficult to see in her problematic bodies the bloodless generic product of which Chandler accuses her. Too much attention has been paid to the resolution of Christie's fictions: the solving of the crime and the concluding ritual of marriage. By reading *before* the ending, however, we might detect the extent to which she pleasurably and mischievously permits free play to the repressed desires and anxieties of her society. The sacred cannot operate without first identifying its taboos, and Christie's 'sacred' texts need to be seen in this context. Alison Light (1991: 64) is right to complain of the absence of Christie from British cultural history, for within these fictions there lies not the empty structures of pure form, but rather a carefully targeted articulation of socio-cultural anxieties, designed to provide a subtly modulated fictional therapy for her constantly evolving readership.

NOTES

1. Miss Marple's harder edges are extensively explored by Shaw and Vanacker (1991), while Alison Light deplores the construction of a nostalgic 'heritage' Christie, divorced from her actual socio-political context. She also succinctly summarises the prejudices of the genre fiction canon:

   It may be respectable to write about Conan Doyle or even Raymond Chandler but Christie remains beyond the pale, the producer of harmless drivel, an unsuitable case for a critic. (Light, 1991: 64)
2. A prime example of woman's deceptive façade is found in *Cards on the Table* (1935), where mild-mannered Anne Meredith undergoes an awesome metamorphosis from 'a timid little creature' (115) into a psychotic opportunist murderer.
3. Hastings's problems with women emerge from his sentimental romanticism. He exemplifies a pre-war Britishness that worships a passive mode of helpless femininity that is all too easily feigned. His gullibility in the face of the feminine, alongside his constant demand for action, aligns him more closely with the conservative traditions of Bulldog Drummond than with the modernity of Hercule Poirot (Light, 1991: 73–4).
4. Whether or not the period from 1918 to 1939 can actually be seen as historically coherent is, of course, debatable. The first half of the century might equally be read as one long period of hostilities, broken only by intermittent 'truces', while the distinction between the 1920s and the 1930s is as nebulous and hard to pin down as that which divides the 'Victorian' from the 'modern'.
5. Orwell's impressions are supported by the observations of the social historian David Cannadine, who comments that 'detective novels, rarely concerned with violent death in the years before 1914 became, at the hands of Agatha Christie and Dorothy L. Sayers, more murderous and macabre' (1981: 231).
6. This detachment is well illustrated by Stephen Knight, who argues that the 'emotionless treatment of death is a constant in Christie' (Knight, 1980: 115, 123).
7. *The Body in the Library* (Miss Marple, 1942); *Murder in Mesopotamia* (Poirot, 1936); *The Mysterious Affair at Styles* (Poirot, 1920); *Murder on the Orient Express* (Poirot, 1934).
8. The value of this corporeal integrity is connected to Alison Light's conception of detective fiction as a 'literature of convalescence'. Both the books themselves and the bodies within them can be seen to have a restorative function within a society recuperating from the national debilitation of cataclysmic war.
9. The faint can also be read as a 'redeemable' death, with resurrection guaranteed. It is not confined to women, and when men are afflicted by this 'feminine' trait, as is the war-survivor Jack Renauld, the phenomenon also suggests the perceived postwar emasculation of men.
10. Cinderella's plucky intervention is followed by the curious reward of marriage to Hastings. As Grossvogel (1983) and Knight (1980) have observed, romance is integral to Christie's fiction, playing a key structural role in the symbolic restoration of order that typically concludes the detective novel. Such a conclusion 'asserts that a new family order can rise from the family disturbed by murder; it has a healing renovating effect similar, in its often bathetic way, to the final sequence in a Shakespearean tragedy when the emergent controller of the

wounded state speaks in calm, ordered tones' (Knight, 1980: 116). Yet there is no doubt that Christie's fictions end with some remarkably curious couplings, and these odd couples suggest that her marriages might also be the bearers of wider signification. Priestman (1991) comments on Christie's penchant for certain character types, including the military gent. This type is something of a dinosaur, uncertain of his role in the new postwar Britain, but a quite disproportionate number of these Colonel Mustards are rewarded at the end of the narrative by marriage to a modern young woman. This curiously sterile coupling represents a bizarre bourgeois revolution, whereby a phalanx of various sensible, lively young women become the backseat drivers of a jaded patriarchy, steering their outmoded masculine counterparts to safe havens in the most distant (and unchanging) outposts of Empire (as Cinderella will do with Hastings).

11. The patterns of crime fiction also echo the fundamental consolatory process embodied in Christianity. In an endlessly repeated ritual, the body of Christ is sacrificed and then miraculously resurrected.
12. I discuss this long period of war-anticipation in Chapters 2 and 3 of *Women's Fiction of the Second World War* (1996).
13. This process began with Christie's interwar contemporaries, writers such as Vera Brittain and Winifred Holtby, but for more recent work on the representation of women in the period see Melman, 1988; Leonardi, 1989; Light, 1991 and Ingman, 1998.
14. Between the wars, and in the aftermath of the suffrage victory, the feminist movement was itself split between the equality feminists of Lady Rhondda's six point group, and those such as Eleanor Rathbone who advocated the assertion of difference, and the need for specific legislation to improve the conditions of women in their traditional roles as mothers. Christie's own life is difficult to fit into either paradigm, although it has been observed that she shows no particular fondness for the career woman. Nonetheless, her independence as a writer and her fascination with travel suggest a woman unlikely to have been satisfied by purely domestic horizons.
15. She is also jealous of her stylish cousin Theresa, and keen to refurbish her wardrobe in order to compete, but this is not presented as the primary motivation behind her actions.
16. Woolf described this freedom from 'loyalty to old schools, old colleges, old churches, old ceremonies, old countries' as the 'fourth great teacher of the daughters of educated men' (1938/1986: 90). In other words, she saw disloyalty to patriarchy as one of the key factors that would enable women, as 'outsiders', to conceive of alternatives to the destructive tyrannies of the status quo.
17. It is worth noting that the 1940 Poirot novel *One, Two, Buckle My Shoe* lays repeated emphasis upon the weariness of Poirot (1940/1993: 187, 193, 215). He suggests his time has passed and that a new generation must take up the challenge of maintaining the integrity of society. The moment of 'modernity' he represented has passed, and perhaps with it whatever claims Christie had to be modern. Christie seems uncertain about the pressure for social change emerging from the context of the Second World War and, in passing Poirot's baton to Tommy and Tuppence, she is, to say the least, making a conservative choice of successor.
18. It should perhaps be noted that, in terms of detection, Tommy and Tuppence Beresford bear more resemblance to Hastings than to Poirot.
19. The particular cultural anxieties opened up by the spectre of the other as proximate are discussed in Chapter 6.

2

When Violet Eyes are Smiling: The Love Stories of Raymond Chandler

> The love story and the detective story cannot exist, not only in the same book – one might also say the same culture. Modern outspokenness has utterly destroyed the romantic dream on which love feeds . . . There is nothing left to write about but death, and the detective story is a tragedy with a happy ending. (Chandler, 1949, quoted in Hiney, 1997: 76)

> [A]n understanding of virtually any aspect of modern Western culture must be, not merely incomplete, but damaged in its central substance to the degree that it does not incorporate a critical analysis of modern homo/heterosexual definition. (Sedgwick, 1990/1994: 1)

> '. . . don't scatter my ashes over the blue Pacific. I like the worms better. Did you know that worms are of both sexes and that any worm can love any other worm?' (Chandler, 1939/1948: 184–5)

Philip Marlowe, the detective hero of Raymond Chandler's hard-boiled American crime novels, has become almost synonymous with the concept of the tough guy. This seminal figure emerged initially from the pulp magazines of the 1920s, and has come in turn to symbolise a particular form of urban American masculinity. But to what extent does the iconic tough guy of legend actually resemble the hard men of Chandler's fiction? In this chapter I want to consider not only the definition of 'toughness', but also the question of what it serves to hide. For Chandler's fiction, like that of Christie, does not entirely conform to its reputation, and on closer examination his studies of urban America seem to resemble detective fiction only in so far as their subject matter is betrayal. These criminal fictions are, first and foremost, narratives of besieged masculinity and love corrupted that seek to explain the paradoxical vulnerability of men within patriarchal society. Arguably the best examples of this paradigm are provided by Chandler's first two novels, *The Big Sleep* (1939) and *Farewell, My Lovely* (1940). These novels, which form the substantial focus of this chapter, together comprise a dynamic engagement with both the formula of detection and the definition of American masculinity. *The Long Good-Bye* (1953), to which I turn in conclusion, is often cited as Chandler's 'mature' postwar masterpiece, yet ultimately it reduplicates rather than develops the paradigms established by the earlier fiction, acting as a long drawn out and painful reiteration of a familiar set of anxieties. These anxieties, which haunt Marlowe throughout his career, are fundamentally focused around desire, and remorselessly reveal the detective as tough guy to be far more defenceless and exposed than his effete classical counterpart.

So what does it mean to be a tough guy in the fiction of Raymond Chandler? In his analysis of 'language as power' in American detective fiction Scott Christianson argues that the tough guy attempts to make sense of a chaotic and fragmented world through the assertion of linguistic control over his environment. He attempts to 'dominate the world, or come to terms with it, by defining it through tough talk, wisecracks, and evocative hard-boiled conceits' (1989: 159). And there can be no doubting the power of Chandler's conceits. The opening of *The Big Sleep* provides a typically complex example of his prose, while also introducing the leitmotif of patriarchal power. In countless ways Chandler's novels work and rework the figure of the powerful and wealthy father betrayed by the 'feminine' – whether that be in the form of wayward daughters, errant wives, or even his own uncontrollable body. This ambiguous figure is seldom central to the action, which is rather situated among the 'middle management' of masculinity – the aspirational would-be inheritors of patriarchal power, who still have everything to lose or gain within a competitive and corrupting symbolic order. The father is instead a character of Chandler's beginnings and endings, the unseen power who must, paradoxically, be both defended and defied. *The Big Sleep* thus opens not with scene-setting, or with a substantial description of Philip Marlowe, but with a series of striking juxtapositions that reveal the detective's relationship to this monstrous power.[1]

Marlowe has been summoned to the home of General Sternwood, a paralysed patriarch whose descent into death has been halted only by his need to set his estate in order. Something of a King Lear figure, the General in Chandler's dystopian vision has been blessed with only two daughters, who unfortunately bear closer resemblance to Goneril and Regan than to the dutiful Cordelia. Marlowe's task will be to contain the threats generated by the instability of these wayward women. On his first visit to the Sternwood mansion, Marlowe finds the General sitting 'like a newborn spider' in the midst of a hellish jungle of hothouse orchids, sinister plants 'with nasty meaty leaves and stalks like the newly washed fingers of dead men' (1939/1948: 13). Marlowe is offered a drink, which the General proceeds to consume vicariously:

> I sipped the drink. The old man licked his lips watching me, over and over again, drawing one lip slowly across the other with a funereal absorbtion, like an undertaker dry-washing his hands. (1939/1948: 15)

The descriptions of the General and his surroundings evoke contradictory images of vulnerability and power. The General himself is as dependent as a newborn baby, but he sits at the centre of a deadly web. The vampiric quality of the old man's gaze reminds us of the vestiges of patriarchal power that cling to his crumbling form despite its frailty – a frailty that is nonetheless emphasised by the ironic simile that follows. Sternwood's transitional status between the living and the dead is metaphorically figured in the image of the expectant undertaker. Tasting and acting by proxy, the old man becomes both corpse and priest, as he passes on to Marlowe the mantle of his parental authority.

This condensed metaphoricity evokes possibilities of meaning far in excess of its apparent brevity, and moves beyond the constraints of dialogic 'tough talking'. Yet this rich language of suggestion is as typical of Marlowe as his witticisms: tough talk is integral to the hard-boiled detective, but it is not all of him.[2] This returns us to the concept of toughness, and the extent to which Marlowe can actually be seen to live up to his own reputation. The question of 'what is toughness' can, on one level, be answered quite simply. Toughness acts as a synonym for and an index of masculinity. Within this context, tough talk might be seen as the act through which masculinity is constituted and reinforced. Tough talk asserts the boundaries of the masculine. But, in the same way that Chandler's hard-boiled conceits far exceed the simple inscription of male power, producing an intricately wrought excess of subtle signification, so the depiction of masculinity comes in Chandler's fiction to exceed the parameters of patriarchal prescription and, in so doing, destabilises the very norms which hard-boiled detection works so ostentatiously to enforce.

Chandler's writing pays detailed attention to the male body. Within the Marlowe novels, the inscription of masculinity is not solely discursive, rather it is always located in the corporeal. Although much of the textual substance is comprised of competitive tough talking between the detective and a succession of cops, criminals, hard men and gangsters, Marlowe actually has little respect for men who are constituted through tough talk alone – as is witnessed by his dismissal of the gambler 'Mendy' Menendez in *The Long Good-Bye*: 'You're not big, you're just loud' (1953/1959: 294). Size, substance, the body – these things matter in Marlowe's world – but, contrastingly, the materiality of the detective's being is most frequently emphasised through markers of vulnerability such as age, alcohol, violence and desire.

These four factors act repeatedly to remind the detective of the limits of his discursive construction. They create a tension between the detective as a verbal icon, and the detective as a middle-aged, battered and hungover man, drawn by desire into yet another disastrous liaison. Thus it is that masculinity within Chandler's fiction emerges from a tension between exteriority and interiority, between the verbal projection of a coherent self and the bodily knowledge of a chaotic, fragmented subjectivity. In *Male Matters*, his acute analysis of masculine anxiety, Calvin Thomas describes men's fear of an embodiment which has always already been displaced on to the feminine. He argues that masculinity's self-assertion is based upon the repression of its corporeal dimension, and the refusal to acknowledge 'the role of the body in the production of thought, speech and writing' (1996: 13). But, although masculinity might claim such a pristine origin, in fact it is faced with a constant struggle to evade the traces of the body:

> Masculinity cannot represent its supposedly immaculate self-construction without giving itself over to discursive productions in which the always potentially messy question of the body cannot fail to emerge. (Thomas, 1996: 13)

That Philip Marlowe aspires to the dream of 'immaculate self-construction' is evident from his extreme biographical reticence. The series of novels repeats rather than develops our knowledge of the detective, whose being is marked both by the absence of a past and an extremely limited acquaintance. Even at his most expansive, Philip Marlowe keeps his history a secret:

> I'm a licensed private investigator and have been for quite a while. I'm a lone wolf, unmarried, getting middle-aged, and not rich. I've been in jail more than once and I don't do divorce business. I like liquor and women and chess and a few other things. The cops don't like me too well, but I know a couple I get along with. I'm a native son, born in Santa Rosa, both parents dead, no brothers or sisters, and when I get knocked off in a dark alley some time . . . nobody will feel that the bottom has dropped out of his or her life. (Chandler, 1953/1959: 79)

Marlowe's masculinity thus stands in splendid isolation, and is regularly reconstituted through tough talk or an equally tough refusal of talk. In each novel he asserts his identity through the verbal combat of aggression or wit, depending on the opposition, or through a stubborn withholding of knowledge. However, the detective also asserts his masculinity through the protection of the weak, both male and female, and through a sentimental, paternalistic romanticism that stands in stark contrast to the isolated existentialism of the tough-guy persona.

In his biography of Chandler, Tom Hiney attributes something of Marlowe's duality to Chandler's own surprisingly delicate sensibilities. Hiney reports that Chandler experienced considerable difficulties in adapting James Cain's *Double Indemnity* for Hollywood consumption. Already struggling against the confines of the notorious Production Code, Chandler's task was further complicated by his own resistance to sexually explicit narrative:[3]

> Synthetic stallions like James Cain have made a fetish of pure orgasms, which the middle classes seem to regard as a semi-

> respectable adjunct to raising a family. The literary glorification of lust leads to emotional impotence, because the love story has little or nothing to do with lust. (Quoted in Hiney, 1997: 142)

Chandler's hostility draws attention to something that has long been acknowledged as an integral part of his own writing, namely the extent to which a chivalric conception of romance co-exists with the depiction of violence, cynicism and urban malaise (Knight, 1980: 137–8; Cawelti, 1976: 177–82). It is a pertinent reminder that, unlike later 'hard-boiled' writers such as Mickey Spillane, Chandler tried at some level to resist the automatic linkage between sex and violence. Indeed, in spite of a considerable quantity of very erotic description, his novels are remarkable for containing hardly any sex at all. What sex there is takes place off stage, suggesting that Chandler is more concerned with the process of desire than with its consummation – particularly in the case of the detective himself.[4] Yet despite the absence of heterosexual sex, Marlowe's world is redolent with the erotic. From where does this mystique emerge? Can tough guys fall in love – and if they can, who or what might form a legitimate object of their romantic desires?

It is difficult to build a case for Chandler's female characters as objects of desire. Although outwardly attractive, they inwardly disappoint on the grounds of either psychosis or neurosis. Chandler is a skilled deployer of both the *femme fatale* and the deadly innocent, but the depiction of these women is devoid of sensuality. Rather, these representations of the feminine are harsh and unforgiving, delineating a female sexuality that is perceived as threatening even as it attracts. The female characters of *The Big Sleep* provide a typical illustration. We might perhaps expect the opening description of Carmen Sternwood, nymphomaniac and murderer, to be less than flattering:

> Her eyes were slate-grey, and had almost no expression when they looked at me. She came over near me and smiled with her mouth and she had little sharp predatory teeth, as white as fresh orange pith and as shiny as porcelain. They glistened between her thin too taut lips. Her face lacked colour and didn't look too healthy. (Chandler, 1939/1948: 10)

And indeed, before long Carmen has revealed a tendency to hiss, a face like 'scraped bone' (1939/1948: 153) and a laugh that reminds

Marlowe of 'rats behind the wainscoting' (68, 151). More surprisingly, however, the other women of the novel fare little better. Although initial descriptions of both 'Blonde Agnes' and Carmen's sister, Vivien Regan, offer the promise of uncomplicated sensuality, on closer acquaintance they turn out to be not far removed from the psychotic Carmen. Before many chapters have passed, Agnes is biting the ankles of the detective and letting out a 'low animal wail' (1939/1948: 87, 93), while Vivien's response to Marlowe's cold shoulder is to tear a handkerchief to shreds with her teeth (1939/1948: 148). Women's position on the perpetual verge of a nervous breakdown makes them an unsuitable site of erotic interest within the text. But if the detective's 'legitimate' heterosexual desire is so seldom either fulfilled or ratified, how and on to what is desire displaced?

The answer returns us to masculinity. Sensuality within Chandler's fiction resides predominantly in the depiction of men. Within these fictions so marked by the absence of satisfaction, the location of the erotic is displaced from its usual locus, the objectified female body, on to the less familiar corporeality of the male. This potentially transgressive strategy of evoking the homoerotic is, however, at least in part deployed as a defence mechanism. By focusing on a taboo – a forbidden object – the impossibility of the consummation of desire is redoubled, and the lack that drives both the narratives of detection and romance is given renewed impetus in the hopelessness of its quest. Georges Bataille suggests that the aim of the erotic is to 'substitute for their persistent discontinuity a miraculous continuity between two beings'; but, he goes on, 'this continuity is chiefly to be felt in the anguish of desire, when it is still inaccessible, still an impotent, quivering yearning' (1962/1987: 19). Chandler's tough guys, in their persistent quest for answers and connections, are defined by their awareness of lack. They show some understanding of the provisional and precarious nature of their existence. This glimmer of comprehension of the 'human condition' is not manifested by those who are only pretenders to the mantle of toughness, characters who attempt to assert their triumph over lack in an excess of empty talk. Marlowe, in his isolation, is haunted by the bodies that surround him, bodies that he knows he cannot possess, but which he seeks, in masculine self-defence (or self-assertion), to explain and contain.

However, the apparent object of his investigations is seldom what actually drives his search. In *The Big Sleep*, for example, Marlowe is ostensibly hired to neutralise the threat posed to Carmen Sternwood by the blackmailing Arthur Gwynn Geiger. However, the subtext of his employment, never officially acknowledged by General Sternwood or by Marlowe, is the search for the missing 'big man', Rusty Regan. Regan is a romantic figure, 'a curly-headed Irishman from Clonmel, with sad eyes and a smile as wide as Wilshire Boulevard', and the General describes him as 'the breath of life to me' (1939/1948: 16). As part of his duty to the metaphorical 'big man' that is the dying patriarch, Marlowe pursues the romantic icon of the literal big man. By the end of the novel this quest has come to dominate the narrative, and the women he was hired to protect are revealed as perpetrators rather than victims of the narrative's criminality.[5]

However, to define the object of the detective's desire as masculine might in itself be seen as a contentious issue. Tom Hiney, for example, acknowledges the critical speculation as to whether Chandler's fiction reveals a 'latent homosexuality', but chooses to take a fairly circumspect approach to the subject. Hiney argues that suggestions of homosexuality 'pointedly failed to make allowances for the genre within which Chandler wrote', concluding that:

> Like westerns, hard-boiled detective stories had always held up strong, handsome and honest men for heroes. That these men were invariably bachelors, and invariably got on best with other bachelors, was a part of the tough genre. (Hiney, 1997: 246)

This strikes me as a fascinating argument. It is not Chandler's fiction, nor his hero, that might be read as homoerotic, but the whole genre within which he was working. Hiney's otherwise informative biography thus evades the issue of same-sex desire within Chandler's fiction, perhaps on account of the singular lack of evidence to suggest any homosexual *activity* on the part of the *writer*. However, as Judith Butler pertinently observes, 'there are structures of psychic homosexuality within heterosexual relations, and structures of psychic heterosexuality within gay and lesbian sexuality and relationships' (1990: 121).[6] The evidence or otherwise of Chandler's life cannot detract from the homoeroticism that characterises his fiction, and the implications of this investment in the homosocial deserves to be considered.[7]

In his essay 'The Simple Art of Murder', Chandler sets out probably his most famous definition of the hard-boiled hero:

> [D]own these mean streets a man must go who is not himself mean, who is neither tarnished nor afraid. The detective in this kind of story must be such a man. He is the hero, he is everything. He must be a complete man and a common man and yet an unusual man. He must be, to use a rather weathered phrase, a man of honour, by instinct, by inevitability, without thought of it, and certainly without saying it. He must be the best man in his world and a good enough man for any world. (Chandler, 1950/1964: 198)

Quite a prescription – and one usually assumed to apply to Philip Marlowe. But does it? Or rather, to what extent is it appropriate? Marlowe is a flawed hero, something he would be the first to admit. In *Farewell, My Lovely*, for example, although his visit to the dissolute and distinctly unlovely Jessie Florian leaves him feeling disgusted both with her and himself, his ethical revulsion is not sufficient to effect a change of strategy:

> A lovely old woman. I liked being with her. I liked getting her drunk for my own sordid purposes. I was a swell guy. I enjoyed being me. You find almost anything under your hand in my business, but I was beginning to be a little sick at my stomach. (Chandler, 1940/1949: 33)

Yet for all his awareness of the corruption and decay that surrounds him, he is not a man much given to personal introspection. When he feels despair, he does not even tell his usual confidant, the reader. *The Lady in the Lake* provides a typical example of Marlowe's alienation. Frustrated and humiliated, he can only describe himself from without:

> I looked at my watch. I looked at the wall. I looked at nothing.
>
> I put the liquor bottle away and went over to the washbowl to rinse the glass out. When I had done that I washed my hands and bathed my face in cold water and looked at it . . . The face under the hair had a sick look. I didn't like the face at all. (Chandler, 1944/1952: 140)

Marlowe is a man of actions and reactions, and his honour emerges not from a clearly defined code of practice, but rather from instinct. As Chandler puts it, his honour is inevitable, but it is also 'without thought'. Marlowe does not define himself as the 'one good man' of hard-boiled legend, and neither should we, as critics, confine Chandler's description of the ideal to the figure of Marlowe. I want, thus, to suggest a shift, and argue that Marlowe is not the 'one good man', but is instead in search of that man. He is looking for and desires this good man, both as an ideal to set in the balance against the void of corruption and despair, and as a lover with whom he might form an idealised homosocial union, located not in the tarnished present, but in another pre-symbolic arena. He seeks exactly that which is prohibited by the laws of masculine self-fashioning: the excess of the body, or what might be seen in Kristevan terms as a 'semiotic' space outside the confines of institutionalised heterosexuality.[8]

Marlowe's tough talk creates a verbal symbolic self that asserts the accepted form of patriarchal masculinity while obliterating all others, including its own vulnerable body. This self-inscription, like the symbolic order of which it is a part, rests upon the unstable and irrepressible foundations of the semiotic: it is, in consequence, both self-creation and self-denial. In his quest for the big man he responds illicitly to the pre-verbal impulses of a 'semiotic masculinity', rooted in the body, and this desiring force, like the semiotic bodies of Agatha Christie's fiction, cannot be wholly contained by the 'text's rational logic' (Grosz, 1990b: 152). It is Judith Butler who offers perhaps the most useful insight into the pervasive melancholy of Marlowe's position:

> To the extent that homosexual attachments remain unacknowledged within normative heterosexuality, they are not merely constituted as desires that emerge and subsequently become prohibited. Rather, these are desires that are proscribed from the start. And when they do emerge on the far side of the censor, they may well carry that mark of impossibility with them, performing, as it were, as the impossible within the possible. As such, they will not be attachments that can be openly grieved. (Butler, 1993: 236)

In his search for the lost ideal man, Marlowe pursues a desire that cannot be articulated in an attempt to compensate for a loss that can never be grieved.

Why, though, do I see the novels as idealising the homosocial at the expense of the heterosexual? Why can't Marlowe find the ideal he seeks in a 'nice' girl, like Anne Riordan? The novels offer little in the way of explanation for the detective's refusal of nearly all offers, and the absence of heterosexual fulfilment is usually attributed by critics to the demands and limitations of the formula. However, Marlowe's desires are sufficiently complex to deserve closer attention. He seems detached, if not actively repulsed in the face of female sexuality. In a somewhat dutiful re-enactment of the Oedipal conflict, Marlowe is attracted to the many beautiful women who litter his path, but always accepts the father's prohibition. In both *The Big Sleep* and *Farewell, My Lovely*, Marlowe's erotic encounters are brought to an abrupt and premature closure by his refusal to transgress patriarchal law. 'Kissing is nice, but your father didn't hire me to sleep with you' (1939/1948: 147) comments Marlowe as he breaks the intimacy of his encounter with Vivien Regan. Similarly, in *Farewell, My Lovely*, the interruption of his embrace with Mrs Lewin Lockridge Grayle by her impotent and aged husband sends Marlowe scurrying back to a distant chair and leaves him feeling cold and uncomfortable: 'I felt nasty, as if I had picked a poor man's pocket' (1940/1949: 120). We are reminded emphatically that this is a patriarchal society in which women, no matter how powerful they might seem, ultimately all belong to somebody.

Moreover, the entire plot of *Farewell, My Lovely* can be seen as an extended exploration of the homosocial structures that facilitate men's ownership of women. Moose Malloy, who literally drags Marlowe into his story at the beginning of the novel, is hunting for 'Little Velma', the woman he left behind when he was sent to jail some eight years previously. Although Moose fairly swiftly disappears from view after committing the casual murder of a black bar-owner, Marlowe nonetheless feels drawn to him and his quest. He has, Marlowe thinks, some right to rediscover Velma, to exert his claim of ownership over her, irrespective of the passage of time. That Velma has since transformed herself into Mrs Grayle is neither here nor there as far as Marlowe is concerned: Moose has a prior claim on her as his ideal woman, the dream that kept him going throughout his years of incarceration.

However, as Marlowe's encounters with Vivien Regan and Mrs Grayle suggest, there is a distinct and significant refusal of risk evident in Marlowe's sexual encounters. This might be seen in Freudian terms as the ego's insecurity, its reluctance to face the inevitability and necessity of change and its fear of its own libidinal energy. In this context it is interesting to return to Chandler's comments on James Cain. Chandler's resistance to what he perceives as Cain's fetishisation of orgasm might be seen as indicative of a different anxiety on the part of his own texts, namely a fear of the self-annihilation associated with orgasm. In 'Beyond the Pleasure Principle' Freud argues that '[t]he pleasure principle seems actually to serve the death instincts'. In a curious paradox of self-preservation, he finds it to be constantly 'on guard against increases of stimulation from within, which would make the task of living more difficult' (Freud, 1920/1955: 63). Freud's conclusion forms a singularly apt description for the sexual self-control that characterises Philip Marlowe. Yet for all his self-containment, Marlowe cannot evade the imperatives of desire, and these repressed impulses return in displaced form. In his 'Three Essays on the Theory of Sexuality', Freud suggests the term fetishism to describe the substitution of the 'normal sexual object' by 'another which bears some relation to it, but is entirely unsuited to serve the normal sexual aim' (Freud, 1905/1953: 153):

> What is substituted for the sexual object is some part of the body (such as the foot or hair) which is in general very inappropriate for sexual purposes, or some inanimate object which bears an assignable relation to the person whom it replaces and preferably to that person's sexuality (e.g. a piece of clothing or underlinen). (Freud, 1905/1953: 153)

Continuing his definition, Freud hypothesises that an element of fetishism is characteristic of all love relations. However, in pathological circumstances it is possible that the longing for the fetish may replace the 'normal aim', and indeed, even become the '*sole* sexual object' (Freud's emphasis, 1905/1953: 154). Without wishing to pathologise Marlowe, it is nonetheless possible to suggest that Chandler's novels are built upon a series of interlocking fetishistic depictions of the male body. *Farewell, My Lovely* acts as a prime example of a paradigm replicated throughout the Marlowe novels whereby individual male body parts act as fetishes for the sexual object, which might be seen as the male body in its entirety. In a structure reminiscent of the Chinese box, or Russian doll, these 'micro'-fetishistic observations exist within a larger 'macro'-fetishistic landscape in which the body of the man, particularly but not exclusively the 'big' man, operates as a fetish for an idealised masculinity which is, ultimately, the impossible object of the detective's desire. Marlowe thus gives intense scrutiny to the specific in the hope that it will lead to the general. Confronting what might be his nemesis in the person of Jules Amthor, Psychic Consultant, Marlowe is struck more by the beauty of Amthor's hands than by the peril of his own situation. Amthor is beautiful:

> He had the palest finest white hair I ever saw. It could have been strained through silk gauze. His skin was as fresh as a rose petal. He might have been thirty-five or sixty-five. He was ageless. His hair was brushed straight back from as good a profile as Barrymore ever had. (Chandler, 1940/1949: 130–1)

However, he cannot ultimately satisfy Marlowe's questing gaze, as his criminality is too 'white collar', too cold and calculating. It cannot appeal to a detective who forgives and forgets only the brutal unpremeditated violence of semiotic masculinity. Consequently, as Marlowe's description continues, Amthor undergoes a fantastical transformation from Jekyll into Hyde, a transformation conceived in the terms of a mythical, legendary atemporality:

> His eyes were deep, far too deep. They were the depthless drugged eyes of the somnambulist. They were like a well I read about once. It was nine hundred years old, in an old castle. You could drop a stone into it and wait. You could listen and wait and then you could give up waiting and laugh and then just as you were ready to turn away a faint, minute splash would come back up to you from the bottom of that well, so tiny, so remote that you could hardly believe a well like that possible.
>
> His eyes were deep like that. And they were also eyes without expression, without soul, eyes that could watch lions tear a man to pieces and never change, that could watch a man impaled and screaming in the hot sun with his eyelids cut off. (1940/1949: 131)

Amthor metamorphoses into a monster, a traditional trial for the questing hero. The mythic quality of Amthor's villainy reminds us that Marlowe is this questing knight in search of an ideal, and in *Farewell, My Lovely* that ideal demands to be read in terms of homosocial, if not of homosexual, desire.[9]

It is important to note that what is at stake, what is possible and what is gained in Marlowe's homosocial bonding and homoerotic encounters cannot be directly equated with his heterosexual encounters. It requires a different set of critical and analytic paradigms to articulate and interpret these textual impulses. Eve Kosofsky Sedgwick has argued that the end of the nineteenth century can be seen as a period increasingly embroiled in the construction of polarised binary categories of identity, a process of 'sexual specification or species-formation' (1990/1994: 9). This new development, she argues, 'left no space in the culture exempt from the potent incoherences of homo/heterosexual definition' (1990/1994: 2). The interpretation of Chandler's work has largely existed within this paradigm, and it is this polarising critical tendency, this insistence on either/or which has made it so difficult to read the fluid, polyvalent sexual signifiers of his fiction. To restore the complexity and ambiguity that mark the bodies of Chandler's fiction, this binarism must be deconstructed.

I want, though, to begin this process by focusing on the most fundamental binarism, that is, the constitutive division between self and other. From the moment that the child is cut off from the ideal imaginary unity of the pre-symbolic dyad, the subject's existence is predicated upon an acknowledgement of loss. For Freud this critical moment is located in the Oedipal crisis, when the law of the father asserts its authority and shatters the child's conception of its symbiotic union with the mother. For Lacan the crisis is located in the mirror stage, where the child makes a crucial misrecognition. Mistaking its image for itself, it believes itself to be complete and unified, when it remains in reality a mass of uncontrollable drives and desires. The gap between the ideal and the real torments the subject, underpinning the impossible desires of adult life. However, for the hard-boiled detective, perhaps the most telling formulation of the subject's precarious status comes from Georges Bataille:

> Each being is distinct from all others. His birth, his death, the events of his life may have an interest for others, but he alone is directly concerned in them. He is born alone. He dies alone. Between one being and another, there is a gulf, a discontinuity . . . We are discontinuous beings, individuals who perish in isolation in the midst of an incomprehensible adventure, but we yearn for our lost continuity. (Bataille, 1962/1987: 12, 15)[10]

The tension between self and other is the axis of eroticism and, Bataille argues, the 'whole business of eroticism is to destroy the self-contained character of the participators as they are in their normal lives' (1962/1987: 17). Here is the risk that so troubles Philip Marlowe. To succumb to the lure of the erotic as embodied by the women he encounters would be to jeopardise the security of his ego. However, within this formulation, Marlowe's fetishisation of the masculine reveals a curious strategy for surviving the threats of a hostile symbolic environment. Marlowe's fascination with the 'big man' can be seen to embody a shift from the threatening opposition between self and other to the security, albeit illusory, of a division between self and *more* self. By shifting the locus of his desire away from the other that is woman, Marlowe seeks security. His desire is for the big man who is both him and not him, the other for whom desire is felt, and yet also the familiar self reflected back in the mirror. While Lacan would assure us of the misplaced nature of Marlowe's trust, within the framework of the narrative, Marlowe's desires manage to navigate a path that successfully evades both the 'little death' of orgasm and the greater death that threatens him as part of his everyday life.

In this movement away from the 'other', Marlowe seeks to replicate the ideal symbiosis of the mother/child dyad – a not unfamiliar textual strategy of the 1930s and 1940s. In British crime fiction the yearning for the pre-Oedipal security symbolised by marriage or home can be seen to emerge from the threat and pressures of the Second World War,[11] but for Marlowe, this urge to retreat emerges from the ongoing hostility and corruption of the hard-boiled urban environment. However, having invested so much in both his own and others' masculinity, the ideal of Marlowe's symbiotic union could only ever be a man – but a man, as the conclusion of *Farewell, My Lovely* will show, whose masculinity is figured less in terms of toughness or aggression than of nurturance. The self-created masculinity of tough talk thus disguises a yearning for the fantasmic security of a pre-symbolic, corporeal origin, more usually associated with the maternal.

Chandler's focus on a semiotic masculinity that is in excess, outside the constraints of linear temporality, and which cannot be contained by the laws of patriarchal society, has the effect of destabilising the binary categories of sex and gender. His writing, which at one level seems only to replicate reductive gender stereotypes, can on another level be seen to undermine the foundational assumption that gender follows automatically upon the unchanging template of sex. In the words of Judith Butler:

> If gender is the cultural meanings that the sexed body assumes, then a gender cannot be said to follow from a sex in any one way . . . The presumption of a binary gender system implicitly retains the belief in a mimetic relation of gender to sex whereby gender mirrors sex or is otherwise restricted by it. When the constructed status of gender is theorized as radically independent of sex, gender itself becomes a free-floating artifice, with the consequence that *man* and *masculine* might just as easily signify a female body as a male one, and *woman* and *feminine* a male body as easily as a female one. (Butler, 1990: 6)

Butler's hypothesis is singularly appropriate for the world of Chandler's fiction where both men and women occupy the full spectrum of gendered positions from delicate femininity to brutal masculinity. Chandler's fiction is also, however, riven with paradoxes. He is capable both of crude biological determinism and of more sophisticated constructions. At the same time as suggesting that sex and gender should not automatically be equated, Chandler is also concerned to revalorise the categories of masculinity and femininity, shifting these terms out of their customary cultural contexts, and establishing his own hierarchy of ethical and physical worth.

Thus, women – in Chandler's world – do not belong in the semiotic, but in the symbolic. They conform to the pattern of a long history of American literature that has cited the domestic as a place of confinement and restraint, a space that threatens to contain and emasculate the free-flowing libidinal energies of American masculinity.[12] As Tony Hilfer has observed, the misogyny of the crime genre is 'a specialized version of the central myth of the American romance: the hero's protection of his personal identity by flight from the entangling alliances of social definition' (Hilfer, 1990: 54–5). In the urban modernity of Chandler's world, women are still expected to inhabit a domestic space, yet their desires are encoded as patterns of order and symbolic stability against which the more 'semiotic' model of masculinity is set. Deviant women, or non-conforming and dangerous women, may also exhibit semiotic tendencies: if they are situated outside the law they frequently display the symptoms of 'semiotic masculinity'. The sexually voracious Crystal Kingsley in *The Lady in the Lake* is a typical example. Not only do her kleptomaniac tendencies set her outside a series of laws her husband is anxious to respect (1944/1952: 14), but her financial independence leaves her free not to 'fuss with the little details like getting married'

(1944/1952: 45). Deviant women, such as the Sternwood girls and Mrs Grayle, are usually characterised by their independent wealth, their roving sexual appetites and the confident occupation of public spaces. They invade masculine space and can arguably be seen to be gendered as masculine. In Marlowe's eyes, however, they are still women, and as such pose a threat to his erotic security. In these terms, Marlowe's desire to save the neurotic Merle Davis in *The High Window* becomes perfectly comprehensible. She is defined by her dependency, constantly repeating a refrain that pays homage to the very woman who has exploited and abused her (1943/1951: 142, 167, 217). We see her only in interior spaces: the tomb-like Murdock house, Marlowe's sanctuary apartment (where she is allowed to inhabit the bed from which Carmen Sternwood was so unceremoniously removed) and, finally, the kitchen of her parents' house, where restored to symbolic femininity, she begins to recover from her neurosis. Her only foray into a public space turns out to be a farce, when she runs to Marlowe claiming to have murdered a corpse. This is a woman who has twice thought that she had taken action, only to be confronted with the reality of her passivity. Whenever she tries to act in her world, she faints. She wanted to kill both Bright and Vannier, but her body failed her, and the actual murders were committed by others more suited to the task. The biological determinism that stalks Merle Davis is one extreme of the complex spectrum of gender positioning that emerges from the Chandler oeuvre.

While gender representation within these novels might thus be seen to exhibit elements of Butler's 'free-floating artifice', Chandler's gender agenda is itself rather more rigidly focused. As his attribution of reward and punishment shows, it is ultimately a particular form of masculinity that is valorised: a masculinity which may be exhibited by women, but which finds its apotheosis in the iconic figure of the 'big man'.

I suggested earlier that Marlowe's quest might be read as the search for one good man, and it is in *Farewell, My Lovely* that this dynamic is most clearly delineated. Although ostensibly seeking the holy 'Grayle' that is Velma, Marlowe seems more strongly driven by a desire to re-encounter the magnificent masculine icon that is Moose Malloy:

> His skin was pale and he needed a shave. He would always need a shave. He had curly black hair and heavy eyebrows that

> almost met over his thick nose. His ears were small and neat for a man of that size and his eyes had a shine close to tears that grey eyes often seem to have. He stood like a statue, and after a long time he smiled. (Chandler, 1940/1949: 8)

The virility of Moose's constant need to shave, a traditional marker of masculinity, is undercut by the evocation of tears – an image that gives a vulnerability to Moose's otherwise monumental appearance. This vulnerability is significant. Moose may be a big man, but he is adrift in a world he scarcely recognises or understands. In *Farewell, My Lovely*, Marlowe's idealised 'big man' is constructed not as a 'tough guy' but as an outsider. Moose's masculinity is not synonymous with the patriarchal structures that form the symbolic order, and he can more readily be conceived as a manifestation of the semiotic. As Marlowe explains to the understandably nervous barman at Florian's, the seedy 'dine and dice emporium' where Moose begins his search for Velma:

> 'He's been away a long time,' I said. 'Eight years. He doesn't seem to realize how long that is, although I'd expect him to think it a lifetime. He thinks the people here should know where his girl is. Get the idea?' (1940/1949: 15)

Moose Malloy represents a form of 'pure' masculinity, outside time, and transgressing spatial boundaries. As Marlowe's early descriptions of a hand big enough to sit in and shoulders the width of a beer truck suggest, Moose is in excess of the symbolic constraints that surround him. His role in the narrative confirms this semiotic dimension. Moose enters the narrative as a semiotic irruption, a substantial return of the repressed, that wreaks havoc on the order around him. Marlowe, the 'innocent' bystander, is literally and metaphorically picked up by Moose, but, having been dragged into the big man's narrative, he seems unable to let the memory rest, and for the remainder of the novel tracks the traces of his presence across the symbolic respectability of LA. Moose frames the narrative of *Farewell, My Lovely*. He only fully emerges from underground at the beginning and the end of the novel, which is otherwise concerned with the opposite end of the social scale. While Marlowe hunts for Mrs Grayle's missing jade and ponders the mystery of Lindsay Marriot's murder, Moose's narrative returns underground, and the reader is only reminded of it by the violent traces of further semiotic irruptions, such as the murder of Jessie Florian. That in the end the repressed 'underlying causality' of Moose's crude criminality should be intimately connected to the artificial gloss of a corrupt symbolic order is singularly appropriate to a narrative in which nothing and no one is quite as they seem.

It is nonetheless disturbing that Marlowe should be so attracted to a man whose first boundary-crossing transgression is the murder of a black bar-owner. As well as being presented as a man out of time, Moose is a character who does not know his own strength. He is like a child both in his single-minded demand for Velma, and in the frequency with which people, like toys, fall apart in his hands. Having crossed the racial boundary separating black from white by entering Florian's bar, Moose seems unable or unwilling to understand his transgression. His invasion is accomplished through a combination of physical force and the unthinking racial privilege that accompanies whiteness. Marlowe tries to break free of Moose's hold over him, and offers support to the terrorised barman. However, for all that Marlowe tries to put this particular big man out of his mind, it is Moose's parting words, 'You ain't forgetting me, pal', that prove prophetic (1940/1949: 16).

The novel, then, is haunted by the spectre of Moose, a beautiful monster in the Frankenstein mould, who only wants to be loved and cannot understand what the world has got against him. As the object of the detective hero's quest, he represents an ambivalent figure, and not one likely to satisfy Marlowe's cravings for one good man. However, it is not until the very end of the narrative that Marlowe stumbles upon a suitable object for his desires. Loitering with intent on the Bay City waterfront, Marlowe's eye is caught by a 'big red-headed roughneck in dirty sneakers and tarry pants and what was left of a torn blue sailor's jersey' (1940/1949: 212):

> He smiled a slow tired smile. His voice was soft, dreamy, so delicate for a big man that it was startling. It made me think of another soft-voiced big man I had strangely liked. (1940/1949: 213)

The connection is obvious and, in Red Norgaard, Marlowe has finally encountered the masculine ideal for which he has been searching. The descriptions of Red are fascinating. Like Moose, he stands outside the corrupting influences of wealth and power – indeed, his honesty has lost him his job as a policeman in the otherwise corrupt Bay City PD – and, like Moose, his size is tempered by 'feminine' characteristics:

> I looked at him again. He had the eyes you never see, that you only read about. Violet eyes. Almost purple. Eyes like a girl, a lovely girl. His skin was as soft as silk. Lightly reddened, but it would never tan. It was too delicate . . . He was not as big as Moose Malloy, but he looked very fast on his feet. His hair was that shade of red that glints with gold. But except for the eyes he had a plain farmer face, with no stagy kind of handsomeness. (1940/1949: 214)[13]

This description is marked by symbols of wholesomeness and honesty. Unlike Amthor, whose good looks outshone even movie stars, Red's beauty is clearly distinguished from the artifice of stage and screen. Classical images of virginal female purity are here transferred to the idealised male, while the whole of his face is associated with the rugged outdoor virtues of the farmer, a description that immediately sets him apart from the novel's norm of urban vice.

Red's 'plain farmer face' also draws attention to the other dimension of his role as the ideal other. Marlowe has struggled through the novel, standing alone against violent assaults and personal betrayals, but in Red he finds not only someone he can trust, but also someone who will help and nurture him in times of crisis. When the hero's resolve is fading, it is Red who offers support and enters into the intimacy of a shared danger. Small wonder, then, that Marlowe should be so attracted to this man. And within the tough-guy framework of the genre, Marlowe's homoerotic intimacy can pass unnoticed. It is acceptable for him to idolise Red precisely because Red is such an edifice of the masculine. Although described as a beautiful girl, the qualities praised are not specific to social constructions of 'femininity', and Red can in no sense be seen as a 'feminised' man. Indeed, his butchness is highly significant, as it is only in its distance from the feminine that the homosocial's descent into the homoerotic is legitimised.

The cumulative effect of the depiction of femininity in Chandler's novels is suggestive of a considerable phobia, and one which extends beyond the chastity of Philip Marlowe. The corruption of blackmailer Lindsay Marriot is evident in the femininity of his surroundings and dress:

> I was looking at a tall blond man in a white flannel suit with a violet satin scarf around his neck . . . I went in past him and smelled perfume . . . We went down three steps to the main part of the living-room. The carpet almost tickled my ankles . . . There was plenty of nice soft furniture, a great many floor cushions, some with golden tassels and some just naked . . . There was a wide damask covered divan in a shadowy corner, like a casting couch . . . It was a room where anything could happen except work. (Chandler, 1940/1949: 45–6)

Not even his heterosexuality can redeem Marriot's deplorable dandyism, while the description of his soft furnishings verges on the pornographic. In the naked cushions and casting-couch divan Chandler evokes a world of decadent sexuality underpinned not by mutual desire, but by exploitative marketplace economics. By contrast, the virtue of Marlowe's plucky 'boy' assistant, Anne Riordan, is evident in the masculinity of her surroundings. Crawling to the 'sanctuary' of Anne's apartment after escaping from the asylum, Marlowe is reassured to discover that '[t]here was nothing womanish in the room except a full length mirror' (1940/1949: 160). However, that it is ultimately femininity rather than homosexuality which offers the greatest threat to the symbolic order is perhaps most clearly illustrated by *The Big Sleep*. Examining the home of Arthur Gwynn Geiger – blackmailer, porngrapher and queer – Marlowe stumbles, like Goldilocks, on to a number of differently signifying bedrooms. Geiger's is 'neat, fussy, womanish', evidence once again of the link between femininity and corruption (1939/1948: 42). That of his lover, by contrast, is described as a 'nice, clean, manly little room' (1939/1948: 99). Marlowe's preference, it is implied, is for the murderous but manly boy over the feminised, degenerate 'fag'.

Within a sufficiently masculine environment, then, it would seem that some degree of same-sex desire is legitimised, and what could be more masculine than danger?[14] In a couple of chapters that can arguably be said to form the most erotic and sensual scenario of the novel, Red and Marlowe take to sea in an attempt to board the boat of crime boss Laird Brunnette (whose feminised name gives a clear indication of his dubious virtue):

> There was just enough fog to make everything seem unreal. The wet air was as cold as the ashes of love.

> Red leaned close to me and his breath tickled my ear. (1940/1949: 221–2)

The proximity of danger incites a confessional mood, with Marlowe admitting that he is 'scared stiff' (1940/1949: 214). The last vestiges of the tough façade break down, and Marlowe attempts to put a jokey frame around his unusual loquaciousness: 'I told him a great deal more than I intended to. It must have been his eyes' (218). Here, as nowhere else, in the private sea space between the corrupt boundaries of Bay City and Brunnette's boat, Marlowe feels able to confess, and with his hand held by the 'strong, hard, warm and slightly sticky' paw of Red, he feels strong enough to carry out his mission (223), which is, ironically, a final desperate effort to locate the elusive Moose. The masculine search for adventure is equally and also a search for the legitimisation of homosexual desire, as it is only within the totally defeminised context of danger that the homoerotic can find any outlet or articulation.

Consequently it would seem that Marlowe's search throughout *Farewell, My Lovely* is not for Velma or Mrs Grayle, but rather for a legitimate object of desire through which he might satisfy his craving for Moose Malloy. Finding Red Norgaard in the climactic moments of the novel satisfies his longing for one good man, and makes possible the completion of his quest. He has sought throughout for Moose as well as Velma, and in a final confrontation that, structurally, is not so far removed from the classical paradigm, he brings the suspects together. What profoundly differentiates Chandler's finale from those of Philo Vance, or Hercule Poirot, however, is the detective's lack of control over the situation. In a bizarre chemical experiment, Marlowe puts Velma and Moose in the same room and waits to see what happens. That this room is also his bedroom, in which he had been dreaming of Red before wakening to the vision of Moose standing over him, only adds to the confusion. Marlowe, the detective, who should be detached, has become voyeuristically over-committed to the conclusion of the Moose/Velma narrative. Unwilling to let the law take its course, he forces a confrontation – the end of the show – and arranges it to take place in the convenience of his own bedroom. That the story ends in murder is no surprise, as Velma proves herself to be both a typical *femme fatale* and the specific Achilles heel of Moose's otherwise invulnerable masculinity (1940/1949: 245).

It might seem, in conclusion, that Chandler's 'love story' has gone the way of all hard-boiled narrative. It has mutated into a story that is 'dark and full of blood' (1940/1949: 246). Moose is dead, betrayed again by Velma, and Marlowe has only the memory of his intimacy with Red to set against the crumbling edifice of a corrupt society. Yet Marlowe's narrative is mendacious. Having told Anne Riordan that his story could have no tidy endings or neat conclusions, in the closing pages of the novel he proceeds quite shamelessly with a project of romantic rehabilitation that reconstructs the narrative as a love story. In a phoenix-like feat of mythologising, the story is even provided with a female lead but, as she is dead, such an elevation of the feminine might, for once, be regarded as safe:

> 'I'm not saying she was a saint or even a half-way nice girl. Not ever. She wouldn't kill herself until she was cornered. But what she did and the way she did it, kept her from coming back here for trial. Think that over. And who would that trial hurt most? Who would least be able to bear it? And win, lose or draw, who would pay the biggest price for the show? An old man who had loved not wisely, but too well.' (Chandler, 1940/1949: 253)

So is this a 'tragedy with a happy ending'? Chandler's description of the detective story is an attractive one, but it is also misleading. For all Marlowe's mythologising, the end of *Farewell, My Lovely* is happy only in so far as it evokes the 'romantic dream on which love feeds'. Nonetheless, in the quests of Moose and Marlowe, Chandler ultimately disproves his own assertion that the love story and the detective story cannot co-exist. Rather his fictions reveal the cohabitation of these two genres, which hard-boiled narrative would traditionally most strenuously seek to deny. Caught between the necessity of masculine self-fashioning and the painful constraints within which that creation must be bound, Chandler's hyperbolic novels end up producing the illegitimate and the taboo. Marlowe's world of masculine excess thus becomes an environment within which the homosocial is celebrated and a legitimised homoeroticism emerges as the love which makes up in body for what it may not speak in name.

THE (VERY) *LONG GOOD-BYE*: A CASE OF *DÉJÀ VU*?

Calvin Thomas reminds us that in 'the long-standing patriarchal ideology in which embodiment and femininity are equated . . . male bodies do not matter' (1996: 15). Yet while writing in a cultural climate within which the only visible bodies were those of women, Chandler paid remarkable attention to the details of the male body and, in so doing, he risked destabilising the patriarchal masculine ideal. As Thomas observes:

> [M]asculinity does not exist outside representation, yet in the process of self-representation it risks losing itself, changing itself, seeping out through its own fissures and cracks. (Thomas, 1996: 16)

Masculinity must be constituted through repeated reinscription and, as Judith Butler suggests, it is this 'citationality' that underpins its authority:

> If a performative provisionally succeeds (and I will suggest that 'success' is always and only provisional), then it is not because an intention successfully governs the action of speech, but only because that action echoes prior actions, and *accumulates the force of authority through the repetition or citation of a prior, authoritative set of practices.* (Butler, 1993: 226–7)

But, 'reiterations are never simply replicas of the same' (Butler, 1993: 226). Reinscription is an inexact science, and each repetition also becomes a multiplication that transgresses the boundaries of the patriarchal template. With each necessary reinscription comes the danger of an*other* inscription: the possibility that the utterance which should have described the self has instead depicted the other. With each new citation men risk seeing the reflection not of masculine self-containment, but of feminine excess. And it is this excess that brings me in conclusion to *The Long Good-Bye.*

Although not the last novel to feature Philip Marlowe, *The Long Good-Bye* is customarily cited as Chandler's swan song, his last great reinscription of the tough-talking hard-boiled ideal.[15] On every level this novel struggles to attain Thomas's 'immaculate self-construction', replaying the tropes of tough talk, stubborn silence and self-imposed isolation. But *The Long Good-Bye* does not only replicate the formula of Chandler's earlier fiction; it also self-consciously reiterates the content, reworking previous plot devices to emphasise the complex process of becoming that produces the masculine and its fictions. In its evocation of both *The Big Sleep* and *Farewell, My Lovely, The Long Good-Bye* becomes an unstable, multilayered and excessive reinscription of an ideal it seems increasingly unable to sustain.

The Long Good-Bye, like *Farewell, My Lovely*, opens with Marlowe's attraction to a man. Although Terry Lennox bears little physical resemblance to the monumental masculinity of Moose Malloy, the lasting fascination of his impact on Marlowe is remarkably similar. The most significant difference between the two opening scenarios would seem to be that, in the later novel, the roles have been reversed. This time it is Marlowe who takes on the role of the big man, picking up the vulnerable Lennox from the gutter of his drunken excess. Here is a prime opportunity for romantic masculine self-definition through the benevolent protection of a weaker, feminised other. The romance, however, is short-lived. After a period of benign companionship, Lennox, like Moose, goes underground. The report of Lennox's death establishes the grounds for Marlowe's quest. This time he will not pursue the literal or semiotic body of the missing man, but rather will seek to restore the symbolic body, that is, Terry Lennox's 'good name'. Through his quest to restore Terry's reputation, Marlowe replaces the reality of the man he knew with an ideal every bit as romantic as his mythologising of Moose Malloy.

Terry Lennox thus becomes an icon of doomed masculinity. Marlowe reads his actions as a noble self-sacrifice to set against the baseness of the world he left behind. The evidence of this residual corruption is, as usual, most clearly evident within the characters of the novel's women, the sexually voracious Sylvia Lennox and the murderous Eileen Wade. Masculinity betrayed is a central trope of Chandler's earlier fiction. However, in *The Big Sleep* and *Farewell, My Lovely* the authentically dead do not run the risk of falling off the pedestals erected by the worshipful Marlowe. Neither the reader nor Marlowe ever has the pleasure of encountering Rusty Regan's Irish charm. He is long dead before the narrative gets under way, shot by Carmen Sternwood, the woman he had scorned, and this textual absence makes his idealisation all the easier. Much the same could be said of Moose Malloy – a man unlikely to improve upon further acquaintance. Fortunately Little Velma shoots him before Marlowe's ardour can cool. Consequently, in returning to life, Terry Lennox comes to provide a masculine illustration of what women have long recognised: the impossibility of living up to an ideal. His bodily self is rejected as being uncomfortably in excess of the tidy obituary which Marlowe had written for him:

> I'm not judging you. I never did. It's just that you're not here any more. You're long gone. You've got nice clothes and perfume and you're as elegant as a fifty-dollar whore. (Chandler, 1953/1959: 320)

Lennox has mutated from masculinity betrayed into that which betrays masculinity. His bodily return has feminised him, while also teaching him that '[a]n act is all there is' (1953/1959: 320). Marlowe, in contrast, still clings to a belief in a fixed ideal of masculinity: the legendary big man. But big men are getting harder to find – a fact that accounts both for the grimmer tone of *The Long Good-Bye*, and for Marlowe's bizarre behaviour in the case of Roger Wade, the novel's other flawed icon of masculinity.[16]

Marlowe's relationship to the author Roger Wade could justifiably be construed as sinister. Wade is a troubled man who cannot finish his latest novel. Part of his problem stems from the psychotic tendencies of his wife, but there is more to his anxieties than the familiar female betrayal. Marlowe is recruited by Wade's wife and his publisher to oversee the reluctant author, but rather than fully accepting or rejecting this commision, he comes instead to haunt the Wade household as an invited but seldom welcome guest. Marlowe comes when he is called, but is always less tractable on arrival, refusing to take action and hovering like a shabby nemesis over the drunken decline of Wade. Rather than helping Wade, Marlowe seems to be testing him, waiting for a sign of masculine greatness – for proof that Wade is, in fact, a real big man. Unfortunately for Wade, Marlowe's criteria of greatness are harsh – and while Eileen Wade and Howard Spencer think he is safeguarding the production of another bestselling novel, Marlowe is instead protecting Wade's right to die. In refusing to complete a debased cultural product and in drinking himself into an easily killable stupor, Wade rejects the corrupted world of his wife's crimes and his publisher's greed, and achieves, in Marlowe's eyes, some dubious form of redemption. And indeed, in death he approximates the masculine ideal sadly tarnished by Terry Lennox's inappropriate return to life.

It is in the eventual ignominious death of the author that Wade comes to act as Chandler's most self-conscious depiction of the pattern which underpins so much of his fiction, namely the struggle for and ultimate impossibility of 'immaculate self-creation'. Wade's role as a writer is crucial here. Each novel that he produces brings him wealth and the power associated therewith, so that his writing could be said to constitute his masculine identity. However, this inscription is an unstable one, for the massive 'body' of Wade's work is the sordid and debased bulk of genre fiction. Wade is a writer of historical romances, and each novel thus becomes a problematic reinscription of the very 'feminine' it seeks to deny. The very thing that makes Roger Wade also repulses him:

> Writers. Everything has to be like something else. My head is as fluffy as whipped cream but not as sweet. More similes. I could vomit just thinking about the lousy racket. I could vomit anyway. I probably will. (Chandler, 1953/1959: 172)

And in Marlowe's eyes Wade is right to be repulsed. Although he likes the man, he loathes the work which produces him: 'I looked at one of his books once. I thought it was tripe' (1953/1959: 79). *The Long Good-Bye*, like all of Chandler's novels, adheres rigorously to the traditional binary divide between a superior, elitist, masculine art, and a feminised popular culture – a paradox that perhaps contributes to the aggressive assertion of toughness within the hard-boiled genre. In Roger Wade, however, masculinity's relation to the abject is made painfully clear. With each new novel, Wade creates and constitutes his masculinity through a very public production of the feminine. And with the assumption that he will produce another novel comes the knowledge that the bodily 'feminine' traces expelled in the process of self-creation can never be wholly eradicated. Writing, which seems on the surface to be the most certain guarantee of the masculine, is also that which most completely ensures its provisional status.

Thus the trajectory of Chandler's own genre fiction also becomes increasingly bleak. No matter how many times he reiterates the prescriptions of masculine conformity, he cannot escape the traces of both illegitimate desire and the abjected body. That which has been repulsed remains an omnipresent threat to the boundaries of masculine self-definition, and, in hard-boiled detection as in the classical clue-puzzle, the excessive traces of those corporeal 'realities' that the narrative would seek to deny come stubbornly and persistently home to roost.

NOTES

1. In the opening pages of *The Big Sleep* Marlowe tells us what he is wearing, describes what he sees around him at the Sternwood mansion, flirts with and is kissed by a passing psychotic

female, and gives a very brief CV consisting only of his age (33) and a tendency to insubordination (1939/1948: 15).

2. Christianson makes a useful distinction between the wisecrack and the hard-boiled conceit, defining the first as a public, specifically dialogic, marker of toughness, and the second as a descriptive mode emerging from the private register of the first-person narrative voice (1989: 156). Stephen Knight, however, sees the distinction as one between private superiority and public insecurity. He compares the 'comfortable control' of Marlowe's private reverie with the frequently immature and aggressive nature of his public utterances (1980: 143–4).
3. The Production Code of 1930 was Hollywood's attempt to evade external censorship through self-regulation, and pre-eminent among its governing principles was the demand that 'no picture shall be produced which will lower the moral standards of those who see it' (Maltby and Craven, 1995: 41–2, 340–3).
4. Marlowe suffers terribly from a literary form of *coitus interruptus*. In *Farewell, My Lovely* his embrace of the holy Grayle is interrupted by her husband (1940/1949: 119), in *The Long Good-Bye* the 'spell' of Eileen Wade is broken by the 'saving' intervention of the houseboy Candy (1953/1959: 180) and, most dramatically, in *Playback*, his first close encounter with Betty Mayfield ends in the oblivion of unconsciousness after a crack on the head with a whisky bottle (1958/1961: 33–4).
5. It is worth noticing that Marlowe's quest is also driven by a sentimental urge to revenge the death of Harry Jones, a little guy whose courage elevates him to big man status.
6. Eve Sedgwick also challenges liberal scholarship's determination to evade the issue of sexuality at all cost. In *Epistemology of the Closet* she provides a witty list of eight popular gay dismissals, of which the most suitable in this case are numbers 6 and 7:
    6. The author under discussion is certified or rumored to have had an attachment to someone of the other sex – so their feelings about people of their own sex must have been completely meaningless. Or (under a perhaps somewhat different rule of admissible evidence)
    7. There is no actual proof of homosexuality, such as sperm taken from the body of another man or a nude photograph with another woman – so the author may be assumed to have been ardently and exclusively heterosexual. (Sedgwick, 1990/1994: 52–3)
7. Although the categories are far from self-contained, some distinction needs to be drawn between the homosocial, the homoerotic and the homosexual. Throughout the chapter I will be using the homosocial to refer to a social order that privileges the bonds between men, whether that be in terms of the economics of exchange (of which women are frequently the object), the inheritance structures and pressures of patriarchy, or the more positive categories of friendship. The homoerotic refers to anything that might connote the possibility of desire between men, specifically the depiction of male characters in explicitly or implicitly sensual modes. The term 'homosexual', by contrast, is reserved for actual acts of physical intimacy between men.
8. The semiotic might be seen as a disruption of narrative order, a textual excess that disrupts symbolic functioning and encodes a yearning for the ideal dyadic unity of the pre-Oedipal phase. Kristeva's concept is discussed in chapter 1, and a useful account is also provided by Pam Morris (1993: 144–8).
9. The tendency of Marlowe's ideals to metamorphose into monsters can also be seen as a byproduct of patriarchal pressure. Discussing Victor Frankenstein's attempt to assert his heroic potential through the creation of a larger-than-life new man, Berthold Schoene-Harwood concludes that 'the masculine ideal has turned into an inexorable imperative perpetuating itself beyond all human control' (2000: 20).
10. Although Bataille's focus falls exclusively upon a hierarchical conception of heterosexual relations, his formulations nonetheless seem singularly appropriate for the homoerotic fantasies of Chandler's detective.
11. Examples include Dorothy L. Sayers's *Busman's Honeymoon* (1937) and Margery Allingham's *Traitor's Purse* (1941). In Sayers's novel the threat of war is one of many pressures which expose Wimsey's vulnerability and drive him to find security in the arms of his new wife Harriet Vane. Marriage becomes a safe haven from an increasingly hostile symbolic order (Plain, 1996). Allingham's novel, meanwhile, offers a more extreme reinscription of the pre-Oedipal. When Albert Campion loses his memory, he becomes totally dependent upon his fiancée Amanda Fitton, who appears to him as a strange and wonderful mother figure,

nurturing him in his hour of need and giving him the strength to save Britain from national calamity (Allingham, 1941/1954: 19, 52).

12. Examples abound, but among the most famous would be Melville's *Moby Dick*, Twain's *The Adventures of Huckleberry Finn* and almost anything by Ernest Hemingway.
13. This, then, is the first appearance of the violet eyes of my title. Their value is twice reiterated over the following pages, most significantly when Marlowe comments, 'I told him a great deal more than I intended to. It must have been his eyes' (1940/1949: 218). However, violet eyes prove rather less trustworthy when part of the female body, as Marlowe discovers to his cost in *The Long Good-Bye* (1953/1959: 81, 87). While Red's eyes act as an index of his inner worth, the devastatingly gorgeous Eileen Wade proves, once again, that female beauty is only skin-deep.
14. This form of homosociality is a frequent byproduct not only of war, but also of prison experiences. In both cases the absence of a legitimate object of desire in the shape of a woman is accompanied by levels of jeopardy and dislocation strong enough to break down taboos regarding same-sex intimacy. However, the similarities end here as structures of homosexuality within prison environments are more frequently connected to the replication of a series of patriarchal power relations, in which the possession of a boy might be equated to the possession of a woman. Bill James's novel *Halo Parade* (1987) effectively illustrates this dynamic through the relationship between an undercover policeman and a crime boss who 'went queer inside' (1987: 360). In a chilling reinscription of heterosexual power relations, the policeman's downfall comes about not through his exposure as a cop, but through his exposure as 'adulterously' heterosexual (391–6).
15. Chandler's final completed novel, *Playback* (1958), has few admirers. It is scarcely more than a long short story and lacks most of the corporeal and epistemological complexity that marked the earlier fictions. Its cruder outline can perhaps best be summarised in the fact that not only does Marlowe get more sex than usual, but also that it is described in comparatively graphic and clichéd detail (1958/1961: 77).
16. Marlowe is at times truly obnoxious in *The Long Good-Bye*. '[S]cowling at nothing' he picks a fight with a stranger in a bar (1953/1959: 83–4) and throughout indulges in an excessive amount of hard-man posturing (35, 65, 115). He is also notably wearier than in earlier adventures (181) and seems to have lost whatever taste he once had for the business: '[s]omething inside me had gone sour' (186). Where once his survival had an edge of optimism, he now seems only to be going through the motions, doggedly persisting in the expectation of no return.

Part II

The 'Normal Science' of Detection

The 'Normal Science' of Detection: Introduction

> [W]e must recognize how very limited in both scope and precision a paradigm can be at the time of its first appearance. Paradigms gain their status because they are more successful than their competitors in solving a few problems that the group of practitioners has come to recognize as acute . . . The success of a paradigm . . . is at the start largely a promise of success discoverable in selected and still incomplete examples. Normal science consists in the actualization of that promise . . . No part of the aim of normal science is to call forth new sorts of phenomena; indeed those that will not fit in the box are often not seen at all. Nor do scientists normally aim to invent new theories, and they are often intolerant of those invented by others. Instead, normal-scientific research is directed to the articulation of those phenomena and theories that the paradigm already supplies. (Kuhn, 1962/1970: 23–4)

The writers considered in Part II are all practitioners of what might be seen as the 'normal science' of crime fiction. They experiment, they explore, they develop and hypothesise; but they do so within the 'preformed and relatively inflexible box that the paradigm [of detection] supplies' (Kuhn, 1962/1970: 24).[1] They push boundaries – but ultimately they do not break or exceed them. This is not to say that these fictions are neither innovative nor radical. In places all the texts of Part II disrupt, destabilise and challenge aspects of the narrative conventions that structure them. Part II reveals that it is possible to stretch the genre to include the 'new' man, the gay man, the female detective and the lesbian policewoman, but perhaps more importantly, these examples also beg the question of whether changes in the subjectivity of the detective can effect a more fundamental challenge to wider socio-political structures.

Many critics of the genre have their doubts. Dennis Porter, for example, argues that:

> Works in the genre always take a stand in defence of the established societal order . . . even when, as in certain hard-boiled novels, they uncover corruption among prominent citizens and public officials. And the cause of such generic 'conservatism' is to be found in the first place at the level of the structure of the action. Like all popular literary genres . . . detective stories combine what might be called deep ideological constants with surface ideological variables. (Porter, 1981: 125)[2]

Porter's point is developed by Peter Messent who cites Sara Paretsky's feminist detective V. I. Warshawski as a specific example. However radical her politics, he argues, as a private eye she is beset by inherent structural problems:

> Paretsky's protagonist directly interrogates the existing social order but cannot finally affect it. Warshawski, like the majority of hard-boiled private-eye protagonists, is caught finally in a kind of in-between world: seeing corruption in, and disliking many aspects of, the environment through which she moves, but serving the interests of the law and the status quo in solving the individual crime and repairing the rent in the social fabric that has occurred. (Messent, 1997: 9)

Messent's argument succinctly encapsulates what would appear to be the limits of detective agency. The PI is a structurally conservative figure whose 'outsider' status is a relative one which fails to challenge the existing order. Rather than reconceptualising structures of power and knowledge, the detective's marginality facilitates a romantic detachment from political and economic reality. Irrespective of his or her oppositional stance and tough talking, the figure of the detective must be content with effecting change on a microcosmic level, providing individual solutions to superstructural problems without ever seriously disturbing the 'deep ideological constants' of power.

However, despite the drawbacks that might be thought to reside in the appropriation of a traditionally misogynist, racist and homophobic figure, the hard-boiled detective has proved remarkably popular with radical writers.[3] In depicting the detective as a relatively empowered voice from the margins, these writers seem attuned to the potential for rehabilitation residing in the apparently conservative form of the genre. Their belief is echoed by critics such as Priscilla L. Walton and Manina Jones who argue that:

> Like popular culture itself . . . genres are neither simply subversive nor intrinsically conservative. Genre, rather, serves as a relational, conventional, and contradictory location that tends to complicate in practice any simple either/or categorization. (Walton and Jones, 1999: 88–9)[4]

Although Walton and Jones eventually become somewhat over-optimistic in their claims for female 'detective agency', it is important to recognise the extent to which contemporary crime writers have attempted to use the form to expose socio-political tensions. By inserting the unfamiliar into the familiar landscape of the crime narrative they construct a critique through 'insinuation', and enable the margins to assume, at least temporarily, a position of centrality. Walton and Jones describe first-person narration as the 'signature effect' of the hard-boiled form, and through this effect, or through focalised third-person narration, the 'other' aquires a voice (1999: 151). Women, racial minorities, gay men and lesbians appropriate the traditional story of the detective's quest for knowledge, and in finding answers are themselves empowered.

It is, I suspect, impossible to resolve the competing claims for the detective's agency or impotence, not least because the argument itself is a manifestation of a much older critical impasse. The debate over the political efficacy of crime fiction restages the conflict between form and content, asking whether radical characterisation and plot construction will inevitably be undermined by the constraints of generic form: namely, closure, resolution, and the restoration of order. Any answer to this dilemma will be dependent upon the texts themselves and must weigh the nature of the internal changes against the integrity and coherence of the formula within which they are contained. In other words, generalisations regarding the radical or conservative trajectory of crime fiction will always be provisional and liable to be exposed by the endless tensions generated by the actual generic product itself, which brings me to the texts that form the focus of Part II. These experiments in 'normal science', although constrained within certain parameters, always retain an explosive potential. They are, after all, *experiments*: their outcome is uncertain and, as it was with the original paradigmatic fictions of crime, it is often around the locus of the gendered and sexualised body that the experiments of contemporary crime are found to be most fraught and volatile.

A familiar dictum holds that the presence of an observer changes the nature of the experiment, and the observation of gender and sexuality within a text does exactly that for the experiment of narrative. When these discourses are acknowledged, the narrative mutates, and the novels of Joseph Hansen, Dick Francis, Sara Paretsky and Katherine V. Forrest are revealed to be not quite as straightforward as they may initially appear. Approaching genre fiction from an alternative perspective disrupts the form/content dichotomy to reveal both unexpected limitations and unimagined potentialities. This shift, however, is not solely a matter of perspective; rather it involves the whole process of reading. In *The Pleasure of the Text* Roland Barthes delineates two systems of reading. The first is a fast reading that 'goes straight to the articulation of the anecdote', while the second mode of 'applied' reading seems, in contrast, to graze. It resists chronology and the notion of reading for 'something to happen' (1973/1990: 12). Genre narrative is assumed to encourage the first mode of reading – a mode that skims past detail in order to attain climax. However, if crime fiction is approached in the spirit of the second mode – a reading of erotic foreplay – then both the text and its pleasures are rendered profoundly different.

In his account of gay culture, *Gay and After*, Alan Sinfield suggests the impossibility of a narrative ever conforming entirely to the categories of the radical or the reactionary:

> The main theme of *The Swimming-Pool Library* is Will's discovery that he is deeply implicated in gay history and not, as he has supposed, free from responsibility and social process. Such a theme – an important one for gay men – does not involve fear and hatred of women, but it does tend to marginalize them. This is not quite 'misogyny', but who you write into your story and who just doesn't seem to count that much is nothing less than the infrastructure of routine gender-chauvinism. For what pushes women to the margins – as with other subordinated

> groups – is not just phobic prejudice or fantasy identification, but the narratives that we live through, in the world and in novels. These narratives are not individual inventions. They depend upon patterns of plausibility that are deeply encoded in culture. (Sinfield, 1998: 106)

Sinfield's comments have considerable relevance for the writers discussed in Part II. In the first instance he identifies a gender exclusivity in some gay writing that undoubtedly applies to the work of Joseph Hansen. Whether this is ultimately a 'problem' or simply the inevitable side-effect of an attempt to reinscribe genre norms is discussed at length in Chapter 3, but the fact remains that in attempting to create a plausible narrative of gay male desire, Hansen ends up further marginalising the narrative potential of women. However, it is Sinfield's 'patterns of plausibility' that resonate most strongly with the concerns of this section. Genre provides the example *par excellence* of a narrative not of 'individual invention'. Thus, in the following chapters four very different writers can be seen to attempt the reconstruction of existing narrative patterns to accommodate alternative identities and modes of investigation, while nonetheless remaining within the bounds of detective plausibility.

Hansen certainly achieves the production of a plausible hybrid form. He makes few changes to the external appearance of the detective: David Brandstetter is cool, rational, laconic and firmly in control. But these stereotypical character traits are set against the rather less familiar features of his homosexuality, his voiced fear of loneliness and his desire for domestic coupledom. The serial narrative focuses as much upon the ongoing negotiation of relationships as on the individual criminal event, and much emphasis is laid upon the importance of friendship. The narrative remains fundamentally homosocial, but, as Sinfield's analysis suggests, it is a long way from the misogyny of its hard-boiled precursors.

In comparison, the novels of Dick Francis are rather less successful in their project of rehabilitating the straight male hero. These novels are best categorised as 'detective thrillers', a hybrid form described by Martin Priestman as one which 'divides our interest between solving a past mystery and following a present action in which the protagonists may confront a dangerous conspiracy alone, or step outside the law, or both' (1998: 2). On first appearance, the various amateur detectives deployed by Francis would seem to challenge traditional modes of heroic masculine agency, but appearances can be deceptive. Chapter 4 suggests that the changes instituted by Francis are largely perfunctory, and his novels ultimately present patriarchal masculinity dressed up in more user-friendly (or, as some critics have argued, more woman-friendly) clothing.[5] However, while Francis effectively comes full circle in his portrayal of heroic masculinity, the tensions, contradictions and desires thrown up en route are remarkable and complex. Francis's novels comprise a tapestry of scenes which constantly (re)articulate a power dynamic of misrecognition. His detective, Sid Halley, is misread by his opponents, who see him as the feminised other and easily assert their authority over him. When Halley reveals his 'masculine' alter ego and is read 'correctly', power relations are reversed and the detective's authority is reinstated. This sadomasochistic performance would not be unexpected in any thriller, as here, more than in conventional detective narrative, the conflict between hero and villain is central. However, within the Sid Halley novels the reiteration of this power dynamic exposes the extent to which sadomasochistic desire underpins all homosocial encounters, not simply those between heroes and villains. The novels of Dick Francis conform to both the generic template and societal norms, but in order to do so they must negotiate the dangerously unstable boundary between homosociality and its transgressive homosexual other.

Chapter 5 is concerned with a very different mode of transgression – that embodied by the female private eye. A female protagonist effectively explodes the homosocial environment of the hard-boiled private detective, forcing a radical reconceptualisation of the investigator's relationship to structures of family and community. The female sleuth has a history dating back into the nineteenth century, but up until the 1980s her sporadic presence within the category of hard-boiled detection had had only a minimal impact. This situation underwent a radical change in 1977 with the publication of Marcia Muller's first Sharon McCone novel, *Edwin of the Iron Shoes*. McCone began her career as an investigator for a San Francisco legal co-operative before going it alone as a private eye, but this nonetheless remains the book most widely credited with initiating the growth industry in female private eyes. Muller's McCone was joined in the 1980s by Sara Paretsky's V. I. Warshawski and Sue Grafton's Kinsey Millhone, and these three writers, along with the countless others who followed them, sought to appropriate the conventions of hard-boiled crime to produce a narrative of autonomous female agency.

Here again it is useful to invoke Alan Sinfield's 'patterns of plausibility'. The novels of Sara Paretsky, which form the focus of the chapter, walk a tightrope between hard-boiled reinscription and feminist revision. V. I. Warshawski must retain sufficient characteristics of the traditional PI to successfully inhabit his narrative but, as a self-identified feminist, she must also subject those conventions to scrutiny and attempt to find new ways of articulating and investigating the social crises embodied in crime. Her tough-talking, wisecracking approach is thus both familiar and new – a female appropriation of 'masculine' discourse. But is such an appropriation anything more than a crude inversion, proving only that women can perform roles of patriarchal dominance as successfully as men? Paretsky's project pushes the genre to its limits in its attempts to bring the detective in from the cold of archetypal isolation, but the desires and needs of a lone pro-active feminist voice remain fundamentally at odds with the demands of hard-boiled narrative, and what begins as a fairy tale of feminist agency is ultimately torn apart by structural contradictions.

The final chapter of Part II turns its attention to what might seem an even more contradictory space for female agency – the police procedural. Katherine V. Forrest's Kate Delafield novels are founded on paradox: a closet lesbian policewoman diligently upholds and enforces the very law that excludes and oppresses her. Delafield is both insider and outsider, pro-active agent and demonised other, and the implications of this dual citizenship are crucial. Walton and Jones argue that the 'female professional investigator novel . . . offers a popular form of novelistic "legal representation," often for interests and issues that fall outside the law' (1999: 207), but Sara Paretsky's novels suggest the extreme difficulty of achieving this representation through the isolated individualism of the private eye. However, the infiltration of the police procedural by a lesbian investigator ironically constructs a space through which much more powerful advocacy can be achieved. Peter Messent suggests that:

> [D]espite the continuing production and popularity of the private-eye story, the generic shift to police procedural has been prompted by a recognition that the marginal position and limited perspective of the PI hero or heroine makes for an ineffectual, and even irrelevant, figure as far as the representation of criminal activity and its containment goes. (Messent, 1997: 2)

Delafield's position may be paradoxical, but she does achieve a significant proximity to power. The radical potential of her character, however, is undermined by one fundamental problem. Her entire agency is predicated upon the denial of her sexuality. Only by effacing that which she also fights to protect can Forrest's lesbian policewoman retain her position within the structures that generate and enforce the law.

The four experiments examined in Part II give rise both to innovatory advances and spectacular retreats, but above all they illustrate the remarkable elasticity of the crime genre. Like lycra it expands to accommodate all shapes and sizes, and like lycra it tends to disguise the lumps and bulges. I am not referring here to Chandler's contention that the second-rate detective story gets published when the second-rate novel does not – although it is arguably the case that genre can facilitate the public display of less than flattering attributes.[6] Rather I am suggesting that under the comfortable cover of genre, writers can display narratives that would not otherwise see the light of day, and, indeed, reach audiences who would not otherwise be reached. Quite what those narratives actually are, however, is rather less easy both to discern and to control.

NOTES

1. Although it is the hard-boiled narrative form that has proved most fruitful for writers wanting to appropriate and develop the genre, my conception of a 'paradigm of detection' is a looser concept embracing the formulae of both classical and hard-boiled fiction. As Part I is at pains to establish, the distinctions dividing these two modes of detection are undercut by unexpected similarities, and by a shared investment in restoring order and reassuring cultural anxieties.
2. Stephen Knight analyses the ideological construction of crime fiction, arguing that 'form and content together create the crucial realisation of a pleasing, comforting world-view' (1980: 5), while Ernest Mandel develops Porter's proposition of a surface/depth dichotomy:

   > It is one thing to question or objectively undermine bourgeois ideology, quite another to reject it consciously and across the board. This becomes possible only if another set of ideas and values can be counterposed to it. Nothing of the kind has occurred, even in the most sophisticated variants of the contemporary thriller. (Mandel, 1984: 124)

   Sally Munt also has serious reservations regarding the detective's role as both 'a representative of society and a critique of it' (1994: 120). These concerns will be discussed in Chapters 5 and 7.
3. Most attempts to explain the predominance of the hard-boiled template in contemporary appropriations of the crime genre focus on the advantages of outsider status and first-person voice. However, the success of the hard-boiled model might also be attributed to an increasing concern with what Kaja Silverman has termed 'the "politics" of desire and identification' (1992: 1). Within the formula of classical detection desire is largely seen from without. The absence of articulated or implied desire in the figure of Hercule Poirot does not make him an ideal template for writers whose conception of subjectivity cannot be divorced from sexuality. Raymond Chandler's fiction, by contrast, offers a very different model. Philip Marlowe's desires drive the narrative, and his perpetual search for idealised figures of both masculinity and femininity make Chandler's hard-boiled style an appealing option for the exploration of identity politics.

4. Walton and Jones's belief in the radical potential of the genre is shared by Maureen Reddy (1988) and Paulina Palmer (1997).
5. David Glover cites Rosalind Coward's contention that Francis's racing thrillers 'are highly popular with women readers precisely because their play upon male dependency via accident or injury imaginarily cedes immense power to women as carers' (1989: 75).
6. 'The average detective story is probably no worse than the average novel, but you never see the average novel. It doesn't get published. The average – or only slightly above average – detective story does. Not only is it published . . . it is read' (Chandler, 1950/1964: 183).

3

Dividing the Men from the Boys: Joseph Hansen's Economy of the Same

> From [Irigaray's] point of view, the philosophers, of whatever persuasion, are comfortably installed in the male imaginary, so comfortably that they are completely unaware of the sexuate character of 'universal' thought. (Whitford, 1991: 103)

> While heterosexuality is necessary for the maintenance of any patriarchy, homophobia, against males at any rate, is not. (Sedgwick, 1985: 4)

> 'If you set out to find a man who isn't a boy anymore', Dave said, 'you're going to be a long time looking.' (Hansen, 1982: 163)

As the investigations of Part I have shown, the process of detection is about the reading of bodies, both living and dead. The detective must decode the desires emanating from and written upon the bodies he or she encounters, and a connection can be traced between the detective's relationship to the physical world and the methodology employed in his or her investigation of the narrative's criminal desires. In the case of Joseph Hansen's serial detective Dave Brandstetter, this paradigm has considerable implications. Brandstetter succeeds as an investigator not through ratiocination nor, like Chandler's Marlowe, through an inherent distrust of wealthy or feminine bodies; rather he succeeds through his ability to read the signifiers of repression. His investigations succeed because he identifies both desire and its denial. He sees through the locked doors of the closet and the myths of the heterosexual family ideal, and in so doing he destabilises the norms of hard-boiled detective fiction. In Dave Brandstetter, middle-aged homosexual insurance investigator, Joseph Hansen has created a 'medium-boiled' transitional phenomenon, and his novels present a paradoxical stage upon which detective fiction's bodies become both more obviously politicised and yet more determinedly attached to the patriarchal structures that underpin popular fictional forms.

Strategies of reinscription are central to Hansen's fiction, and at the centre of these scripts is the body – specifically, the male body. As Roger Bromley has observed, 'the death or disappearance of a father, son, or husband is almost always the precipitating moment of the text, as it is in the "classic" mode' (Bromley, 1989: 103). However, as Bromley goes on to suggest, 'what follows is an inquiry into the ideological bases of norms of gender and sexuality. In these texts, destabilisation is not simply a matter of plot, but the basic ordering principle of the narrative.' To a certain extent these claims are indisputable, at least as far as the 'norms of gender and sexuality' are concerned. Hansen undoubtedly enquires into the ideological basis of heterosexuality, but his challenge is in many ways as blinkered as the edifice it attacks. These novels present a critique of one gender and one sexuality – both of which are male. Ultimately these novels are concerned not with the rewriting of gender categories, but with the definition, deconstruction and reconceptualisation of masculinity. Wherever he travels and whatever he investigates, Dave Brandstetter encounters and himself espouses a system of values and assumptions that are uncompromisingly and exclusively masculine.

These criticisms, however, are not intended to invalidate Hansen's project, nor to deny the effectiveness of these novels. Hansen is the author of twelve Brandstetter novels, published between 1970 and 1991. The novels comprise a 'real time' sequence underpinned by two central motifs: death, and the corruption of the American Dream. The series begins with Brandstetter's 'spiritual' death through grief for his lost lover, Rod. This loss is a prelude to the detective's rebirth through the reawakening of desire, but Brandstetter's first attempt at a new relationship seems doomed to failure. Doug Sawyer looks like Rod, but is not Rod – a fundamental failing that Dave can never quite forgive. However, in the fourth novel, *The Man Everyone was Afraid Of*, Dave meets Cecil, a young black media student, and it is this relationship that will form the emotional bedrock of the series. Cecil's extreme youth causes problems at first. The couple are forcibly separated by Cecil's older brother, and it is not until the sixth novel, *Gravedigger*, that Cecil is old enough to escape the imperatives of heterosexual patriarchy and become Dave's full-time lover.

The advent of Cecil also acts as an irritant upon the racial wound of American society and facilitates Brandstetter's exposure of the hypocritical sham that is white heterosexual American family life. Indeed, the American Dream could arguably be seen as the master criminal or arch villain of Hansen's narrative. Intimately connected with the novel's death motif, the American Dream is remorselessly exposed as a cancer – eating away at any possibility of a tolerant co-operative society. Irrespective of superficial plot details, each Brandstetter novel reveals the ideal of the happy, white, heterosexual family to be built upon a web of deceit and denial. The more ostentatiously 'ideal' the family, the deeper the roots of sexual deceit are likely to run. As the series progresses, Brandstetter evolves from insurance death claims investigator to private eye, but throughout his cases uncover the realities of poverty, racism and social exclusion. He also tackles corporate greed, religious fanaticism and right-wing paranoia; but above all, he decodes desire, acting as an undercover agent exposing the closet culture of 'straight' America.

Not surprisingly, after twenty years of hard labour policing the Augean stables of the American Dream, Brandstetter is exhausted. The final novels of the sequence emphasise his age and return to the ache of loneliness that characterised the opening fictions. Although he continues to work, he yearns for the company of his lover to stave off the intimations of mortality inherent in the ageing and death of his friends. The novels feature an ongoing community of characters, and in the penultimate novel, *The Boy Who Was Buried This Morning* (1990), it is the death of Dave's friend, the restaurateur Max Romano, that completes the circle of grief. The rejuvenating effect of the relationship with Cecil is undermined, and Cecil, like Dave's father, Carl, before him, must watch over the bereaved Dave, coaxing him back into a life for which he no longer has much of an appetite. Finally, and unusually, the ultimate death of the series belongs to the detective. In the appropriately titled *A Country of Old Men* (1991), the supposedly retired Brandstetter works on in order to take his mind off the changes that surround him, and the narrative is brought to an abrupt end when its focaliser, Dave, is consumed by the pain and darkness of a heart attack.

Over the course of the twelve books this narrative trajectory is crisply and succinctly conveyed. The novels are short and the prose is typically characterised by a terse metaphoricity. Carefully balanced syntax and extensive use of alliteration give a poetic intensity to the writing, as is evident in this achingly powerful depiction of grief:

> The bleakness was in him. After only three months he and Doug were coming apart. The dead were doing it – Doug's dead, a French boy, skull shattered at a sun-blaze bend on the raceway at Le Mans; his own dead, a graying boy interior decorator, eaten out by cancer in a white nightmare hospital. He and Doug clung tight, but the dead crept cold between them. Neither he nor Doug knew how to bury them and in their constant presence they treated each other with the terrible, empty gentleness people substitute for love at funerals. It was no way to live and they weren't living. (Hansen, 1973/1996: 1)

This quotation forms the second paragraph of the second Brandstetter novel, *Death Claims* (1973), and is typical of the treatment of death within the early books. An opening paragraph lays repeated emphasis on the 'bleakness' of Dave's perspective, a bleakness that dominates despite the suggestion that the bay before him 'might have been dabbed there by Raoul Dufy' (Hansen, 1973/1996: 1). The detective's vision of life has been indelibly marked by the experience of death, and the boundary that divides the two states is seen to be fragile and permeable. The ghostly haunting of the living by the dead is a not unfamiliar trope within crime fiction, but Hansen's depiction has a careful vividness not often evoked in popular writing.[1] The painful whiteness of the bright sunshine described in the first paragraph is developed as a memory in the second paragraph, evoking not only the clinical horror of the hospital but also the incongruous sunshine of the French boy's death. Brandstetter has become not only an investigator but a carrier of deaths, burdened with the grief of his own loss and that of his partner, Doug.

This paragraph is also crucial in its conception of the detective's lost object. Both interior designer and racer are described as boys, lost boys at that, forever trapped in the ideality of adolescence. The figure of the boy attains almost iconic significance in the Brandstetter novels, and it is important to recognise that the male body as object of desire is as significant a textual marker as Bromley's slaughtered patriarchs. Roger Bromley has effectively illustrated the extent to which the novels emerge from an assimilationist, liberal dynamic that might be seen to undermine any claim to political radicalism (1989: 115–16). However, while the ostentatious politics of the novels remain muted, the politics of desire within these texts cannot be so easily explained or contained. Objects of desire will inevitably be freighted with cultural meanings within a serial narrative that encompasses moments of radical change within American conceptions of self and sexuality.

Transgressive desire is always disruptive and potentially dangerous. American history makes this inevitable. It was not until 1973, coincidentally the year in which *Death Claims* was published, that the American Psychiatric Association and the American Psychological Association finally decided that homosexuality was not an illness (Altman, 1982: 5). This belated depathologising of homosexuality acts as a pertinent reminder of the context within which these early investigations were conceived and published.[2] While the object of the detective's affections remains firmly masculine, Brandstetter's relationship to the ideological 'norms' of American society will always be an unstable and disconcerting one.[3] As Dennis Altman has observed:

> [I]n our society the depiction of sexuality is always in heterosexual terms, and any affirmation of homosexuality is an attack on the prevalent values. Hence to declare the validity of homosexuality, to reject the judgement that it is sick, evil, a maladjustment, a deviance, or a perversion, is a political statement, and the assertion of a homosexual identity is as much a political act as was the assertion of a Czech or Romanian identity in the nineteenth century. (Altman, 1982: 3–4)

Brandstetter's laconic, unquestioned and guilt-free homosexuality is, from the outset, established as a 'norm' to set against the predominantly dysfunctional examples of heterosexuality that crowd the texts. When his father takes advantage of Rod's death to claim that Dave's homosexuality might have been only a 'passing phase', his conventional platitudes are swiftly and succinctly debunked. Any paeon to family values would sound hollow coming from a man married as many times as Carl Brandstetter (ten, by the time of his eventual death in *Skinflick*), yet Dave's most telling rejoinder is not an accusation of hypocrisy, but an affirmation of desire. In response to

Carl's question 'Why be a middle-aged auntie if you don't want to?', Dave simply replies, 'Did I say I didn't want to?' (1970: 100–1).

These texts can be seen then as confident assertions of a transgressive sexual agenda, but in one key dimension this must be recognised as an agenda with tunnel vision. Throughout all the novels, one constant remains: the absence of woman. And thus it is not so much in his depiction of a monogamous 'liberal' homosexuality that Hansen's assimilationism is most evident, but in his unquestioned replication of patriarchal norms. Brandstetter's potentially disturbing otherness is rendered comfortable and unthreatening through the adoption of a familiar binary relational structure, and through the creation of a greater or 'other' other. This other is not necessarily demonised, but its difference exists primarily to confirm the superiority of the subject, which here, as usual, is represented by a particular mode of patriarchal masculinity.

The world of David Brandstetter is fundamentally and unquestioningly homosocial. It is man who forms the units of social signification, becoming the yardstick against which value may be measured:

> The waterwheel was twice a man's height, wider than a man's two stretched arms. The timbers, braced and bolted with rusty iron, were heavy, hand-hewn, swollen with a century of wet. Moss bearded the paddles, which dripped as they rose. The sounds were good. Wooden stutter like children running down a hall at the end of school. Grudging axle thud like the heartbeat of a strong old man. (Hansen, 1973/1996: 12–13)

Irrespective of sexual orientation, it is the things that men say and do that matter, and it is in this context that the limits of Hansen's agenda become apparent. What Hansen's novels offer is very far from being a reinscription of gender, or of sexuality and sexual roles; rather they depict what Luce Irigaray has described as an 'economy of the same'. Irigaray's critique of western philosophy detects a 'sexual indifference' in which one sex, the male sex, holds a monopoly on value (1985: 69), and this concept is easily applicable to the popular cultural product of Hansen's novels. In the world of Dave Brandstetter, women simply do not signify. This is not misogyny in the traditional sense. Female sexuality presents no obvious threat; it is not concrete enough to threaten anything. Rather, it represents marginality at its most extreme and its most evasive – the marginality of invisibility. Within this fictional framework, women attain new heights of superfluity, and should a man fall from the heights of homosexuality into the triviality of heterosexuality, it is he rather than the woman who will be punished, as is the case in *Fadeout* (1970). Women become the ultimate in passive signifiers. They are not evil, they tend not to be the murderer, some of them are even quite 'nice', but they have no function within the narrative, nor within the moral or aesthetic world of the detective.

Defending her critique of Freudian psychoanalysis, Luce Irigaray argues that:

> Woman herself is never at issue in these statements: the feminine is defined as the necessary complement to the operation of male sexuality, and, more often, as a negative image that provides male sexuality with an unfailingly phallic self-representation. (Irigaray, 1985: 70)

But Hansen has enacted a further displacement that removes women even from their role as mirrors to the male psyche. With women thus erased from the scale of cultural and sexual signification, the traditional binary oppositions supposedly essential to cultural understanding are disrupted. To fill the gap left by this displacement, Hansen's texts offer an alternative opposition. In a world where the only significant relationships are between men, the founding binary is no longer that of man/woman, but that of man/boy. This transition does not emerge from an exact concurrence between women and boys; rather it is a qualitative shift, recognising an alternative mode of identity formation. Irigaray's economy of the same delineates a gender hierarchy that privileges masculine self over feminine reflection of that self. Accordingly, Hansen's hierarchy replaces feminine reflection with masculine resemblance. The boy does not simply mirror the man, he also acts as a reminder of what the man has been. He becomes a distorting mirror that reflects eternal youth and virility at the same time as it presents raw material to be shaped in the patriarchal process of man-making. The boy/man dyad becomes an all-sufficient narcissistic paradigm for masculine development. This structure of self-fashioning bears a marked resemblance to the Greek example cited by Eve Sedgwick in *Between Men*:

> Male homosexuality . . . was a widespread, licit and very influential part of the culture. Highly structured along lines of class, and within the citizen class along lines of age, the

> pursuit of the adolescent boy by the older man was described by stereotypes that we associate with romantic heterosexual love . . . with the passive part going to the boy. At the same time, however, because the boy was destined to grow up into manhood, the assignment of roles was not permanent. Thus the love relationship, while temporarily oppressive to the object, has a strongly educational function . . . Along with its erotic component, then, this was a bond of mentorship; the boys were apprentices in the ways and virtues of Athenian citizenship, whose privileges they inherited. (Sedgwick, 1985: 4)[4]

Not surprisingly, Hansen's novels provide copious examples of this mentoring dynamic. Over the course of the series, for example, Dave's banker friend Mel Fleischer nurtures Japanese student Makoto from incomprehensible immigrant to flawless French lecturer, from rollerskating teenager to conservative professional (1988: 57). A slightly less radical transformation is enacted on Kovaks, the 'wild man' turned 'brilliantly gifted potter', adopted by phone company executive Ray Lollard (1991: 126). Here, however, the Athenian model is brutally disrupted by AIDS, as the final appearance of the couple anticipates not patriarchal inheritance but Kovaks's premature death. Many of the later novels evoke this disruption in their titles. *Early Graves* (1987), *The Boy Who Was Buried This Morning* (1990) and *A Country of Old Men* (1991) all suggest the disintegration of the 'natural' order. A generation has been lost and the values of a particular mode of patriarchal gentility seem increasingly threatened by the modern world.

Boys, then, are different from girls because they at least have the potential to turn into men. What is not clear from Hansen's novels, however, is whether this potential is inherent within all boys, or whether some boys are destined never to grow up and to remain eternally in the childhood state equated with femininity. Perhaps, though, it is less a question of essentials than an issue of nurturance. As the mentoring model suggests, men are made and not born – but how is this man-making to be achieved in contemporary society? Peter Middleton argues that the relationship between men and boys, like that between men and women, is one of separate spheres. Traditionally, men's role in the workplace has meant their absence from the home, with the result that 'the defining activities of manhood are largely invisible, even as the scope and power of this masculine world are everywhere evident' (1992: 41). Boys are excluded from the sphere of the manly and given a comic-book world in recompense for their lack:

> Men don't want boys in their world, so they give them a surrogate one because their admission into the world of manhood would force unacceptable changes. Men would have to care for the boys and this would mean sharing power with women and children, and transforming those laws which call comic manhood into being. For men, manhood must remain a separated condition, not one of emergence and dependency. (Middleton, 1992: 42)

Within such a framework, Hansen's novels offer radical possibilities. Boys are admitted, even welcomed, into the sacrosanct world of the male, and a duty of care is undoubtedly placed upon the men who look after them. Less radical, however, is the language of ownership and possession that accompanies the boys' adoption (Hansen, 1982: 78–9; 1988: 58–9). For most of the boys that feature in the Brandstetter novels, manhood requires a *very* long apprenticeship.[5]

Yet however long and ill-defined these apprenticeships, the ultimate trajectory of the Brandstetter novels suggests that boys must eventually become men, if only because of the stigma of femininity that attaches itself to the 'lesser' half of any binary relation. Boys may be only quantitatively different from men, but if they stay that way too long they risk becoming qualitatively different, too. Hansen's novels are seldom kind to ostentatiously 'feminine' men. Even *Skinflick*'s sympathetically drawn transvestite, Randy Van, must transform himself into a boy to win the prize of Dave's desire (1979/1980: 159–62), while the charms of youthful femininity are depicted as corrupt and degrading when carried into adulthood or old age (1970/1980: 102; 1984: 34–5).

Given the ongoing power of femininity to repell and disgust, it is inevitable that even Hansen's Athenian model of homosocial patriarchy will incorporate a degree of uncertainty. The boy is both object of desire and something which must be transcended, improved upon, left behind and transformed. Consequently, in the early novels, *Fadeout* and *Death Claims*, in which the 'boy' operates as a 'feminised' object of desire, he is to a certain extent seen as an immature object choice. The key task to be achieved by both the detective and the peripheral characters is to relate man to man.[6] Yet as the novels progress, contradictions emerge within this developmental framework, and by the time of the later *Gravedigger* (1982), the nature of this responsible adult masculinity has been brought into question – challenged by the detective's own regeneration through the love not of a man, but a boy.

DIVIDING THE MEN FROM THE BOYS: HANSEN'S EARLY OBJECT LESSON

Given the detective's dual role as death-claims investigator and desiring subject, the centrality of the body to these fictions is inevitable. *Fadeout*, the first Dave Brandstetter novel is, above all, concerned with the lost or absent body. The detective examines the supposed death of small-town superstar Fox Olson, unwilling to pay out his company's cash until the victim's missing body surfaces from the swollen river into which it has apparently disappeared. This case is Brandstetter's first since the death of his long-term partner, Rod, and his loss pervades the book, turning this into a novel in which the traditional narrative of investigation (the case of Fox Olson – dead or alive?) is at least partially usurped by a narrative of grief. The detective seeks the lost object of his desire and is in turn sought out by the ghosts of that loss. Psychologist Colin Murray Parkes comments that ghosts form a characteristic component of bereavement. Survivors search for the person that, rationally, they know is lost, oscillating between the comfort of memory and its pain (Parkes, 1972/1986: 64–72, 77–96). This pattern is evident in both the frequent visions of Rod's dying that haunt Brandstetter's investigation (1970: 7, 44), and in the number of characters who physically or emotionally evoke the various lost loves of the narrative. Dave's dead lover, Rod, bears a remarkable resemblance to Fox Olsen's lost love, Doug Sawyer, who in turn bears a remarkable resemblance to Olsen's substitute love: his wife, Thorne (1970: 92).

Returning to work after his bereavement, the detective seeks to exorcise the ghosts of one death by explaining another, but the irony is that in this case it will be a resurrection. For all its preoccupation with death, this is a novel in which the body itself is remarkably evasive, and within this evasion the narrative offers an unexpected fantasy. Moving beyond detective fiction's customary dream of an explanation, *Fadeout* offers instead a vivid fantasy of resurrection. As the title itself suggests the boundary between two states of being is a permeable one, and the events of the narrative confirm this. Olsen's supposedly dead body is missing, and although his death was in fact a carefully staged rebirth, he remains an absent presence at the centre of the narrative; as does his mystery visitor, Doug Sawyer. When Sawyer at least is discovered, it transpires that he too carries a lost-and-found dynamic. He has lost Fox Olsen, but found Jean-Paul, lost Jean-Paul only to rediscover Olsen, lost Olsen, but, finally, as the narrative closes, he finds Dave. Yet, by the end of this confusing game of hide-and-seek, the detective has found the object of both his quests – a body (Fox Olsen) and a lover (Doug Sawyer). In the fantastical world of detective fiction, lost objects *can* be found, bodies *can* be resurrected: death is not real.

Significantly, these patterns of death and rebirth are fundamentally intertwined with a discourse of sexuality. Since losing Doug Sawyer to the Second World War, Fox Olsen had been living the double life of a 'passing' heterosexual. This heterosexual self has to 'die' to facilitate the rebirth of his 'authentic' homosexual identity. And briefly Olsen achieves a return to his prelapsarian happiness, as he frolics with Doug Sawyer on the beach of their youth. However, within the logic of the narrative, Olsen had fallen. He had compromised and denied his homosexuality, for which sin he was punished initially by the loss of his creativity, and ultimately by death.[7] Neither Dave nor Doug, however, have ever committed the sins of repression or denial, and, thus, at the end of the novel, it is the detective who, having rescued the damsel in distress, is rewarded with the promise of curative romance. As the novel draws to a close, the dead boy, Rod, is metamorphosed into the living man, Doug:

> He stood bewildered in the middle of the room. The jacket was not American made. Nor the bulky sweater under it. Nor the slacks. They'd all been slept in. On pine needles. He turned, and Dave felt shock in the pit of his stomach. The eyes were shiny opaque, like stones in a stream bed. Rod's eyes. He was the same size and build as Rod, same dark color, same long head. Another man, but like, very like. Even to the voice. (1970/1980: 148)

Thus it would seem that Hansen subscribes to the ideal of an authentic sexual identity that characters repress or ignore at their peril. Hansen's novels are littered with the corpses of closeted gay men, killed, usually, by some agent of the heterosexual world into which they had tried to insinuate themselves. As in all discourses of exclusion, the penalty for passing is more extreme than any punishment meted out to those clearly identifiable as 'other'. Yet although the narratives of *Fadeout* and *Gravedigger* firmly condemn the passing homosexual, in the early novels at least, Dave is both uncomfortable when the markers of his identity are clearly read and hostile to 'other', more obviously feminine, modes of homosexuality: 'Dave didn't like being tagged. Not by Kohlmeyers's kind' (1970/1980: 103). Dave is not above passing himself if it will gain him information, and with his well-heeled appearance, the role of the all-American male is easily assumed (1970/1980: 94–5). Nonetheless, it seems that in *Fadeout* Hansen firmly subscribes to a belief in an essential sexual identity (100, 103), even if that identity is itself subject to subdivisions, and offers a variety of possible roles.

Given that the majority of Hansen's crimes emerge from the repression or denial of an authentic gay sexuality, the problem for Brandstetter becomes one of detecting this authenticity. He must learn to read the bodies he encounters for the markers of sexual identity. And it is here that the narrative's concern with sexuality re-encounters its obsession with death. The concept of the detective as death-claims investigator poses the novel as an interrogation of grief, establishing the authenticity of mourning as the authoritative index of culpability. And paralleling the enquiry into grief's authenticity is the discovery that at the root of the mystery is the question of sexual authenticity. Thus the crime at the centre of *Fadeout*, the crime that must be and is uncovered, is Olsen's repression of his homosexuality. The uncovering of the murderer is both less central and less satisfying than the unravelling of the emotional ties that contributed to Olsen's tragedy. Through his capacity to read the signs of Olsen's desire, Brandstetter reveals the heterosexual paradise constructed around an ideal of Olsen as an inauthentic and fraudulent sham. Dave knows that something is amiss from the moment that he first sets eyes upon the disturbing picture of the phallic chute that hangs over the hearth of heterosexual bliss. From such small cracks in the façade of conformity, Brandstetter begins to garner the clues that will expose the American Dream as a sham.

The enhanced capacity of the homosexual detective to read and interpret sexual signs should come as no surprise. Harold Beaver observes that:

> [T]o be homosexual in Western society entails a state of mind in which all credentials, however petty, are under unceasing scrutiny. The homosexual is beset by signs, by the urge to interpret whatever transpires, or fails to transpire, between

> himself and every chance acquaintance. He is a prodigious consumer of signs – of hidden meanings, hidden systems, hidden potentiality . . .
>
> Homosexuals, like Masons, live not in an alternative culture but in a duplicate culture of constantly interrupted and overlapping roles. (Beaver, 1981: 104–5)

Yet, significantly, Beaver also stresses the provisional nature not just of homosexuality but of all sexual identities, which are, he argues, constructed out of the need for the constitutive oppositions typical of binary reasoning. The homosexual thus emerges from a historically specific need for a structure of otherness that would further legitimise a bourgeois, heterosexual, matrimonial norm (1981: 100–3). In Hansen's novels, however, the familiar binary oppositions have been displaced – a radical intervention that, superficially at least, facilitates the inscription of a challenging counter-cultural narrative of resistance. Yet, on closer inspection it becomes clear that this is no paradigm shift. While the signifiers may have changed, the structure of signification remains the same. Hansen's texts construct a series of alternative binary oppositions, of inversions and reconfigurations, that effectively expose the frailties of heterosexual hegemony, but which are nonetheless simultaneously embedded in a fundamental and unquestioned patriarchal fallacy.

The central paradox of the Brandstetter novels thus resides, as Beaver's masonic metaphor suggests, in the duality of Dave's position. Although his sexuality remains stigmatised, and his object choice illegitimate, Dave cannot plausibly be read as the excluded other. The job at Medallion Life symbolises his acceptance by his father, and the wealth and comfort accruing to him from his economic status in turn ensures his acceptance by the conceptual father of patriarchal society. Irrespective of his transgressive sexuality, Dave represents the powerful figure of the patriarchal inheritor.[8] Hansen has conferred status and authority upon his detective, with the result that these fictions seem concerned less with the radical undermining than with the nostalgic rehabilitation of patriarchal structures.

Nostalgic rehabilitation is a serious business, and one that demands levels of responsibility supposedly characteristic of adult masculinity. Rather than standing outside the law as romantics or revolutionaries, Hansen's homosexuals are seen to be the true upholders of patriarchal tradition. It is the homosexual man who truly understands and appreciates beauty, and who is established as having a privileged relationship to a concept of high culture. Significantly, Fox Olsen, the repressed homosexual, is trapped in the hell of popular mainstream success, when in reality he craves a superior world of classical music, serious prose and homosexual desire. This high art versus popular culture divide is partially replicated in Dave's relationship with Rod, whose populist tastes confirm his arrested development, that is, his cultivation of a feminised or boyish immaturity:

> Rod would have cheered . . . At home, he'd have grabbed corn chips and beer from the kitchen, kicked off his shoes, settled with food, drink, books in a corner of a couch, feet tucked under him like a girl. He'd have shouted with laughter. He'd have jumped up repeatedly to show Dave this photo of Ann Sheridan sultry in five-inch wedgies, that photo of Barbara Stanwyck in a square-shouldered mink, a Luger smoking in her hand. And Dave? He'd have hunched down lower and grimmer in his chair, trying to focus on *The New Republic* or *Scientific American*. (Hansen, 1973: 58–9)

At this stage of the detective's career, then, it would seem that Hansen is firmly opposed to the Peter Pan dynamic that tempted Olsen to relive his past. The boys are lost, and should stay that way. 'He's a grown up' says Dave, justifying his relationship with Doug to his sceptical friend Madge (1973: 35), and it is not until the fourth Brandstetter novel, *The Man Everyone Was Afraid Of*, that the seeds of a challenge to this binary are sown. In the closing pages of this novel, Dave meets the first significant challenge to his authority as a white, liberal patriarch, when the brother of his new boy lover, Cecil, confronts him and prohibits him access to the object of his desire. Two novels later, in *Gravedigger*, Cecil returns – old enough now to do as he pleases, and to force the increasingly patriarchal Dave into a reconception of what it means to be a father.

REDISCOVERING THE INNER BOY: HANSEN'S LATER CHANGE OF HEART

'If you set out to find a man who isn't a boy anymore . . . you're going to be a long time looking' (1982: 163) explains Dave to Anna Westover, a woman who has singularly failed to understand the rules of Hansen's homosocial universe. Yet the reader might also be forgiven a moment's confusion, as this seems a blatant contradiction of the binary opposition that has dominated the previous novels. Dave *is*, or has been until now, the man who isn't a boy anymore. Throughout *Fadeout* his adult masculinity was juxtaposed against the boyishness of Rod; he did not get on with the boys who were Rod's friends, and he discourages the amorous boy Anselmo by telling him that he is a 'morose bastard' (1970: 116). Hansen's founding binary opposition would appear to be undergoing a transformation. Increasingly the duality is internalised, suggesting that the capacity to be a boy remains within and it is up to the man whether he chooses to exhibit it. Or, more precisely, whether he has the chance to rediscover it. The trope of rediscovery is strong – in *Fadeout* it is largely confined to Olsen, but in *Gravedigger* the pattern incorporates not only the missing patriarch Chass Westover, but also Dave himself, who changes radically in the rejuvenating company of Cecil:

> *The man behind the counter was a woman old and gray*. The lines of the nonsense rhyme jumped into his mind and he had to suppress a grin in the storefront office of Momentum Truck Rentals in Santa Monica . . . But he had no right to grin. He was gray himself and, if not as old as she was, still old. Cecil was making him forget that, making him remember that silly verse from his childhood. (Hansen, 1982: 51)

The arrival of Cecil Harris complicates the paradigms of masculinity established in the early Brandstetter novels. Although the balance of power suggested by the age/youth binary suggests a replication of the butch/ femme dynamic of Rod and Dave's earlier relationship, Cecil's actual role is somewhat different. It is his presence, his role as an appropriate other, that finally exorcises the ghosts of Brandstetter's grief, and although it might seem that Dave has found another 'boy', Cecil is very far from being a replica of Rod. The differences between the two are subtle and complicated by race, as Cecil's blackness throws Dave's whiteness and its privileges into sharp relief. When the villain of *Gravedigger* wants to frame Cecil, his task is made ludicrously easy by dominant ideological presumptions about black criminality (Marriott, 1996: 187–8). However, it proves equally easy for Dave to get Cecil out of jail – his whiteness and wealth combining to ease the path of justice. Inevitably their cohabitation runs the risk of evoking a colonial dynamic. The spectre of racial patronage haunts Brandstetter's adoption and 'education' of the younger Cecil, a character who in many ways seems designed to ease white fears of black masculinity. The myth of black sexual excess that so terrorises white America is confounded by the presentation of a young, thin, sensitive gay boy. However, in this context, the term 'boy' itself becomes newly problematic. In terms of sexuality, it acts as a useful signifier of difference, but in conjunction with race it mutates into a painful reminder of historical trauma. I will, however, continue to use the term as a designation for Cecil, as in Hansen's gay landscape it is not the markers of race that are used to distinguish between the boys and the men, and to suggest that Cecil's blackness is simply assimilated by a 'superior' (white) gay civilisation would be to oversimplify the construction of both black and gay subjectivities within the novels.

Although Hansen's novels foreground sexuality as a determinant of identity, the texts seem aware that identity cannot be reduced to a singular 'truth'. Hansen also seems sensitive to the exploitative potential of the Cecil/Dave relationship and acts to defuse this through Cecil's active choice of Dave as lover and partner. Hansen also refuses to leave the lovers in paradise for long. Their idyllic reunion is almost immediately problematised by the intervention of outside forces. Although Miles Edwards's attempt to separate them is prompted by selfish motives, his attack has sufficient social force to shatter the couple's prelapsarian world. Edwards undermines Cecil's confidence by accusing him of being a 'kept boy' – a description designed to open racial wounds by evoking the master/slave dynamic. What had once been a desirable cohabitation now bears the stigma of dependency:

> Cecil shook his head impatiently. 'You don't need my help. You don't need anybody's help. Got along fine on your own all this time. Kept boy, that's what I'd be.' He jerked his head to indicate the laughing people at the other end of the room. He pitched his voice up, pursed his mouth, fluttered his lashes. 'What do you do, young Cecil? Do you act, do you interior decorate, do you style women's hair?' He changed voices. 'No, ma'am – ah jus' sleeps with Mistuh Brandstettuh.' (Hansen, 1982: 59)

Cecil wishes to resolve the situation by taking a job, Dave wants to keep his lover by his side, and agreement is eventually forged between them in a scene that ironically echoes the battles of women's liberation. Cecil, like many heroines before him, must struggle to escape the restrictions of the romance plot.

In an article on the impact of AIDS upon gay narratives, Derek Duncan has argued that:

> [T]he very nature of the 'coming out' narrative reinscribes the notion of the gay man as a feminised subject . . . For women writers, one way of contesting the oppressive ends of femininity was to write beyond marriage, and to interrogate what happened next. In the context of gay writing and experience, the challenge was to chart what happened after coming out. (Duncan, 1994: 159)

The plot of heterosexual romance ends in marriage or death, and the coming-out novel ends at the closet door; but the serial generic form adopted by Hansen enables him to evade, or at least displace, the imperatives of closure and resolution. While the specific crimes of each novel are solved, it is evident that larger issues, such as the growth of religious fundamentalism or AIDS, cannot be so easily contained. Similarly the personal development of the detective is ongoing, and it is here, primarily, that Hansen is able both to undermine the hegemonic authority of Dave's whiteness and begin his re-evaluation of what it means to be a boy.

Cecil Harris is the boy who will become 'both a son and a lover, a husband and a wife' (Schoene-Harwood, 2000: 175). In *Gravedigger*, the semiotic significance of the 'boy' undergoes a radical transformation. While never losing a 'feminine' dimension encoded as dependency and emotionality, the boy nonetheless becomes a patriarchal apprentice, awaiting initiation into the rites and responsibilities of patriarchal manhood. Cecil, like Dave, is a patriarchal inheritor. He will enter and inherit the business of being a man, just as Dave took on the mantle from his father, Carl. Dave's accession to full patriarchal status is emphasised in *Skinflick* and *Gravedigger* through the changing nature of his relationship to his stepmother, Amanda. As Amanda grieves for Carl, Dave becomes a father to her, taking a paternalistic interest in her future that extends to the vetting of a potential husband in *Gravedigger*.

PRESERVING PATRIARCHY: THE BATTLE FOR THE BOYS

Yet, for all Hansen's reinscriptions and revalorisations, the homosocial landscape is still subject to a fundamental binary division between men and boys. In a fascinating article on the construction of American masculinity, Michael S. Kimmel argues that 'manhood is neither static nor timeless; it is historical' and proceeds to trace the evolution of contemporary masculine paradigms. Kimmel distinguishes between the modes of masculinity characteristic of the late eighteenth and early nineteenth centuries – types defined as the 'Genteel Patriarch' and the 'Heroic Artisan' – and the predominant modern version of American masculinity, which he calls 'Marketplace Man':

> The story of the ways in which Marketplace Man becomes American Everyman is a tragic tale, a tale of striving to live up to impossible ideals of success leading to chronic terrors of emasculation, emotional emptiness, and a gendered rage that leaves a wide swath of destruction in its wake. (Kimmel, 1994: 124)

Kimmel's schema has significant repercussions for a study of Hansen's fiction, which is rooted in an idealisation not of modern marketplace masculinity, but of its older patriarchal precursor.

Kimmel describes the 'Genteel Patriarch' as a responsible man of property, 'refined, elegant, and given to casual sensuousness' (1994: 123) – all qualities that apply to both Carl and Dave Brandstetter. Coexisting with the genteel patriarch in Kimmel's model is the 'Heroic Artisan'. Strong and independent, 'the Heroic Artisan taught his son his craft, bringing him through ritual apprenticeship to status as master craftsman' (1994: 123). For Hansen, however, these two modes of masculinity are not separate and complementary, but rather are inextricably linked. The two have become entwined into one idealised form that might be termed heroic patriarchy. Carl Brandstetter's relationship to Dave certainly encompasses both forms. Although exhibiting all the qualities of the genteel patriarch, he is nonetheless the heroic artisan who would pass on his life's work to his son and heir, Dave. And despite leaving Medallion Life, Dave undoubtedly inherits the portable property of the twentieth century – wealth – alongside a sense of craft and skill that is recognised in his developing media reputation as a PI and crime solver.[9] Similarly, when Dave meets Cecil he, in turn, assumes the composite role of the heroic patriarch: desiring to pass on to Cecil not only the skills of the trade, but also the cultural values embodied in the aristocratic ideal of patriarchy.

This is the model of masculinity that predominates in Hansen's serial fiction, and what makes the 1982 novel *Gravedigger* such a pivotal narrative is that it is here that Brandstetter's masculinity is most seriously threatened. The threat takes the shape of the predatory bisexual Miles Edwards, whose behaviour remorselessly reveals him to be a prime example of 'Marketplace Manhood'. Hansen's resistance to this capitalist construction is evident in his depiction of Edwards's predominant qualities: greed and competitiveness. Kimmel's definition of marketplace masculinity emphasises the acquisition of culturally valued commodities alongside tangible proof of that acquisition (1994: 124–5), and the first commodity that Edwards is seen to acquire and parade within the novel is Dave's stepmother, Amanda. Dave's first impressions are coloured by an unexpected degree of jealousy, as he feels his paternal relationship to Amanda coming under threat. However, it is not until Edwards begins to undermine Cecil's confidence and credibility that it becomes evident that he is a threat to Dave. Exhibiting behaviour that could be described as a form of 'herd' masculinity, Edwards identifies Dave as the dominant male, and thereafter attempts to seduce and feminise him. Edwards's laying down of his body in Dave's bed is not a sacrifice at the altar of an older, wiser masculinity, but rather an attempt to recuperate Dave into an alternative mode of masculinity. Edwards wants to be closer to the source of power because he is secure in the knowledge that ultimately he will usurp that power – and it seems particularly significant in this context that *Gravedigger* lays considerable emphasis on the issue of Dave's age (1982: 89, 119, 157).

Another characteristic of Kimmel's marketplace masculinity is its 'relentless repudiation of the feminine' (1994: 125), and in *Gravedigger* this can be seen to undergo a bizarre transformation. The feminine is here appropriated and incorporated into the homosocial economy of the Dave-Cecil-Edwards triangle, while the traditional repository of femininity, Amanda, is rejected even from the unenviable position of being a mere object of exchange. This is 'between men' – she simply does not count. 'What's Amanda got to do with it?' responds Edwards when his behaviour is challenged by Dave. 'Amanda and I are all right, we're fine. This is something separate and apart' (1982: 115). Within this revised structure of signification, the role of object is instead occupied by the feminised Cecil, against whom Edwards schemes and plots in order to ensure his access to the big prize, which is Dave. Marketplace manhood is thus figured as a threat to the benevolent heroic patriarchy embodied by Dave. This structure has, over the course of *Skinflick* and *Gravedigger*, evolved into a parodic version of the heterosexual all-American family. Dave's stepmother, Amanda, has effectively mutated into his daughter, while the youthful black Cecil is being groomed as the new inheritor to Dave's liberal family ideal.

It is thus particularly interesting that the threat of marketplace masculinity should be embodied in the figure of the bisexual. The bisexual would seem to symbolise all that is wrong with modern masculinities, and in *Gravedigger* the two key bisexual characters, Miles Edwards and the largely absent Charles Westover, are depicted as immature and destructive – child-men who go bad, or even turn dangerous, when they cannot have everything they want. The parallel with capitalism is evident, but the model is also significant for an understanding of Hansen's overall developmental schema. With bisexuals now available to fill the role of 'other', boys can move up the hierarchy. The adoption of a boy is no longer the sign of an immature object choice; rather it is indicative of responsibility. The older man selects a boy who will himself become a worthy inheritor of the patriarchal mantle. Cecil's youth and relative femininity is rendered positive in comparison with the voracious promiscuity of the bisexual, whose inability to practise restraint and monogamy becomes the marker of his immaturity and lack of suitability to inherit. Significantly, when Edwards is exposed, he reverts to the childhood from which he never really emerged. Dishevelled and sullen, he is defended by his aged father, 'a sick and shrunken looking man who moved like an invalid' (1982: 156). Meanwhile, the much wronged against Cecil evidences the health of the Brandstetter family line, maturing into an appropriate apprentice of heroic patriarchy. Finding no pleasure in revenge, he proves himself a true inheritor (1982: 157).

Cecil, then, is a more 'serious' figure than Rod could ever have been. He is obsessed with news (a 'news junkie') – indicative of his engagement with the public world of the symbolic order, whereas Rod was an interior designer (as Amanda appropriately becomes), indicating their roles as inhabitants of a separate, private sphere – the feminine. Admittedly Dave is a phenomenally domesticated man, but this is depicted as an accomplishment. The theory of dishwashing that he memorably expounds in *Skinflick* does not represent a feminisation of the hero, but is rather a paeon to male self-sufficiency, in which the female is rendered redundant (1979/1980: 147–8). So Cecil is less of a boy than Rod, and Dave is more boyish in the presence of Cecil, but Cecil remains the feminised figure of the two:

particularly on account of his tears. Although he holds himself together admirably through the crisis, the aftermath provokes an appropriately feminine bodily collapse (1982: 150). Indeed, tears become a defining feature of Cecil's character for much of the following novel, *Nightwork* (1984). Having been severely wounded at the end of *Gravedigger*, he cries frequently with frustration at his dependent status in *Nightwork*. Nonetheless, he continues to fulfil the dual role of feminised boy and masculine inheritor, confirming his legitimacy in the final scenes as he saves Dave's life by killing a man, before once again bursting into tears (1984: 170).[10]

The claim made by Jeffrey Weeks and others that masculinity is achieved by warding off the threats represented by femininity and homosexuality begs a further question (Gutterman, 1994: 225). What happens if that normative model of masculinity is itself homosexual? The answer, as far as Hansen's fiction is concerned, would seem to be very little. The dualistic frameworks through which identity is conceived are not fundamentally changed, and while heterosexuality may be temporarily displaced from its customary centrality, patriarchy remains firmly in place.[11] Perhaps this fluctuation tells us something. By creating an opposition between the usually homogenous discourses of patriarchy and heterosexuality, Hansen undoubtedly disrupts familiar binary oppositions. However, the lack of destabilisation and change consequent upon this disrupted opposition would seem to suggest that changing one element of a binary opposition will never suffice as a strategy for change. As long as one element of a rooted structural binary remains in place, another other can always be found. Men and women, men and boys, men and bisexuals: only when both poles are displaced from their fixed signifying positions might it be possible to see a truly radical change in our understanding and conception of identity.

In his recent interrogation of masculinity, David Gutterman draws attention to the concept of 'branded contingencies', which might be seen as the foundation stones of a culturally constructed identity (1994: 225). And it is patriarchy that is revealed by Hansen to be the fundamental 'contingency branded into' his characters' sense of self and other. However, Gutterman also draws attention to the extent to which all selves are ultimately intersecting selves, and that no agency is ever fixed or stable. Even Brandstetter, visiting the ghetto in *Nightwork*, can find his authoritative identity thrown into disarray. No private investigator ever moves far from a recognition of the performative nature of identities, and Hansen's rewriting of the script of homosexual exclusion ultimately, and shockingly, becomes a re-enactment of the American Dream it sought to displace. Dave's accession to patriarchal authority confirms the fantasy that the all-American patriarch is not an impossible role for any male – not even a 'middle-aged auntie' (1970: 101).

Consequently, the categorising of these fictions as either radical or reactionary is fraught with critical difficulties. The Brandstetter novels challenge the priorities of formula fiction through their foregrounding of illicit desire, but the landscape that they depict is nonetheless fraught with paradox. Whether the novels are seen to be composed of shifting subjectivities, or of essentialist affirmations of 'deviant' sexualities, these radical dimensions remain fundamentally undercut by a founding absence. The performative world of Dave Brandstetter is ultimately the world of the renaissance stage. Gender and sexuality are up for grabs, but Irigaray's economy of the same remains firmly in place, and irrespective of script or staging, when it comes to the performance, all the women's roles are played by boys.

NOTES

1. Diverse examples of the bereaved might include Katherine V. Forrest's Kate Delafield, P. D. James's Adam Dalgliesh and Dorothy L. Sayers's Lord Peter Wimsey, a character haunted by the ghosts of his wartime experiences.
2. A context which is perhaps qualitatively rather than quantitatively different from the present. In America, homosexual activity remains illegal in a significant number of states, and a deeply disturbing 'backlash' against left-wing politics and minority rights is evident in the rise of the 'Patriot Movement'. An impressive account of the social and cultural implications of the 'white male as victim' is provided by David Savran's *Taking It Like A Man: White Masculinity, Masochism, and Contemporary American Culture* (1998).
3. I would stress, however, that Brandstetter is not, and never becomes, an outsider. As I will discuss later, his status rests firmly on the privileges of race, class and gender, which in western patriarchal society usually more than compensate for stepping over the boundary between the homosocial and the homosexual. Nonetheless, as a homosexual, he is always subject to some degree of risk. When his father dies in *Skinflick*, Dave is not in a position to take over the insurance company that is his inheritance on account of a homophobic boardroom backlash. He walks away from the conflict, but his new career as an independent investigator acts as a pertinent reminder of the precipice that awaits the overconfident homosexual (1979/1980: 39).
4. Contrasting modes of gender construction are not confined to antiquity. R. W. Connell observes that:

   > Masculinity does not exist except in contrast with 'femininity'. A culture which does not treat women and men as bearers of polarized character types, at least in principle, does not have a concept of masculinity in the sense of modern European/American culture.
   >
   > Historical research suggests that this was true of European culture itself before the eighteenth century. Women were certainly regarded as different from men, but different in the sense of being incomplete or inferior examples of the same character (for instance, having less of the faculty of reason). (Connell, 1995: 68)

   Shakespeare puts it more succinctly when he has Rosalind comment that, 'boys and women are for the most part cattle of this colour' (*As You Like It*, III, ii, 402–3). However, recent Renaissance scholarship has uncovered a more complex picture. Jean Howard agrees that gender and its signifiers were far from fixed: 'If dominant medical discourses . . . saw only male genitalia in both men and women and so, in some sense, authorized the view that there was only one sex, the Bible provided authority . . . for a two-sex gender system . . .' (1988: 422). Nonetheless, she goes on to argue that multiple gender discourses should not be mistaken for a tolerant view of gender flux:

> [T]he Renaissance needed the idea of two genders, one subordinate to the other, to provide a key element in its hierarchical view of the social order and to buttress its gendered division of labour . . . This simply means that gender difference and hierarchy had to be produced and secured – through ideological interpellation when possible, through force when necessary – on other grounds. (Howard, 1988: 423)

5. Just when it seems as if Cecil has finally achieved maturity – in his successful career and his care of the ageing Dave – we are given an abrupt reminder of his relative boy-status when he is tricked by a wily politician and bursts into tears. Dave, by contrast, seems never to have been a boy. His narrative effectively begins in the aftermath of the Second World War, and war has long been a pre-eminent maker of men. This 'fathering', combined with his grief, puts Dave on the 'fast-track', catapulting him into an emblematic state of idealised adult masculinity.
6. An imperative that includes Dave's long-standing lesbian friend, Madge, a character who attains the status of 'honorary man'.
7. Hansen, unlike Freud, has little faith in sublimation. Olsen's repression of his homosexuality does not bring forth creative genius elsewhere. Quite the opposite is the case: repression cramps his ability, reducing his talent to a parody of its original potential. His work is a triumph of middle-brow mediocrity, ironically celebrated by the undiscerning American mainstream.
8. Although Dave parts company with Medallion Life upon the death of his father, his status as a private individual is ensured by the wealth he inherits – wealth that facilitates his continued promotion of 'civilised' cultural values and guarantees his authority as effectively as ever did the institutional backing of corporate status. Dave most definitely does not inhabit the down-at-heel world of the traditional private eye. Indeed, in terms of his supremely confident subjectivity, he might better be defined as a private 'I': central rather than marginal, a figure who seems designed to reassure detective readers of the survival of those moral and cultural codes which had seemed so embattled in the world of Philip Marlowe.
9. The later novels contain countless references to Dave's burgeoning public reputation. An early example is found in *Gravedigger*:

   > He took out his wallet and handed the boy a card. The boy read it and looked startled. 'Brandstetter,' he said, and smiled. 'Hey, sure. I saw you on TV – Tom Snyder or somebody. You solve murders when the police can't do it.'
   >
   > 'The police are busy,' Dave said. 'I'm not busy.' (Hansen, 1982: 3)

   Hansen's police, unlike Chandler's, are seldom corrupt or stupid, but they are always overworked. In *Skinflick*, the hard-pressed LAPD Lieutenant Ken Barker has all the right ideas, but no time to explore them. He does not have time to solve crime, only to police it, and in such a climate the PI becomes an economic rather than a moral necessity. Civic justice is effectively privatised.
10. In the novels after *Nightwork* in which Dave increasingly comes to feel his age, a subtle transformation occurs. Gradually, almost imperceptibly, Cecil becomes the primary care-taker, a kind of father figure who watches over the no-longer omnipotent Dave. Dave, meanwhile, becomes more reckless, showing a disregard for his own safety that might be read either as a refusal of age, or as a fatalistic acceptance of age that bears the imprint of the the death drive. This evolution is evident in such developments as Cecil's rescue of Dave in *Obedience* (1988). Cecil's actions are now competent and efficient, and no longer marked by tears.
11. It could also be said that the system remains 'heteronormative', although it is no longer marked by heterosexual behaviour.

4

Wounded Masculinity and the Homosocial Bond: Fathers and Lovers in the Novels of Dick Francis

'Homosocial' . . . describes social bonds between persons of the same sex; it is a neologism, obviously formed by analogy with 'homosexual,' and just as obviously meant to be distinguished from 'homosexual.' In fact it is applied to such activities as 'male bonding,' which may, in our society, be characterised by intense homophobia, fear and hatred of homosexuality. To draw the 'homosocial' back into the orbit of 'desire,' of the potentially erotic, then, is to hypothesize the potential unbrokenness of a continuum between homosocial and homosexual – a continuum whose visibility, for men, in our society, is radically disrupted. (Sedgwick, 1985: 1–2)

Sensations of a pleasurable nature have not anything inherently impelling about them, whereas unpleasurable ones have it in the highest degree. (Freud, 1923/1961: 22)

The prospect of a human body being rendered helpless, put under slowly increasing stress, so that the maximum amount of sensation can be run through skin, nerves and muscle, will always seem horrifying to some readers, not a fascinating attempt to bring out the body's stamina and grace. (Califia, 1988: 25)

The novels of Dick Francis raise significant questions of loss and desire within a series of narratives in which the homosocial is always posited as the most significant bond. They also appear with awesome regularity at the top of the British bestseller lists. His thirty-seven novels to date are, in terms both of genre and consumption, truly 'popular' fictions – a pre-eminence achieved, it would seem, through the repeated deployment of a remarkably consistent model of the 'wounded' hero. Unlike the majority of other writers considered by this study, Francis has avoided the creation of a serial detective, choosing instead to produce a more or less successfully cloned series of individual heroes. The most notable exception to this rule is Sid Halley, who appears in three novels and will form the primary focus of this chapter. All manifestations of the Francis hero, however, can be seen to inhabit a common psychic landscape, exhibiting such characteristic traits as isolation, integrity, reticence, pride and endurance. Indeed, so potent is the Francis hero's capacity to endure that early commentators described the fictions as sadomasochistic.[1] The term is certainly appropriate to the formula adopted by Francis, whose texts inhabit a borderline between the detective novel and the thriller, a genre which traditionally boasts an investment in the power relations of s/m.[2] However, this connection begs important questions. Is the conflict between sadistic villain and enduring hero simply the deployment of a generic convention, or do the novels contain a more complex narrative of power that is profoundly rooted in gender issues? What are the implications for both gender and genre of a construction of heroic masculinity that situates agency not in action, but in stasis, silence and seemingly passive endurance?[3]

Francis's novels exist at a crossroads. They occupy an uncomfortable boundary between the radical and the reactionary, resulting in a disturbing refusal to fit the categories of either crime or its revision – yet both as popular fictions and as criminal fictions they have been subject to remarkably little critical attention. It is hard to account for this cursory consideration. Certainly the phenomenon of mass popularity is itself difficult to explain, but the symptoms of Francisphobia might also emerge from the contradictions within the novels themselves.[4] The accusations of sadomasochism can interestingly be counterpointed against Carolyn Heilbrun's claim that these fictions, if not actually feminist, have at least 'gone far along the road of antistereotyping' (Heilbrun, 1991: 250). To what extent, then, are Francis's fictions typical of the thriller genre? And can a change in the male hero's relationship to agency actually impact upon the fundamentally conservative patterns of the chase and confrontation narrative?

The problem of generic reinscription returns us to the more critically acclaimed work of Joseph Hansen. Undoubtedly there are considerable and significant differences between the writers, not least of which is the distinction between the urban American context of Hansen's work and the Britishness that pervades Francis's novels, irrespective of their setting. Yet both writers can be seen to undertake a mission to rescue patriarchy and its homosocial structures from the ravages of late capitalism. Although Hansen's increasing concern with the politics of sexuality and race is in marked contrast to the politically conservative trajectory of Francis's writing, they share a series of key values in their determination of what makes a man, and as such both display aspects of a condition which Thomas B. Byers has dubbed 'pomophobia'. This postmodern 'dis-ease' is defined as 'a set of deep and persistent fears on the part of a formerly dominant order that has begun to recognize that it is becoming residual' (Byers, 1995: 6), giving rise to a whole range of cultural anxieties regarding changing economic pressures, the blurring of gender boundaries and the breakdown of the traditional masculine subject.[5]

The pomophobic anxiety of Francis and Hansen makes for unexpected connections beneath the superficial difference of their works. As I suggested in the previous chapter, Hansen's 'radicalism' is undermined by his investment in a classical, and somewhat utopian, model of benign patriarchy which must be defended against the encroachments of the irresponsible and excessive 'Marketplace Man'. Francis shares this investment in what might be termed the 'good-enough' father, with the result that the liberalism of Hansen is ironically welded to the conservatism of Francis through a shared mission of patriarchal regeneration. To achieve this end, both writers begin their projects by using loss as a means to disable, and thereafter reconstruct, the hero. As with the early Brandstetter novels, Francis's fictions of the 1960s are marked by powerful depictions of loss. The hero is confronted not only by threats from without, but also by grief, disillusionment and self-doubt – enemies from within that render him unsuccessful, isolated and depressed.[6]

Although later Francis heroes have tended to be more economically and emotionally secure, it remains the case that all Francis heroes must face some form of loss, and they must also always occupy a position of relative otherness within their particular social environment. This otherness may be predicated upon class, education, occupation or physical difference, and represents a potentially misleading form of wounded masculinity. Within the framework of the story, the hero must usually defeat a villain who misrecognises the hero – seeing only the trappings of the feminised other – and therefore underestimates the character's capacity to endure. Alongside this narrative, the hero must negotiate his personal life, which will usually involve the identification, but not necessarily the attainment, of a female lover, and the ongoing development of a relationship with a male significant other. This division is not designed to suggest that the Francis hero is bisexual, as that would suggest a system embracing a spectrum of desire that might equally be manifested in male or female object choice. Rather, the distinction evokes the work of Luce Irigaray, who pertinently asks, 'Why is masculine homosexuality considered exceptional, then, when in fact the economy as a whole is based upon it?' (1985: 192). Although the woman may act as an obvious textual locus of desire, it is the relationship with a man, often but not exclusively a surrogate father, that forms the bedrock of the hero's emotional life. In the words of Irigaray:

> [A]ll economic organisation is homosexual. That of desire as well, even the desire for women. Woman exists only as an occasion for mediation, transaction, transition, transference, between man and his fellow man, indeed between man and himself. (Irigaray, 1985: 193)

This scenario is perhaps most succinctly put in play by *Odds Against* (1965), *Whip Hand* (1979) and *Come to Grief* (1995): the three novels featuring Francis's serial detective, Sid Halley.[7] Halley is a particularly intense amalgamation of all the forms of otherness suggested above. An ex-jockey of working-class origins, he is illegitimate, orphaned, small in stature, unremarkable in appearance, painfully divorced and disabled by a particularly brutal racing fall that crippled his left hand and ruined the career for which he had sacrificed his marriage. When he first appears in *Odds Against* he is flat on his back in hospital, shot in the stomach as a result of his own carelessness, and swamped by the enormity of all he has lost. Halley's otherness is complex – not least because his other predominant characteristic is the desire to win. This ambition had taken him out of his disadvantaged beginnings to the top of his profession, and as champion jockey he had acquired status, wealth and a wife from the ruling elite.[8] His 'fanatical' (1995: 6) obsession with winning had, however, resulted in the total investment of his identity in the role of jockey. In consequence the beginning of *Odds Against* establishes him as a hero without an identity. The loss of his career was equally the loss of his self. His subjectivity is in limbo and he exists in a void awaiting what in *Come to Grief* is described as the 'slow lingering birth of a detective' (1995: 6).

In a fascinating article challenging the dominance of the penis/phallus equation in cultural conceptions of masculinity, Arthur Flannigan-Saint-Aubin demands a reconsideration of the male body as a 'metaphoric locus' and source of identity (1994: 246).[9] Within this context he describes the construction and affirmation of masculine identities within phallogocentric patriarchal societies as a constant struggle. Masculinity is 'something to be achieved and to be experienced as a triumph over nature' (1994: 241). In *Odds Against*, the impetus to achieve this triumph emerges from a combination of the near-death experience that opens the novel and the torture scene that ends it. Pain, from the outset of the Halley novels to their conclusion, is associated with life. Pain brings clarity of vision, while its absence is characterised as numbness and inertia. It stimulates the senses, ironically empowering those who endure it. Freud observes in 'The Ego and the Id' that:

> Sensations of a pleasurable nature have not anything inherently impelling about them, whereas unpleasurable ones have it in the highest degree. The latter impel towards change, towards discharge, and that is why we interpret unpleasure as implying a heightening and pleasure a lowering of energic cathexis. (Freud, 1923/1961: 22)

As Halley comments after having been whipped with chains, 'I had noticed before that sometimes when the body was injured the mind cleared sharply and worked for a while with acute perception' (1979/1981: 227). The endurance of pain thus becomes a mode through which masculinity can be constantly and reliably reconstituted and reaffirmed.[10]

By the end of *Odds Against* Halley has lost the remains of his left hand, but has found a new and suitably painful arena within which he can exercise his constitutive desire to win – namely, detection. The loss of the hand, however, cannot be straightforwardly assimilated. The hand is a powerfully gendered symbol of agency. Indeed, as

Luce Irigaray would attest, not simply masculine agency but the very foundations of phallic sexuality are dependent upon 'the action of some power, function, or organ' (Irigaray, 1985: 211). In Irigaray's account of female sexuality, 'When Our Lips Speak Together', women's pleasure is self-sufficient and self-actuating; it is only men who require the assistance of an outside agent to stimulate them. Significantly Irigaray's philosophical love letter also contends that there is '[n]o event that makes us women . . . Your/my body doesn't acquire its sex through an operation . . . Without any intervention or special manipulation, you are a woman already' (1985: 211). As Flannigan-Saint-Aubin has observed, the same cannot be said for men. Patriarchal masculinity is by definition phallic and erect, and thus demands the triumph of exertion over natural inertia – a mode of identity formation which inevitably gives an emasculatory dimension to the loss of a hand.[11] It is not, therefore, surprising that Halley should spend much of the second novel, *Whip Hand*, coming to terms with this new loss. It dominates both his sense of self and the novel, which opens with a vivid, erotic, dream of racing:

> Winning was all. Winning was my function. What I was there for. What I wanted. What I was born for . . .
>
> I could still feel the way I'd moved with the horse, the ripple of muscle through both of the striving bodies, uniting in one. I could still feel the irons around my feet, the calves of my legs gripping, the balance, the nearness to my head of the stretching brown neck, the mane blowing in my mouth, my hands on the reins.
>
> There came at that point, the second awakening. The real one. The moment in which I first moved, and opened my eyes, and remembered that I wouldn't ride any more races, ever. The wrench of loss came again as a fresh grief. The dream was a dream for whole men. (Francis, 1979/1981: 7)

This dream encapsulates the aching void of all human subjectivity in its evocation of the ideal unity with another, but in Halley's case, the absence of wholeness is particularly fraught. Although now clearly committed to his new career as investigator, the loss of his bodily integrity is always present on the margins of his consciousness. It represents a force that must constantly be negotiated and which threatens to overwhelm him. In this configuration, the physical bond with the horse experienced in racing assumes a pre-symbolic dimension. The wordless communication between the body of the man and the body of the horse represents a semiotic space of absolute plenitude that is wrenched away from Halley, forming an original, inescapable loss. This is the pain that dominates irrespective of context, as is revealed later in the novel when the stunned Halley returns to consciousness after having been attacked and abducted. His returning memory lets slip a telling series of priorities: 'I had not been racing. I had one hand. I had been abducted . . .' (Francis, 1979/1981: 87). The loss of the horse/mother and the prohibition of the castrating father (a threat made 'real' by the loss of the hand) are foundational sources of pain that easily overshadow the immediate inconvenience of abduction.

The novels thus chart a process of coming to terms with loss that is both completed and reconstituted in the final episode, the appropriately entitled *Come to Grief* (1995). Although Halley finally resolves the bodily conflicts that have assailed him throughout the previous two fictions, the plot of *Come to Grief* opens a new psychic wound for the detective, who now must grieve for the loss of the friend he loved, but who betrayed him. This is Francis's most complete example of the thriller's familiar homoerotic conflict between hero and villain, and it would seem to be this betrayal of the homosocial that alone has the power to displace his physical wounds from the centre of Halley's consciousness. In this third novel Halley's close friend Ellis Quint mutates into the archetypal sadistic villain, culminating in one of Francis's most paradoxical affirmations of the homosocial bond. After speaking of the love and comradeship he feels for Sid, Ellis cheerfully sets about the pleasurable business of mentally and physically torturing him (1995: 218–29). Once again, the enduring hero triumphs, but as he himself concludes, the victory is a hollow one: 'I had the win, but there was no one standing in the stirrups to share it with' (1995: 279). As this conclusion suggests, homosociality has been of fundamental importance throughout the trilogy, and the most significant example of this is the fascinating 'counter-romance' between Halley and his father-in-law, Rear-Admiral Charles Roland, RN. All Halley's relationships with women are secondary to this 'romance', with the result that the novels persistently refuse the script of normative heterosexuality. In the wake of Halley's failed marriage it is Charles who supplies approval, advice and security, and it is to his ironically maternal arms that the wounded hero inevitably retreats: 'I could think of only one place to go. My only haven, in many past troubles' (1995: 4); 'I paused a fraction, searching for the simplest words that would tell him what I felt for him. Found some. Said them. "This is my home"' (1979/1981: 126).

The bonds between men that form the substance of the Halley trilogy reveal some striking similarities with those that characterise the Brandstetter novels. Between these two seemingly diverse narratives there lie shared conceptions of social order, the value of patriarchy and the meanings of masculinity, as well as a foundational deployment of a binary division between the male subject and his female other. Once again, Kimmel's 'Genteel Patriarch' and 'Heroic Artisan' must combine forces to defeat the threat represented by 'Marketplace Man'. Charles Roland was born to the 'refined and elegant' role of the genteel patriarch, while Halley is admirably fitted to the role of the heroic artisan, that is, the working-class man made good through skill and dedication to his craft (Kimmel, 1994: 123).[12] Similarly the villains of both *Odds Against* and *Whip Hand* can be characterised as marketplace men. In *Odds Against* the corruption of Howard Kraye's sadistic masculinity is underlined by his conspicuous consumption; his voracious acquisition of quartz and racecourses shows no sense of an elegant sufficiency. Meanwhile, the aspirational status of *Whip Hand*'s Trevor Deansgate is evident in his decision, on his journey from rags to riches, to adopt the name of a Manchester shopping centre. As in Hansen's *Gravedigger*, a conflict is established between the 'true' and 'false' disciples of patriarchal ideology:

> He had a way of speaking to me that acknowledged mutual origins, that we'd both come a long way from where we'd started. It was not a matter of accent, but of manner. There was no need for social pretence. The message was raw, and between equals, and would be understood. (Francis, 1979/1981: 89)

However, although there are extensive structural similarities between the two writers' depiction of patriarchy, in the heterosexual landscape of Francis's novels it is a rather more traditional pattern of homosociality that emerges. While Hansen's novels displaced women into a state of insignificance and opened up an entirely new range of binary oppositions among men, Francis tends to rely, at least superficially, on the familiar opposition of female irrationality (animality) versus masculine rationality. Elements of this division are evident in the erotic racing dream, quoted above, in which the evocation of 'the ripple of muscle through both of the striving bodies, uniting in one' could as well be applied to man and woman as man and horse. Indeed, in *Whip Hand* women veer dangerously close to being equated with horses. Although the love interest, Louise McInnes, thankfully evades this fate, the hysterical Rosemary and the embittered Jenny are repeatedly figured in animal terms. Coming to Halley in search of help, Rosemary is depicted as a quivering bundle of instincts. Like a horse she senses something is wrong, but can offer no rational explanation for her feelings, and her fears are condemned as menopausal fantasies. Halley's ex-wife, Jenny, however, is a 'tiger', who likes nothing better than giving her ex-husband a good 'mauling' (1979/81: 20, 84). Her energy is atavistic and disrupts Halley's rational façade: 'Where once we had clung together with delight and passion, we now, if we chanced to meet, ripped with claws' (1979/1981: 23). With Francis, as it was with Hansen, the love of men is figured as a higher love, and while Halley's mind is gratified and absorbed by the homosocial nurturance of Charles, his body aches for both the horses and the woman he has lost. Women, in *Whip Hand*, are in a no-win situation. They are depicted as craving security – indeed, this was the cause of Sid's marriage breakdown – while men, such as Halley and the manic balloonist, John Viking, take risks. However, within this novel, and in *Come to Grief*, it is men, not women, who actually provide the safe havens of domesticity, and this 'appropriation' of a role traditionally associated with the feminine, while superficially positive, in fact leaves women with only one possible function, namely that of becoming recreational objects of sexual desire.

Why, then, have these novels been read as proto-feminist? Perhaps in part because of the deceptive form of the wounded hero, who lulls both villains and readers alike into a false sense of security. Not only the hero, but also the writer, might be seen to disguise traditional forms behind the semblance of 'new' man mildness. The Francis hero's predominant crime-fighting methodology is the hiding of a steely resolve behind a mask of inoffensive, unthreatening anonymity. Such a technique owes something of a debt to golden-age detectives, such as Allingham's Campion and Sayers's Wimsey, who disguised their razor-sharp minds behind façades of asinine, upper-class idiocy – but as with these characters, the question remains as to whether the superficial feminisation of the hero can actually effect any change upon a discourse that continues to privilege patriarchal conceptions of 'truth' and justice. The tension between form and content underlies all attempts to both rewrite and analyse genre formations, and it is important to accept that these formations are both more fluid and more adaptable than we might think. Crime fictions, and the crimes they contain, are subject to mutation and deviations that make it impossible to say any one novel is wholly 'feminist', 'radical' or 'reactionary'. Consequently it seems possible to assert that for all of the sexism that characterises the novels, Francis's engagement with configurations of masculinity is not mere window-dressing. Indeed, the novels suggest that Francis has identified, exploited and, to a certain extent, reconceptualised a series of potent fantasies from the wider cultural sphere, all of which are themselves profoundly implicated in the construction and maintenance of gender ideologies.

The golden age is not the only model evoked by the Francis hero's strategy of disguise. A rather more famous exemplar of this technique is, of course, Superman. Behind the unassuming façade of the innocuous Clark Kent lies the superhero – the man with the strength to withstand anything and everything – and part of Francis's remarkable success might well be attributed to his ability to redeem and reconfigure the comic-book paradigm for adult consumption. The fantasy of a secret self dominates the Halley novels and, in *Come to Grief*, as Sid lies, once again, in a hospital bed, the scene is set for the superheroic revelation:

> 'I have to explain that *I* am not as I seem. When people in general look at me they see a harmless person, youngish, not big, not tall, no threat to anyone. Self-effacing. I'm not complaining about that. In fact I choose to be like that because people then *talk* to me, which is necessary in my job . . .
>
> But Ellis knows me better. Ellis calls me cunning and ruthless, and I probably am.' (Francis, 1995: 263)

The comic-book parallel continues into the description of Ellis Quint, who, unlike the marketplace men who were defeated in the first two novels, is truly a villain of stature: a Lex Luthor to Halley's Superman:

> 'Ellis is not what he seems, either. Davis Tatum thinks him a playboy. Ellis is tall, good-looking, outgoing, charming and *loved* . . . But he's not only that. He's a strong, purposeful and powerful man with enormous skills of manipulation. People underestimate both of us for various and different reasons –

> I look weak and he looks frivolous – but we don't underestimate each other.' (1995: 264)

Sid Halley, then, is the unsuspected man of steel (1979/1981: 110; 1995: 165), but the implications of this identity are not as straightforward as they might seem. As indicated above, Arthur Flannigan-Saint-Aubin draws an important distinction between two contrasting modes of masculinity: the all too familiar phallic mode, and an alternative configuration which he designates the 'testicular':

> [A] man is experiencing the testicular mode when he is nurturing, incubating, containing and protecting. The testicular masculine is characterized by patience, stability and endurance. (Flannigan-Saint-Aubin, 1994: 250)

However, the testicular, like the phallic, has both positive and negative attributes, and these negatives are designated as the 'testerical'. Testicular masculinity offers a useful template for understanding the composition of Sid Halley. Significantly, Flannigan-Saint-Aubin includes 'lack of direction and inertia' in his anatomy of the testerical, a description that evokes the aimless Sid of *Odds Against*. This suggests that the trilogy could be seen to encompass Halley's efforts to regain the equilibrium of the testicular from the undesirability of the testerical. But such a reading reckons without the ongoing power of the 'unequivocally phallic' patriarchal ideal, within which 'the construction of a masculine identity and the experience of masculinity are indeed contingent upon a denial of the testicular/testerical' (Flannigan-Saint-Aubin, 1994: 250). Flannigan-Saint-Aubin uses Superman and his alter ego Clark Kent to illustrate these paradoxically interdependent masculinities, but his analysis could as well describe the bifurcated subjectivity of Sid Halley:

> Whereas Superman is the phallic 'Man of Steel,' it is Clark Kent who has 'balls.' He is testicular and potentially testerical; he is mild mannered, enduring, ever present. Superman is episodic; he 'rises' to the occasion 'like a speeding bullet' and then disappears with only a trace of his former self. Clark Kent 'hangs in there' until the Man of Steel, driven by crises, springs into action. (Flannigan-Saint-Aubin, 1994: 252–3)

The Halley novels' appropriation of the Superman ideal also contains an element of irony that is most self-consciously explored in *Whip Hand*, where the entire plot could be said to hang on the question of whether or not Sid Halley *is* Superman.[13] The entire premise of the Superman series is based upon the misrecognition of Clark Kent: nobody thinks he is Superman. Much the same could be said of *Odds Against*, in which Halley is undervalued and misrecognised, his super-powers unsuspected until it is too late. *Whip Hand*, by contrast, inverts this pattern, and Halley finds himself in the uncomfortable position of being mistaken for Superman when he is in fact merely mortal. 'I'm no superman' he asserts in the opening pages of the novel, 'I just snoop around a bit' (1979/1981: 12), but his protests are to no avail. His steel constitution has become the stuff of urban legend, and this alone is enough to invite attack.

If the foundations of parody can be said to lie in repetition, then the plot of *Whip Hand* can clearly be seen to verge upon the parodic. Typically the thriller is concerned with the battle of wills between hero and villain, rather than the process of detecting that villain, but here the concept of detection is rendered utterly superfluous as not only Deansgate, but a whole series of villains make pre-emptive strikes on the hero, hoping that by nobbling Clark Kent they will save themselves from the wrath of Superman. The absurdity of his reputation does not go unremarked by Halley. Although our hero is tied up at gun-point, an adversary nonetheless reaches for a protective crowbar 'as if he thought that somehow I could liberate myself like Superman and still attack him' (1979/1981: 90). Yet, ultimately these comic inversions are themselves deceptive, for however the narrative might try to mislead us, the fact remains that Francis *is* rewriting the comic-book tradition, and Sid Halley *is* Superman, as his ultimate defeat of both marketplace man and Ellis 'Lex Luthor' Quint reveals. In *Whip Hand*, though, it is we, the readers, rather than the hapless villains, upon whom the deception is primarily played, as Francis pulls no punches in his efforts to make us believe that Halley really has lost his power.[14]

But what exactly is Halley's power and how does it relate to wider structures of power within the novels and the thriller genre? It would be impossible to deny that the structure of the thriller genre encodes a model of sadomasochistic desire in the symbiotic relationship between hero and villain. The form is dependent upon reversals of power: the hero must first be beaten before he (and more recently she) can assume the dominant position. Without this relationship the thriller as a genre simply could not function. If, instead of indulging in sadistic foreplay to performatively celebrate the (f)act of their domination (while conveniently giving the resourceful hero time to regroup), villains simply killed those who threatened them, the genre would implode.

In the case of Sid Halley, however, the primary identification is with the masochistic rather than the sadistic end of the spectrum. Masochism is a central trope of the trilogy and its complex configurations connect it repeatedly to the homosocial structures of the novels. As Eve Kosofsky Sedgwick has indicated, homosocial structures may be characterised by intense homophobia (1985: 1–2), creating an impossible tension between desire and its prohibition. The homosocial society is at heart a paradoxical one, built precariously upon the repression of its foundational desires. It is not surprising that such a construct should be masochistic. Indeed, as Kaja Silverman argues, male masochism is 'as much a product of the existing symbolic order as a reaction against it' (Silverman, 1992: 213). Silverman's extensive examination of masochistic desire contemplates the possibility that masochism might facilitate the negotiation of 'a different psychic relation to the Laws of Language and Kinship Structure than that dictated by the dominant fiction' (1992: 213). However, her optimism is not shared by David Savran. In a summary that is singularly appropriate to the structure of the Halley novels, he concludes that masochism:

> represents no more nor less than a scandalous eroticization of patriarchal relations, a desire for the father that is transformed into a desire to submit to the cruelty of the father's will and all he represents . . . Masochism functions, in short, as a mode of cultural reproduction that simultaneously reveals and conceals (through the mechanism of disavowal) the homoeroticism that undergirds patriarchy and male homosocial relations. (Savran, 1998: 32)

Masochism, for Savran, confirms rather than challenges patriarchal power. It acts as 'a kind of decoy' enabling narratives of masochistic masculinities to 'characteristically conclude with an almost magical restitution of phallic power' (1998: 37).

The Halley novels, like most thrillers, indeed conclude with such a restitution of phallic power, but this power is not necessarily invested in the figure of the detective. Although the hero who has successfully withstood the torments of the text is vindicated and rewarded, his emergence from a position of 'feminine' submission can at best be seen as partial. Halley may defeat the villains who threaten the stability of patriarchal structures, but his victories are subdued and often marked by a burden of guilt. *Whip Hand* provides an illustration through Halley's investigation of Lucas Wainright, the corrupt father figure at the head of the Jockey Club, which here as elsewhere in Francis's work acts as a microcosmic representation of the patriarchal symbolic. In order to defeat Wainright, the bad father, Halley must enlist the support of Charles Roland, the good father, to authorise and validate his claims (1979/1981: 240, 242). Only in the name of the father can the son triumph over the father. Halley's personal struggle to affirm his masculinity will inevitably be overshadowed by the duty he owes to patriarchy, which operates here as a sadistic superego to the masochistic ego of the individual male subject, who must constantly struggle to be a good-enough child and obey the laws of symbolic fatherhood.[15]

The Oedipal structures which underpin the relationship between Sid and Charles suggest that Halley's condition is ultimately closest to what Freud terms moral masochism. In 'The Economic Problem of Masochism' (1923), Freud suggests that moral masochism is psychic rather than sexual, emerging from an unconscious sense of guilt, which he argues is 'an expression of a tension between the ego and the super-ego'. The super-ego, he reminds us, combines the pressures of the external world with the introjection of the subject's parents and their prohibitions. The super-ego retains 'essential features of the introjected persons – their strength, their severity, their inclination to supervise and to punish' (1923/1961: 167). The moral masochist's behaviour can thus be seen to emerge from a reanimation of the child's Oedipal conflict – the dual desire to be beaten by and to have 'a passive (feminine) sexual relation' with the father (1923/1961: 169). The intense bond between Halley and his father-in-law is implicated in just such a structure as Freud outlines: 'We parted as usual without physically touching. Eye contact said it all' (1995: 20). The relationship can scarcely be articulated, let alone consummated. It is absolutely integral, and yet dependent upon obedience to certain rules of conduct (particularly the non-display of emotion).[16] It is the impossibility of ever living up to this ideal that might be seen to underpin the constant reworkings of Halley's suffering. In a moment of crisis he describes Charles as his 'rock' (1995: 116) and the metaphor could not be more appropriate. Halley is chained to an utterly solid foundation that symbolises security at the same time as being uninhabitable, unyielding and unforgiving.

For Sid Halley, then, the cyclical engagement with suffering and pain is part of an essential and constitutive need to prove his masculinity. He must endure to gain the approval of the novel's good fathers – the non-articulation of desire might be seen as a suffering in silence – and he must jeopardise himself in order to preserve their laws and challenge the false creeds of corrupted patriarchy. That Halley suffers physically is obvious. He is shot in both *Odds Against* and *Come to Grief*, he loses his left hand and breaks his right arm, he is whipped, knocked unconscious and, in true thriller style, variously tormented while tied up by sadists. However, in defining moral masochism, Freud was as much concerned with psychological as physical blows, and throughout all three novels it is verbal assaults that cause the hero most pain, while at the same time providing him with the most effective impetus for change.

Succinctly paraphrasing Freud, Kaja Silverman argues that 'the moral masochist's cheek is the ego. That is the erotogenic zone of choice, the site where he or she seeks to be beaten' (1992: 188–9). Examples abound of the verbal flaying of Halley, who in *Come to Grief* is subject to a tabloid slur campaign. Beyond this public assault, however, lie a series of private verbal assaults, many of which emerge from his ex-wife, Jenny, whose comments, while vicious, are often singularly perceptive. Here she is blaming Sid for the breakdown of their marriage:

> Your selfishness, your pigheadedness. Your bloody determination to win. You'll do anything to win. You always have to win. You're so hard. Hard on yourself. Ruthless to yourself. I couldn't live with it . . . I can't live in the sort of purgatory you make of life for yourself. (Francis, 1979/1981: 233–4)[17]

One of the most significant verbal assaults, however, comes not from Jenny but from Charles, who at the beginning of *Odds Against* conducts an humiliating public character assassination of Sid:

> 'That,' he said, 'is my son-in-law.' His tone was light, amused, and infinitely contemptuous; and it jabbed raw on a nerve I had thought long dead. I looked at him sharply, and his eyes met mine, blank and expressionless. (1965/1967: 34)

The attack that follows plays on all of Halley's multiple 'othernesses': his class, his education, his disability, and its purpose is the construction of the Superman smoke-screen, 'the destruction of me as a man in the eyes of his guests' (1965/1967: 37). However, it is significant that Charles does not warn Sid of his intentions; the attack comes out of the blue and is genuinely painful. Here Charles can be seen to have recognised the dangerous 'testerical' inertia into which Sid had fallen in the wake of his multiple losses and, appropriately for his role as father, his actions in this scene teach Halley the value of pain as a stimulant. But the scene carries further significance. From the moment that Halley declines to protest at Charles's abusive treatment, the beating becomes performative. It evolves into a model of consensual sadomasochistic practice, played out between the hero and his partner. It moves beyond the duties of masochism to its pleasures, exploiting the performance of dominant and submissive roles within an existing relational dyad.[18]

Odds Against can thus be seen to display three contrasting modes of masochism. The thriller's deadly sadomasochistic conflict between hero and villain, played out in the torture of Halley by Howard Kraye, is complemented by the 'pleasurable' sadomasochism of the homosocial bond with Charles. These in turn are accompanied by the first symptoms of Halley's moral masochism, a condition which by the second novel has become if not chronic, then certainly acute. It is in *Whip Hand* that Halley's need to authenticate his existence through pain is most fully exploited, and he proves himself to have been an apt pupil of the regenerative lesson taught by Charles. So much so that he no longer needs the father for confrontation, but has instead displaced his multiple anxieties on to the investigative process.

Towards the end of *Come to Grief*, Ellis Quint observes that '[n]o one has yet invented anything you've found actually unbearable, have they, Sid?' (1995: 222), but in *Whip Hand* Trevor Deansgate comes pretty close when he threatens to shoot off Halley's other hand. This threat devastates the hero:

> All the fear I'd ever felt in all my life was as nothing compared with the liquefying, mind-shattering disintegration of that appalling minute. It broke me in pieces. Swamped me. Brought me down to a morass of terror, to a whimper in the soul. And instinctively, hopelessly, I tried not to let it show. (Francis, 1979/1981: 91–2)

I discussed earlier some of the weight of signification associated with the hand, and throughout all three novels Halley struggles to negotiate the threat to his subjectivity embodied in its disablement and loss. Elizabeth Grosz, discussing the relationship between corporeality and subjectivity, argues that 'the subject is incapable of adequately integrating the fragmented sense of its corporeality provided by its senses with the completion, cohesion and totalization of the visual image of the body' (1990a: 83). The subject is, then, always already unstable, its integrity and functionality dependent upon a precarious sense of bodily cohesion. The shattering of Halley's bodily 'wholeness' inevitably has a profoundly destabilising effect upon the cohesion of his ego. The problem is not resolved by the artificial arm he acquires (in spite of the degree of agency it restores); indeed, the new arm creates new problems, occupying as it does an interstitial space between self and other. Although the new arm cannot be hurt as flesh can, its dismantling by Ellis Quint causes Halley acute psychological pain (1995: 220–2). The limits of his body have been destabilised, the arm is both him and not him, and as such his relationship to the prosthesis can best be described as abject. Julia Kristeva suggests that the abject is neither subject nor object: '[w]e may call it a border; abjection is above all ambiguity' (1982: 9) – a definition expanded by Elizabeth Grosz:

> The abject is undecidably inside and outside the body (like the skin of milk), dead and alive (like the corpse), autonomous and engulfing (like infection and pollution). It is what disturbs identity, system and order, disrupting the social boundaries demanded by the symbolic. (Grosz, 1990a: 90)

The trilogy might thus be read as a struggle against abjection, a progression towards bodily accommodation. The three novels chart a movement from the loss of a hated, dysfunctional, but nonetheless integral, body part (the disabled hand) to the partial acceptance of lack evident in *Whip Hand*. This is a phase of remarkable insecurity as is illustrated by Halley's response to Deansgate's threats. Finally, in *Come to Grief*, Halley achieves a masochistic pleasure in the 'borderline phenomenon' that is his arm (Grosz, 1990a: 95). For the first time he allows another to come into intimate contact with the corporeal locus of his identity crisis:

> The touch of her fingers on the skin of my forearm had been a caress more intimate than any act of sex. I felt shaky. I felt more

> moved than ever in my life . . . I stretched out my left arm and fastened the hand on her wrist. (Francis, 1995: 275)

The eroticisation of this particular psychic pain has, however, been a long time coming, and at the point of Deansgate's threat (almost the exact mid-point of the trilogy), Halley's response comprises a combination of both testicular and phallic masculinities. This reformulation of self opens up the possibility of a radical reconceptualisation of masculinity – a possibility which is, however, fairly rapidly foreclosed. Acknowledging that Deansgate's threat of (further) emasculation has indeed deprived him of something central to his sense of self, Halley contemplates the state of his identity. However, this self-examination reveals that it is not the 'phallic' self that he sees as damaged by this psychological emasculation, but rather something that Flannigan-Saint-Aubin would more closely associate with the testicular: 'The analytical reasoning part of my mind might be marching straight on, but what had to be called the soul was sick and dying' (Francis, 1979/1981: 99).

A phallic 'front' is, then, deployed (almost without volition or control) to disguise and protect the psychic wound – a defence mechanism identified by Victor Seidler as typical of patriarchal masculinity. Seidler suggests that men 'learn to trust only ourselves because it is too risky to reach out towards others' (1997: 60), and in his anatomy of masculinity the archetypal male is wholly isolated, unable to communicate what residual feeling might have survived the childhood conditioning to repress. Yet Halley is not in this position. Unlike the archetypal detective outsider, who might admirably fit the pattern outlined by Seidler, he has a network of significant others who offer him nurturance, and upon whom he can and does depend. Seeing that something is seriously wrong with Sid, Chico Barnes tries repeatedly, if clumsily, to get him to speak about it: ' "You're a big boy now," he said . . . "You want to cry on Daddy's shoulder?" '(1979/1981: 105). This is where the attempt to graft testicular masculinity onto a phallic generic form collapses. It is also the point at which the limits and conditions of homosociality that I outlined above become most painfully obvious. Halley cannot respond to Chico's 'testicular' offer of support because of the double bind facing men within patriarchal homosocial structures. The offer of homosocial nurturance is made in the absolute expectation that it will be refused. Indeed, it almost acts as a warning – a euphemistic injunction to paper over the cracks in the masculine façade – because, as the relationship with Charles reveals, the continuation of the testicular environment is actually dependent upon the exhibition of phallic restraint. To be part of the homosocial, Halley must be the dutiful son, and he values this homosocial bond more than he values the heterosexual bond he could experience if he exhibited more testicular, or 'feminine', qualities. Ironically, if he were less of a man, he could *have* a woman. The conclusion of Jenny's comments on the breakdown of the marriage is telling:

> I need a husband who's not so rigidly in control of himself. I want someone who's not afraid of emotion, someone uninhibited, someone weaker . . . I want someone who can break down. I want . . . an ordinary man. (Francis, 1979/1981: 234)

Women, in this case Jenny, are perceived as wanting men to be disloyal to patriarchy, and in staying silent about his physical and emotional wounds, Halley chooses the rigid self-control of homosociality over the loss of self that might emerge from the 'femininity' of heterosexuality.

Ultimately, then, Halley's endurance becomes phallic rather than testicular, and his silence becomes a symbol of power. In the final confrontation with Deansgate, Halley is almost completely silent. In a remarkable closing scene, he speaks only once, leaving the first-person narration to assert this mutinous silence in a series of abrupt statements: 'I didn't say anything', 'I said nothing', 'I didn't answer' (1979/1981: 254–5). This reassertion of his silence confirms Halley's sadomasochistic relationship to life. He keeps on taking the punishments doled out to him because he will not say stop – and ironically the one time that he does break his silence, in the first confrontation with Deansgate, the absence of pain proves more unbearable than its presence. Indeed, Halley is as unable to endure kindness as he is able to endure pain. Kindness in fact can be seen to *cause* him a very different, arguably 'feminised' pain. This paradoxically unbearable agony is evident in his response to Jenny's kind words in *Come to Grief*. In a description that evokes the impact of Deansgate's threats, Halley is once again 'liquefied inside' (1995: 166). Thus, without the familiarity of pain he loses his fundamental masculine identity as most potent endurer, as the one whose spirit can bear everything, irrespective of the torments heaped upon his body.[19]

Arthur Flannigan-Saint-Aubin poses a crucial question: 'Is and how is a non-patriarchal conception of masculinity possible?', and this dilemma is central to the work of Dick Francis. Time and time again this becomes the question that the novels ask, struggle with, and ultimately fail to answer. Instead of re-creating the hero, reconstructing him in a non-patriarchal mode, Francis's novels augment the hero, attempting to graft testicular or feminine characteristics on to what remains at heart a phallic structure. The hero exhibits a series of paradoxical binary oppositions: internal doubt against external strength, outer gentleness versus inner steel, homosociality both in opposition to and in alignment with heterosexuality. The paradoxes cannot be tidily contained or rendered coherent, and the Francis hero is left with a subjectivity that manages to be both radically decentred and conservatively coherent. It is difficult to determine whether such a duality represents a staging post within the evolution of popular cultural masculinities, or a smoke-screen disguising the same old phallus. Patriarchy itself is certainly untroubled by these narratives, but the male subject within patriarchy is beginning to show the cracks. The novels challenge the generic norms that set passive femininity against the unquestioned agency of pro-active masculinity, but they do so at a cost, both to the suffering hero and the women he encounters. It seems that to change the genre, the form and function of the detective protagonist must undergo a wholescale reconception, but in Francis's novels these fundamental structures continue unchanged. Instead a superficial update occurs in which the potentially radical displacement of the macho hero is achieved through the further displacement of the usually female, but always feminised, other. Until this other is able to assume the protagonist's role, the prospects for generic emancipation seem bleak – and we as readers should not be led into a false sense of security by Superman's innocuous disguise.

NOTES

1. In the third edition of his bestselling history *Bloody Murder*, Julian Symons seems keen to distance Francis from this reputation, commenting that 'the often remarked sado-masochism of the stories is absent, or much less noticeable, in recent work, and too much has been made of it' (1972/1992: 289). However, this sanitisation of Francis seems completely at odds with the evidence of the texts, all of which indulge in the remorseless physical or psychological punishment of their long-suffering, patiently enduring heroes.
2. Typical examples of the sadomasochistic thriller might include any of Ian Fleming's James Bond novels, but *Casino Royale* is particularly implicated in the s/m exploration of power, pain, pleasure and endurance. An equally famous, and perhaps more notorious, example would be James Hadley Chase's *No Orchids for Miss Blandish*, a text described by George Orwell as 'a daydream appropriate to a totalitarian age' in which 'only one motive is at work throughout the whole story: the pursuit of power' (Orwell, 1944/1965: 78, 70).
3. I am grateful to Berthold Schoene-Harwood for reminding me that masculinity is also possessed of a defensive dimension – it can be the resolute and unyielding fortress as well

as the active assailant. However, in the case of the Francis hero, attention is simultaneously drawn to both protective shell and soft underbelly. The Francis hero's fortress-body is a leaky one that emphasises the precariousness rather than the invulnerability of masculinity.

4. Account might also be taken of the canons and hierarchies that form as readily within genre studies as without. Here, as in the world of 'high' culture, popularity often exists in inverse proportion to critical acclaim.
5. Byers's entertaining essay uses James Cameron's film *Terminator 2* to illustrate cultural anxieties surrounding 'fears of late capitalism, fears of theory, fears of feminism, fears of any swerving from the path of "straight" sexuality' (Byers, 1995: 7). The triumph of Arnold Schwarzenegger's 'old-fashioned' Terminator T-101 over the monstrous fluidity of the shapeshifting, ungraspable T-1000 is read as an attempt to revalorise a traditional conception of masculinity that is firmly fixed, and capable of *doing* rather than *being* everything.
6. Typical examples include *Rat Race*'s (1970) Matt Shore, a divorced, debt-ridden airline pilot with a nose-diving career, and *Blood Sport*'s (1967) Gene Hawkins, the depressive hero *par excellence*. Hawkins begins his novel in a suicidal state, and although his lot is mildly tempered by love, he only continues to live out of a masochistic sense of obligation towards a character who saved his life. Francis's early fictions are generally bleaker in outlook than his later novels, and it is for this reason that I speak of a conservative 'trajectory' in his writing. The early novels, although conciliatory in tone, are nonetheless marked by a sharp awareness of the class hierarchy that structures the microcosm of the racing world.
7. Although thirty years divides the first novel from the last, the fictional timescale involves a period of approximately five years. A separate article could, however, be written on the evolution of gender politics between 1965 and 1995, and the changing register of discourses on femininity within the three novels gives rise to some curious and uncomfortable dislocations.
8. It should be noted, however, that within the world of racing, the status of even a champion jockey cannot be considered on a par with that of those who run the racing establishment. Jockeys might be seen as analogous to servants on horseback, and this paradoxical lack of the status which might otherwise accompany his wealth and success is particularly evident in Halley's first appearance back in 1965.
9. In 'The Male Body and Literary Metaphors for Masculinity', the fundamental question underpinning Flannigan-Saint-Aubin's analysis is what happens to our understanding of masculinity when we remember that men are not wholly phallic, they also have balls?
10. The impossibility of achieving a secure identity, and the necessity of constantly reasserting masculine agency, is also made clear by Judith Butler's account of citational authority: 'there is no power, construed as a subject, that acts, but only, to repeat an earlier phrase, a reiterated acting that *is* power in its persistence and instability' (Butler, 1993: 225).
11. I am grateful to my students at the University of St Andrews for pointing out the gender assumptions that underlie the depiction of disability within *Odds Against*. Halley's rehabilitation occurs in part through his encounter with the disfigured Zanna Martin. The two cases are offered as parallels, with the loss of Martin's looks being compared to the loss of Halley's hand/career, a painful reminder of the extent to which the 1960s considered that a woman's career *is* her appearance.
12. For a wider discussion of Kimmel's terminology see above, Chapter 3. In the first two books, Halley also shares a significant homosocial bond with the much younger Chico Barnes – but here, inspite of the similarity in their ages, it is Halley who tends to act the genteel patriarch to Barnes's reliable artisan.
13. Superman is not the only iconic figure to be reappropriated by Francis, whose style undoubtedly owes something of a debt to the sparse narration of Ian Fleming. The Francis hero can plausibly be read as a form of domestic James Bond, whose outlandish and excessive figure has, quite literally, been cut down to size.
14. At key points in both *Odds Against* and *Whip Hand* Halley's first-person narration becomes distinctly unreliable (1965/1967: 212–15). The reader is encouraged to trust a voice that allows access to the intimacy and immediacy of its doubt and pain, and is in consequence caught out when strategies of steely deception are not mentioned until after the event.
15. The pressure to conform to patriarchal demands is undoubtedly powerful, not least because patriarchy can be seen to exhibit the characteristics of what Freud terms 'sadism proper': namely, 'the destructive instinct, the instinct for mastery, or the will to power' (1923/1961: 163).

16. As Charles drives the battered Sid home from a particularly bruising s/m encounter with Ellis Quint, Sid ventures to suggest that he has had a hellish day. Charles's response rigidly reinforces the boundaries of their relationship: 'He frowned, glancing across in distaste. "Has hell arrived, then?" He hated excess emotion. I cooled it.' (1995: 246).
17. Jenny frequently points out the masochism inherent in the life of a jockey – the pain of injury, the refusal of food and sex (1979/1981: 64) – all for the sake of winning. Halley's entire life can thus be seen to have been in thrall to the pleasures of pain. Through the painful mastery of his own body, Halley achieves the archetypal masculine reward of being the best.
18. Rather appropriately, after the performance is over, the physically weak Halley is put to bed by Charles 'in his quick, neat, naval manner' (1965/1967: 39).
19. Silverman devotes a substantial part of her analysis of masochism to its Christian manifestations (1992: 195–201), and it is difficult not to see Halley's taking of the sins of others on to his body as implicated in this tradition.

5

V. I. Warshawski and the Little Red Shoes: Sara Paretsky's Feminist Fairy Tales

I dressed carefully for my meeting with Darraugh Graham, in black wool with a white silk shirt and my red Magli pumps. Close to, you can see where the leather has become frail with age. I tend them anxiously, with polish and waterproofing, new soles and heel tips: to replace them would take almost a month of rent money. They bring me luck, my red Magli pumps. (Paretsky, 1994/1995: 17)

She put on the red shoes . . . then she went to the ball and began to dance! The shoes would not let her do what she liked: when she wanted to go to the right, they danced to the left; when she wanted to dance up the room, the shoes danced down the room, then down the stairs, through the streets and out of the town gate. Away she danced, and away she had to dance, right away into the dark forest . . .

On and ever on she danced; dance she must even through the dark nights. The shoes bore her away over briars and stubble till her feet were torn and bleeding; she danced away over the heath till she came to a little lonely house. She knew the executioner lived here . . .

Then she confessed all her sins, and the executioner chopped off her feet with the red shoes, but the shoes danced right away with the little feet into the depths of the forest. (Andersen, 1906/1993: 65–7)

In Hans Christian Andersen's famous fairy tale, Karen's brutal punishment is meted out for a number of crimes against patriarchy. The archetypal female vice of vanity drives her to sacrilege: she wears the red shoes to her confirmation. This initial crime is then compounded by the sin of wilful disobedience, when she puts on the forbidden shoes to go to the ball, and, as if this were not crime enough, she dances while her benefactor is dying. The impoverished Karen had been adopted by an old lady who 'could not see very well' (1906/1993: 64). Indeed, her vision was so bad she could not see the danger encoded in the red shoes and, when illness strikes, suffers for her failure to police her wayward charge. Karen judges that the old lady cannot possibly live, and so she commits what is perhaps the ultimate female crime against patriarchy – she behaves selfishly, putting her own pleasure before thought of others. For this catalogue of behaviour that is both unfeminine and yet stereotypically female, Karen is duly punished with exhaustion, amputation and expulsion from church and community.

Andersen's story concludes with Karen's dutiful submission to God's will. Her rehabilitation into the community is short-lived, however, as 'God's mercy' so fills her with joy that her heart breaks and her soul rises, footloose and fancy free, to heaven. The outsider has been reincorporated in the most definitive of manners: the transgressive woman is dead. Sara Paretsky's serial narrative, featuring private investigator V. I. Warshawski, thankfully evades such a conclusion, but Paretsky's feminist reappropriation of the crime genre is no less problematic for that. The V. I. Warshawski novels attempt to mould the hard-boiled detective narrative into a feminist fairy tale – a narrative that rehabilitates the 'wayward girls and wicked women' of legend, at the same time as it pays homage to the generic template of tough-guy fiction. Yet although the fictions superficially seem to succeed in creating a fantasy of feminist agency, in fact the project is riven with contradictions, creating a series of detective fairy tales that reinstate rather than overthrow the rigid systems of rule, reward and punishment that characterise Andersen's moral universe.

Across the nine books that comprise Warshawski's detective career to date, the detective is punished, like Karen, for the sins of selfishness and sacrilege. She has abandoned her husband and put her career first, rendering herself an outsider to the power and rewards of patriarchal belonging. She has confronted the patriarchy as it is embodied by church, state, family and capital in countless variations on the symbolic transgression of wearing red shoes to a confirmation. Time and again, she will not do as she is told, irrespective of the consequences (1994/1995: 74). As the novels progress, she is also punished for betraying the woman who 'adopted' her, Lotty Herschel. When Lotty is injured as the result of what she perceives as Vic's selfish disregard for the safety of others, a chasm opens between them, destroying what had previously been the security of an intimate and nurturing female friendship. I will return to a consideration of Warshawski's transgressions, but in the first instance they serve to illustrate that Vic, like Karen, is perceived as uncontrollable – and, by extension, dangerous.

However, it is not primarily for these parallels that I have chosen to open with the story of the red shoes.[1] Although there are many grounds for comparison, Andersen's story ultimately resonates because of the nature of Karen's punishment. For the crime of disobedience she is subject to the punishment of perpetual motion. She may not rest and must constantly dance, through night and day, in isolation and in pain, until the contradictions of this dance of death drive her literally to the executioner's axe. And this, equally, will be Warshawski's punishment for the crime of challenging the patriarchal status quo.

The red shoes are thus a redolent signifier within Paretsky's novels. Warshawski has a considerable investment in her red Magli pumps. On one level they symbolise some generally unobtainable aura of quality – something denied her by her blue-collar background and her rejection of marriage and establishment wealth. They stand in contrast to her everyday uniform running shoes, and are possessed of 'magic' transformative powers that enable her to assume an alternative persona when she wears them. These magical propensities are also encoded in their indestructability. In *Killing Orders*, for example, they survive both fire and mafia kidnap, returning safely to their owner against all odds (1985/1987: 158, 171). On another level, however, the shoes represent a dimension of the detective's complex relationship with her dead mother. The Italian shoes which encode a particular model of femininity are inextricably linked to the beautiful Italian mother with whose imagined desires and prohibitions Warshawski finds herself in constant dialogue.

Reading the red shoes through the dark lens of Andersen's fairy tale also opens up a framework of obsession and compulsion, a realm of frenzied, unreflective and potentially self-destructive activity. V. I.

Warshawski is arguably the most hard-boiled 'feminist' detective in print, and it is perhaps her example that best illustrates the difficulty of appropriating this particular set of generic conventions for feminism. As Warshawski struggles to contain the paradoxes of her position as a woman detective, she increasingly risks collapse through a frenzied hyperactivity as far removed from agency as its opposite – the passive dependency of the female other. In *Guardian Angel* she observes, in a rare moment of self-analysis: 'I was floundering from action to action, not knowing in what direction I was going' (1992: 217), while her lifestyle is effectively summarised in one sentence from the final novel, *Tunnel Vision*: 'I longed for a bath and the drink I'd turned down at Sal's, but once home I resumed my headlong dash through the day' (1994/1995: 43). This frenetic overactivity stems from a desire to evade her greatest fear: dependency. After a series of cataclysmic struggles and confrontations, *Guardian Angel* finally sees Warshawski gain succour in the arms of black police sergeant Conrad Rawlings, but only two pages later the defences are firmly back in place: 'I could call Conrad, but it would be a mistake to start a relationship in a state of dependency' (1992: 283). Vic's dread of being contained within the prescriptive role of normative North American femininity drives her constantly to reject offers of friendship, support and assistance and, as the series progresses, comes to situate her in complete opposition to the cooperative detective methodologies developed by a number of lesbian feminist writers.[2] Although the characters have changed, and female stereotypes have been overturned, the formula remains ominously familiar, and the psychic complexity of Warshawski needs to be set against this seemingly crude feminist role-reversal to establish exactly what the novels contribute to the regeneration of the detective genre. Is Warshawski's fear of becoming the passive female other so great that it causes her to become alienated from the community of 'outsiders' that surrounds her? And can the heterosexual female detective, however oppositional her stance, ever really threaten to destabilise a patriarchal system in which she is also profoundly implicated through structures of desire?[3]

To begin to answer these questions it is important to acknowledge the extent to which V. I. Warshawski changes over the course of her eight-volume narrative. These novels are underpinned not only by Warshawski's personal development and the evolution of her relationships with certain key friends, but also with an ongoing engagement with the family romance. While the novels of Dick Francis examine the ties that bind fathers and sons, Sara Paretsky's novels can equally be seen to explore the fate of patriarchy's daughters. Francis's sons seem fated to inherit the masochistic mantle of patriarchal duty, but what, if anything, is the daughter's inheritance? How might the daughter negotiate her loyalty to both father and mother? Can the daughter exist outside these formative relationships? As Paretsky, and Warshawski, struggle to find answers to these dilemmas, the novels undergo a complex evolution which suggests that, ultimately, there is no place for the patriarchal daughter. She cannot inherit, and if she does not evolve into mother or lover, then her marginality (and death) is guaranteed.

Indemnity Only, published in 1982, introduces us to Victoria Iphigenia Warshawski, known to her friends as Vic, but to everyone else as V. I., or Ms, Warshawski. The private names behind the initials link her to her mother, while it is the *nom du père* that identifies her in public. Her name is important both for its calculated androgyny, and for its unpronounceability. A character's willingness, or refusal, to address her correctly is used as a gauge of trustworthiness (1982/1987: 22, 127), and the 'difficulty' of her name provides an early example of her ungraspability. Neither the concept nor the signifier of the female private investigator can be assimilated by a patriarchy rooted in binary gender stereotypes, as is indicated by Warshawski's first meeting with the novel's love interest, Ralph Devereux:

> 'My name's V. I. Warshawski. I'm a private detective and I'm looking into Peter Thayer's death.' I handed him a business card.
>
> 'You? You're no more a detective than I am a ballet dancer,' he exclaimed. (1982/1987: 26)

Indemnity Only also tells us about her immigrant background as the only child of a Polish-American policeman father and an Italian refugee mother. Both of these parents are dead, and the orphaned status of Warshawski can be seen to hark back to interwar models of the detective as existing in a familial vacuum.[4] However, this status is deceptive, and Paretsky constructs a curious transitional model that manages both to have its family and eat it. Although Gabriella and Tony are dead, they are very far from forgotten, and Vic's negotiation of almost every aspect of her life is shaped by the spectral presence of her absent parents. Warshawski is haunted in particular by the ghost of her mother. Painful memories of her early death form a bedrock of grief for the detective, but this difficult haunting is supplemented by a form of sustenance from beyond the grave as the voice of Gabriella urges her never to give up. The legacy of her father is less immediate. Although she has inherited his ideals, his ghost is most commonly invoked by her institutional nemesis, the 'honest cop' Bobby Mallory. Mallory uses the memory of his friendship with her father as legitimisation for his attempts to control her, and to criticise her career as a detective: 'Tony would turn in his grave if he knew what you were doing . . . You've made a career out of something which no nice girl would touch' (1982/1987: 33–4). Finally the novel introduces us to the characters that set Vic apart from the template of hard-boiled detection: her friends.[5] Most significant amongst these is her best friend and, arguably, her surrogate mother, Lotty Herschel, a Jewish doctor who fled her native Vienna to escape the Nazis.

The second and third novels in the series introduce us to what is left of Vic's family, as well as the complex network of guilt and obligation that ties her to the past. *Deadlock* (1984) deprives Vic of her only pleasant relative, her ex-hockey player cousin Boom Boom, and sketches in the Polish-Catholic ancestry of her father. *Killing Orders* (1985) switches to her mother's history, as Vic goes reluctantly to the aid of her hideous Aunt Rosa, a wicked stepmother figure who neatly complements the ugly sisters or aunts of her father's family (1984/1987: 10, 13; 1985/1987: 10). Vic's mother and father continue to haunt the narratives of all her investigations, if not in plot, then in the dreams and anxieties that drive her, and in the internal dialogues through which she arrives at her decisions. However, from the fourth novel *Bitter Medicine* onwards, it is her friends and acquaintances who become the psychic impetus that drives the narrative.

V. I. Warshawski is a woman who has lost more friends to violent crime than Philip Marlowe has encountered *femme fatales*. The comparison is not entirely flippant. Marlowe is a man without either friends or family. His encounters with others are predominantly framed within the space of one narrative. Even those friends who stand outside the category of the *femme fatale*, and with whom some degree of intimacy is achieved – such as Red Norgaard and Anne Riordan – disappear in the cold light of a new quest. Superficially Warshawski appears to be the complete opposite. She is blessed with a plenitude of friends, but it seems that her punishment for such riches must be a constant cycle of grief and guilt as friend follows friend to the morgue.[6] Thus it is that in spite of her ongoing friendships, something of the hard-boiled loner survives in the spirit of

Warshawski. Her actual circle of intimacy is not great (Lotty, her nurse Carol Alvarado, the reporter Murray Ryerson, an assortment of cops, and in later novels her downstairs neighbour, Mr Contreras), and she trades sexual partners with few regrets, revealing yet another point of comparison with her predecessors. In an excellent essay on female friendship in Paretsky's novels, Rebecca Pope has observed the lack of continuity that characterises Vic's heterosexual encounters in comparison to her relationship with Lotty. Lotty can indeed be seen as the bulwark between Vic and complete isolation, but as the novels progress, their relationship becomes increasingly fraught with tensions. These tensions are the tip of the iceberg that threatens to sink Paretsky's project of feminist reappropriation, suggesting, as they do, that 'family' and detection cannot occupy the same conceptual space. The project of rewriting hard-boiled narrative, turning one of the many tools of patriarchal gender stereotyping against the master narrative, seems in danger of collapsing under too great a weight of expectation. You can make the woman as powerful as the patriarchy she opposes, but can you control the implications of this acquisition of power? And is such power actually desirable?

For Sally Munt the implications of such a super-power confrontation are somewhat problematic. In *Murder by the Book?* she argues that novels such as Paretsky's represent 'the tendency to . . . rebel within an overall conformity':

> Feminism is injected in order to enrich, temporize, and affirm the literariness of detective fiction, and its roots in a notional politics of liberal humanism . . . Without wishing to castigate these writers for colluding with masculine forms, the production of these counter myths does not sufficiently analyse the myth-making process: what must be called into question are those literary constructs like the subject, or the idea of the humanist self. (Munt, 1994: 58)

Warshawski certainly manifests a powerful investment in the traditional liberal values of justice and the concept of individual rights, and these attitudes tend in the end to prevent Warshawski from offering any radical revision of the structures of otherness that shape contemporary North American society.[7] However, this criticism overlooks the problems experienced by the detective in the process of establishing the counter-myth of feminist agency. The tensions within and around Warshawski expose the terrifying extent of the forces ranged against any manifestation of the female agent, and as the novels progress, they increasingly suggest the impossibility of presenting the detective as an embodiment of humanist rationality. Warshawski's investigations do not present the triumph of rational legality over the deviant forces of criminality. Rather they represent a violent semiotic assault on an irrational and destructive patriarchy that disguises its menacing prejudices behind a façade of propriety. And perhaps the most painful and potentially self-destructive factor for the detective within this mess resides in the fact that she is constantly driven by a desire to make sense and order out of chaos.

In the final two novels of her series, *Guardian Angel* and *Tunnel Vision,* Paretsky seems painfully aware of the contradictions inherent in her creation. Indeed, the narrative trajectory of the novels is almost unremittingly pessimistic as Vic argues with, confronts and alienates friends and enemies alike. These escalating tensions suggest an undermining of the myth-making process undertaken in the early novels, and an evolution within the series from the confident predictability of a Disneyesque fantasy to a Grimmer (sic) conception of the feminist fairy tale. In her monumental study *From the Beast to the Blonde,* Marina Warner discusses what she terms the 'double vision' of the traditional tale. Fairy tales deploy the fantastic precisely in order to contemplate the real. They exhibit no fear of paradox, nor of the monstrous impossibilities they recount:

> The prodigies are introduced to serve this concealed but ever-present visionariness of the tale, and serve it well by disguising the stories' harshly realistic core . . . The enchantments also universalize the narrative setting, encipher concerns, beliefs and desires in brilliant, seductive images that are themselves a form of camouflage, making it possible to utter harsh truths, to say what you dare. The disregard for logic, all those fairytale non-sequiturs and improbable reversals, rarely encompasses the emotional conflicts themselves: hatred, jealousy, kindness, cherishing retain an intense integrity throughout. The double vision of the tales, on the one hand charting perennial drives and terrors, both conscious and unconscious, and on the other mapping actual, volatile experience, gives the genre its fascination and power to satisfy. (Warner, 1994a: xvii)

The prodigy that is V. I. Warshawski offers a multiplicity of interpretative possibilities. She is both fairy godmother and Cinderella, superwoman and waif, tireless campaigner for justice and a woman on the verge. Her adventures present a sharp political engagement with the injustices of contemporary American society wrapped up in the fantasy of a woman powerful enough to effect change. The paradoxes encoded here indeed suggest a 'disregard for logic' that opens up the transgressive space of a fairy tale within the framework of the detective narrative.

Bitter Medicine, the fourth Warshawski novel, offers perhaps one of the best examples of the feminist fairy tale in Paretsky's oeuvre. Within the novel Vic manages simultaneously to fulfil the roles of both fairy godmother and the orphaned Cinderella, while at the same time gesturing towards a more co-operative mode of investigation. The story begins once upon a time in a land far, far away (the suburbs outside Warshawski's familiar Chicago), when Vic is forced to take a critically ill pregnant teenager to a hospital more concerned with its brochures than its patients. Both the teenager, Consuelo, and her baby, disturbingly baptised Victoria Charlotte, die as a result of medical negligence, but the real villain is identified not as the individual doctor responsible for the delay in treating her, but rather a system that denies the provision of healthcare to those who cannot pay and persistently discriminates on grounds of race and gender. Consuelo is effectively killed by this discrimination, but she was initially rendered pregnant and vulnerable by a different monster, the ogre of family expectations. *Bitter Medicine* more than any of the early Warshawski novels emphasises the extent to which women are the primary victims of patriarchal capitalism, but it is nonetheless ruthless in its exposure of women's complicity in their own oppression. It is the enormous weight of her mother's demand that she 'go out by [her]self to Gringoland and win prizes for them' (1987/1988: 15) that drives Consuelo into an ill-advised pregnancy. There is a bitter irony to her paradoxical non-escape. Her fear of family expectations leads her to construct another (fatally) self-destructive fantasy based upon misplaced expectations of romance. In her desire to escape, she transforms the obnoxious Fabiano into a reluctant Prince Charming, and thereby finds 'a perfect exit from the pressure and the glory heaped on her since birth by the rest of the family' (1987/1988: 12).

The mother/child motif dominates *Bitter Medicine*, depicting in various guises both the paradigm of the child that destroys the mother, and that of the mother who destroys her child. In the first instance Consuelo's death in childbirth reopens a series of repressed psychic anxieties for the detective. It is not until the much later *Tunnel Vision* that Warshawski finally confesses that her mother's death had been 'the cataclysmic event' of her life, from which she has in some ways never recovered (1994/1995: 117), but the power of this cataclysm is nonetheless painfully evident in *Bitter Medicine*. The boundary between past and present fragments into a series of nightmare translations as Vic finds Consuelo and Gabriella blurring one into the other:

> I hadn't seen Consuelo since she'd passed through the double steel doors six hours ago. In my mind she appeared as I'd last seen my mother, small, fragile, overshadowed by the machinery of an indifferent technology. I couldn't help picturing the baby, a small V. I., unable to breathe, lying with a shock of black hair, lost in the medical maze. (Paretsky, 1987/1988: 40)

> I slept restlessly, haunted again by Consuelo's baby . . . The streets in South Chicago were flooded and I made my way to my parents' house with difficulty. When I came into the living room, a crib stood in the corner with a baby in it. She lay very still, not moving, staring at me with large black eyes. I realized it was my child, but that she had no name, that she would come to life only if I gave her my name. (Paretsky, 1987/1988: 49)

Irrespective of the 'truth' of her mother's death, Vic feels guilt and responsibility, and becomes the 'vampire' child complicit in the hospital's consumption of her mother. In a patriarchal society the mother is expected, either literally or metaphorically, to make a gift of her life to the child, but such a gift will inevitably be contaminated by regret and anger, leaving the child with a burden of guilt.

Set against the consumption of the mother by the child is the mother who destroys her child through the imposition of impossible desires. This is clearly established in the case of Consuelo and her mother, and, as I shall suggest later, it emerges as one of the factors that contribute to the 'breakdown' of Warshawski in the final two novels. However, in *Bitter Medicine* the maternal tension between symbiosis and mutual destruction (both Consuelo *and* the baby die) is symbolically figured through the abortion debate and the attack on Lotty's clinic that forms a dramatic set piece at the heart of the novel.

Significantly, Lotty's clinic is a community health centre. It provides both abortions and ante-natal care for women on the margins of society, symbolising women's right to control over their own bodies within a society that persistently seeks to deny them this right. Nearly all the men of the novel are implicated in the appropriation of women's bodies. Fabiano crudely trades the dead body of Consuelo for a hospital pay-off and a flashy car (1987/1988: 72), while Dieter Monkfish, the caricature anti-abortionist, makes a profession out of the usurpation of women's choices. We are also reminded of Vic's boyfriends past and present who have demanded the right to protect her, and refuse her right to be the judge of the risks to which she submits her own body. Even Bobby Mallory is implicated through his conservative gender politics. He makes no bones about repeatedly telling Vic that her place is in the suburbs, making a career of procreation.

In this context, the failure of the police to protect Lotty's clinic acts as a reminder of the extent to which women's issues are still not regarded as worthy of attention. The political thrust of the novel is squarely aimed at a society which distinguishes between first- and second-class citizens along the lines of race and gender, a point which is further emphasised by the widely voiced fear that the novel's other victim, the murdered doctor Malcolm Tregiere, will not receive the justice of a fair investigation because of his colour. In terms of the fairy tale's revision of patriarchal narratives, it is thus important to see Vic not only as a fairy godmother, but also as a newly pro-active Cinderella. This is a Cinderella who manages her own transformations, and is utterly disinterested in romance. She does not want to marry the prince, nor even to be the prince – rather she hopes to change the entire story. Besides which, Vic's lover in *Bitter Medicine,* the young doctor Peter Burgoyne, turns out to be less of a prince than a frog. In a pleasing inversion of the crime genre's *femme fatale,* Burgoyne lays down his body in an attempt to distract Vic from her investigation into the hospital's activities. Vic takes him up on the offer but, in yet another refusal of gender stereotypes, is ultimately unmoved both by his betrayal and his later suicide. He was, she concludes, 'a lightweight' (1987/1988: 282).

There is a further sense in which Lotty's clinic might be seen to form the symbolic core of *Bitter Medicine*. The project represents a community or society of outsiders in the sense imagined by Virginia Woolf, who presciently argues in *Three Guineas* that corrupt patriarchal structures could not be transformed from within. Asked by a correspondent to join a society for the prevention of war, Woolf responds that she cannot, and goes on to argue that real hope for change lies not in the assimilation of the energies of newly enfranchised women, but rather in women's resistance to the patriarchal status quo. Women must work together to imagine and initiate alternative modes of organisation. They must be 'outsiders', 'anonymous' and 'indifferent' to the power and prestige of belonging:

> It seems both wrong for us rationally and impossible for us emotionally to fill up your form and join your society. For by so doing we should merge our identity in yours . . .
>
> We can best help you to prevent war not by repeating your words and following your methods but by finding new words and creating new methods. We can best help you to prevent war not by joining your society but by remaining outside your society but in cooperation with its aim. (Woolf, 1938/1986: 121)

Woolf's ideas have profound implications for the character of Warshawski, who seems to vacillate uncomfortably between modes of patriarchal infiltration and opposition. In her search for the truth, Vic alternates between two fundamentally contradictory methodologies. Confronting the hospital managers and government officials whose sins of omission, or commission, are ultimately responsible for the deaths of both Consuelo and Malcolm Tregiere, Vic claims the authority of one powerful institution in order to intimidate another:

> 'I'm a lawyer, Mr Coulter. I'm a member of the Illinois bar in good standing – you can call the bar association and find that out. And what I really want is the report on the death of Consuelo Hernandez and her infant daughter.' (Paretsky, 1987/1988: 216)

Yet her approach to her ex-lawyer husband, Dick, and his plea of client confidentiality, is in marked contrast to this assertion of belonging. This time her claim is one of 'freedom from unreal loyalties' (Woolf, 1938/1986: 90):

> 'Yes. Confidential to you. But, sweetheart, I'm not a member of your firm. Nor of your person. I have no obligation – legal, mental, physical, or ethical – to protect their privacy.' (Paretsky, 1987/1988: 221)

In the service of her investigation Warshawski oscillates between belonging and marginality. She occupies both of the problematic polarities that characterise the identificatory possibilities presented to women. In *About Chinese Women* Julia Kristeva argues that woman can only gain access to the agency of the symbolic order through identifying with the father, but, in so doing, she denies herself the pleasure and comfort of both the mother's body and her own:

> We cannot gain access to the temporal scene, that is to the political and historical affairs of our society, except by identifying with the values considered to be masculine (mastery, superego, the sanctioning communicative word that institutes stable social exchange) . . . we have been able to serve or overthrow the socio-historic order by playing at being supermen. A few enjoy it: the most active, the most effective, the 'homosexual' women (whether they know it or not). Others, more bound to the mother, and more tuned in to their unconscious drives, refuse this role and sullenly hold back, neither speaking nor writing, in a permanent state of expectation, occasionally punctuated by some kind of outburst: a cry, a refusal, 'hysterical symptoms'. (Kristeva, 1974/1986: 155)

Kristeva's description of an unconscious homosexuality resonates strongly – particularly in the light of the argument proposed by Rebecca Pope that for women in opposition to a heteropatriarchal norm, transgressive desires and identifications will always surface in some form, irrespective of their actual choice of sexual partner. *Guardian Angel* concludes with a dream about Gabriella and Lotty that awakens Vic from the intimacy of a night with her lover Conrad. For a brief moment, argues Pope, the novel's subtext has broken through: 'the explicitly erotic and heterosexual scenario dissolves and uncovers the mother-daughter relation that heterosexual relations have displaced' (1995: 168).

Nonetheless, the wider scenario outlined by Kristeva is that of an impasse between the two compromised strategies of mastery and its refusal. Kristeva, however, believes it is possible to evade this destructive binary. She argues for the power of 'listening', and demands the recognition of 'the unspoken in all discourse' (surely the archetypal role of the detective!) before concluding with a statement of the need for:

> A constant alternation between time and its 'truth', identity and its loss, history and that which produces it: that which remains extra-phenomenal, outside the sign, beyond time. An impossible dialectic of two terms, a permanent alternation: never one without the other. It is not certain that anyone here and now is capable of this. (Kristeva, 1974/1986: 156)

Certainly not V. I. Warshawski – for as the novels progress, it seems increasingly the case that the feminist detective hero must disintegrate under the attrition of this 'permanent alternation' and the contradictory pressures of her position.

Bitter Medicine depicts Vic as a fairy godmother, or as the superman of Kristeva's analysis. She responds constantly to the demands of a dependent community of outsiders who believe she can use her magic powers to make things better. Lotty Herschel, Consuelo's sister Carol and Malcolm's lover Tessa all demand that she be their agent and enter the hostile symbolic order to avenge the deaths of those inadequately served by prejudiced structures of justice (1987/1988: 56). However, the demand that she enter the world of the oppressors leads inevitably to inappropriate expectations and creates tension within the community of outsiders. A conflict of interests emerges between the outsiders' demand for an 'ethical' investigation and Vic's belief that she must 'fight fire with fire'. The gulf dividing equality feminism from separatist feminism seems unbreachable, and threatens to destroy the fantasy of justice (1987/1988: 112). But in this novel, ultimately, the fairy godmother succeeds. Rather than going it alone, Vic draws on the strengths of the community of outsiders (the press, the 'good' doctors, a black policeman), and together these forces effect a public exposure of patriarchy's dirty linen.

Thus, *Bitter Medicine* stands out among Paretsky's novels as a successful feminist fairy tale, and as an effective reappropriation of the crime genre. But even at this mid-point in her literary career, the pressures of Warshawski's position as feminist/detective are becoming evident. Vic is initially reluctant to get involved in the case, and throughout the investigation she is subject to bouts of exhaustion and corporeal collapse that act as counterpoints to her usual frenzied activity. From the outset of the series Vic has been depicted as someone who drives herself to the limit. Time and again as she heads home to the pleasures of bath and bed she is intercepted, denied rest and recuperation. Frequently the only way for her to escape is literally to opt out of her life – to check anonymously into a motel where she can rest uninterrupted (1987/1988: 250; 1992: 289, 312). *Guardian Angel* includes a chapter entitled 'Step Aside, Sisyphus' (1992: 112), which clearly aims to signpost the intolerable pressure of operating within the symbolic order. By maintaining a network of supportive friends, Vic has attempted to create an alternative site within which she might be nurtured and restored, but increasingly her 'constant alternation', her perpetual motion, threatens instead to render dangerously permeable the barrier between the symbolic and its others. By the time of *Guardian Angel*, Vic's crime-fighting forays into 'enemy territory' begin to look more like manifestations of a Freudian death drive than a strategy which might genuinely disturb 'the mutual understanding of the established powers' (Kristeva, 1974/1986: 156).

Guardian Angel is the seventh Warshawski investigation, and it reveals a notable change of tone in the detective's narrative. Vic has always been prone to anger – 'I could feel my head vibrating with rage' (1987/1988: 22) – but *Guardian Angel* reaches new heights of fury. The novel is quite remarkably confrontational. Driven by her anger over the gratuitous killing of a 'senile' neighbour's dogs, Warshawski moves from one highly charged encounter to another like the proverbial bull in a china shop. She collides with the vested interests of industry (Diamond Head Motors and Paragon Steel), the legal profession (once again, her ex-husband, Richard Yarborough) and yuppidom (her upwardly mobile neighbours, Todd and Chrissie Pichea). This is not the subtle and well thought-out strategic power-play that characterised the conclusion of *Bitter Medicine*, but rather a chaotic hitting out, not only at enemies but also at friends. In the first half of the novel Vic quarrels with Mr Contreras, Murray Ryerson, her lawyer, Freeman Carter and, most significantly, Lotty. Warshawski has become a significantly angrier character than was even the case in such fraught early adventures as *Killing Orders*, in which the murder of a close friend and the burning down of her flat might be seen to give justifiable reason to her rage. In *Guardian Angel*, however, she is quite literally consumed by rage. Her body becomes an explosive force that she struggles to contain: 'My finger shook as I stabbed their polished brass doorbell', '[t]he impulse to smash in his face was so strong that I just pulled my fist back before it connected', 'my neck muscles had turned so stiff from rage that when I got to my own front door I was trembling violently' (1992: 83, 85, 85).

These semiotic eruptions of violence speak powerfully of repression. Vic desires 'direct action' that would cut through the court orders and injunctions which protect not the vulnerable poor and elderly, but those who conspire to prey upon them. These lawless emotions also emphasise the instability of the boundary between the two poles of Vic's existence: she cannot always remember the rules. However, although Vic does on one occasion indulge in a fantasy of satisfying her almost orgasmic rage – '[f]igure out how to replace that stuff, I thought, panting as I pictured myself trashing it' (1992: 352) – her violence ends up predominantly directed against herself:

> I found a bench at a bus stop across the street and sat there, taking in great gulps of air. I was still shaking with fury, pounding my right fist against my thigh. People waiting for the bus backed away from me: another crazy on the loose. (Paretsky, 1992: 322)

Her anger at a character's careless racism makes her choke (1992: 295), while the 'end of active rage' experienced in conversation with Dick leaves her 'exhausted' (322). In an encounter towards the end of the novel she announces that '[f]ury so had me in its grip, I could barely see' (431), emphasising again the intense corporeality of her ire. The detective's body, it seems, is becoming as vulnerable to internal crisis as it is to external assault. Warshawski threatens literally to come apart at the seams:

> When we'd hung up I stood in the middle of the room with my hands pressed against my head, trying to keep the boiling inside from spilling out through my temples. (Paretsky, 1992: 284)

It is not simply the boundary between her private and public lives which has become permeable, but her very subjectivity, leaving her very far from being the rational liberal humanist subject described by Sally Munt.

Discussing Paretsky's work in more detail, Munt observes the considerable attention that is paid to dress and clothing within the novels:

> As a fantasy of empowerment, Warshawski's style reassures the female reader that 'dressing up' enables you to do the job. The fetishization of clothes in Paretsky's work implies the 'draggish' imperative of femininity, signalling its artifice. Or is the reason

> perhaps more mundane – could Warshawski's constant need to change her clothes be a reflection of the many identities necessary to her survival as a woman in a multi-roled and predominantly masculine environment? (Munt, 1994: 47)

There is, however, a further dimension to Warshawski's wardrobe – namely, its destruction. Her outfits may be lovingly selected, but they are unlikely to survive a typical day at the office. Obviously the repeated beatings and regular immersions in Chicago's less than sanitary waterways take their toll but, ironically, the violence inflicted upon Warshawski's clothing is as likely to come from within as without. Vic does not simply change clothes for disguise or masquerade, frequently she does so because her silk shirts and chic jackets have been destroyed by her body. The rage that drives her receives another corporeal manifestation in the blood, tears and, in particular, sweat that regularly leave her in need of a new sartorial skin (1987/1988: 238, 250, 254, 313; 1992: 246, 342, 355).

Guardian Angel, like *Bitter Medicine*, is marked by examples of the detective's bodily collapse, but again a transition is evident from the earlier novel. Whereas before it was outside agencies that stood between Vic and her well-earned rest, now the punishment is self-imposed. After each new crisis, she denies herself rest: 'I resisted the longing for a bath', 'I was tempted to climb into my own bed . . . but there was just too much to do', '[m]y bones were aching with exhaustion. I negotiated the distance . . . by sheer willpower' (1992: 79, 181, 240). Rather than submitting to her bodily needs, Vic seems driven to expunge them. She vomits after lying to the ailing Mrs Frizell in hospital, and again after waiting anxiously for Mr Contreras to emerge from a dangerous situation (1992: 97, 375). Increasingly it seems that she can only maintain her corporeal and moral integrity through the violent expulsion of the forces that threaten it. Teetering on the brink of the abject, Vic throws out the baby with the bathwater and forcibly thrusts away all and everything that might encroach on the imperilled boundaries of her identity.

Throughout the transitions of *Guardian Angel* one factor remains constant: the haunting of Warshawski by her mother's ghost. But why is it that Gabriella no longer seems able to sustain her daughter, or stabilise her volatile emotional equilibrium? Perhaps because the early novels told only part of the story. *Bitter Medicine* depicts Gabriella solely as muse and victim, but by *Tunnel Vision* a fuller portrait has emerged of a woman whose frustrated ambitions and independence were channelled into the training of her daughter as a survivor. One of the few mementos of Gabriella that Vic carries (somewhat miraculously) throughout the novels is a set of red Venetian glasses, but as the glasses are gradually eroded through fire and violence, so their influence begins to change. In early novels they soothe her, but in *Tunnel Vision* the glasses bring 'not comfort but agitation' (1994/1995: 132):

> Looking into the ruby of the glass I could see my mother's fierce dark eyes. Gabriella had been like some wild bird, choosing a cage as a storm haven, out of bewilderment, then beating her wings so fiercely she broke herself against the walls. If that was what compromise brought, I didn't want it. (Paretsky, 1994/1995: 132)

Warshawski is the child who never ceases to mourn for her mother and, as a modern-day Cinderella, she should expect to find that absent mother to be a source of strength. Marina Warner suggests that '[v]ariants on the tale from all over the world give the mother's ghost some kind of consoling and magical role in her daughter's ultimate escape from pain' (1994a: 205), and in the early novels it would seem that Gabriella does indeed do this for Vic. However, as the books progress, it becomes harder to see Gabriella as a source of nurturance and plenty; rather she becomes a symbol of the law, attempting to impart to her daughter a strategy for survival in the symbolic order. Gabriella's code states that to be dependent is to be weak, and to be weak is to be vulnerable, but this rule is so rigid that it threatens to enforce self-destruction rather than preservation, particularly since it conflicts with, and denies Vic access to, the contrasting mode of *paternal* nurturance. Perhaps believing that the daughter's desire for the father will leave her exposed, Gabriella even reveals a Freudian streak, effectively placing an injunction upon her daughter's development of heterosexual relationships: an injunction that receives a comical airing in *Bitter Medicine* when Vic discovers she cannot have sex in the presence of her mother's Venetian glasses (1987/1988: 121–2). Although Vic remains sexually active, as soon as any relationship threatens to become intimate and co-dependent, her Pavlovian fear of dependency kicks in, and once again she must face the trauma of loss.

In 'Beyond the Pleasure Principle' Freud distinguishes between the unpleasant sensations of anxiety, fear and fright. He identifies fright as the root of traumatic neuroses which manifest themselves in the patient's dream life:

> [D]reams occurring in traumatic neuroses have the characteristic of repeatedly bringing the patient back into the situation of his accident, a situation from which he wakes up in another fright. (Freud, 1920/1955: 13)

Gabriella's death begs to be read as the 'traumatic accident' of Vic's life, as the death that underpins all her investigations and which drives her relentless search for explanation. In my earlier discussion of Agatha Christie, I related the psychic work of the *fort/da* game to the historically specific cultural attraction of the crime genre, but Freud's example is equally pertinent to the case of the individual detective. Observing the child's response to the 'loss' of the mother, Freud writes:

> At the outset he was in a *passive* situation – he was overpowered by the experience; but, by repeating it, unpleasurable though it was, as a game, he took on an *active* part. (Freud, 1920/1955: 16)

Freud also suggests that the repeated throwing away of the toy might be seen as a form of revenge for the betrayal of the mother's departure. By cutting off ties before they can be cut by others, the child asserts a defiant independence and invulnerability to the pain of loss. Certainly this desire to translate passivity into action can be seen as paradigmatic of the impulse behind feminist detective narratives. However, in the case of V. I. Warshawski, the repetition of loss comes increasingly to far outweigh the pleasures of recovery, and her narrative speaks not of empowerment but of self-destruction.

Warshawski repeats the trauma of maternal loss by constantly rejecting those closest to her, keeping them at a distance so that she cannot again be subject to the pain of bereavement. This dynamic is made explicit by her lover, Conrad Rawlings, at the end of *Guardian Angel*. After Vic has expressed her fear that Lotty will abandon her as her mother did, Rawlings responds:

> 'So you have to keep everyone around you on pins and needles all the time? Is that it? So guys like me, or even the old man

> downstairs, don't get enough of a hold on you to leave you in the lurch?' (Paretsky, 1992: 438)

But what is intended as a strategy of self-preservation seems instead to bear witness to what Freud terms the 'mysterious masochistic trends of the ego' (Freud, 1920/1955: 14). The masochism of Paretsky's novels is far removed from that which characterises the work of Dick Francis. Although Vic is subject to a plethora of beatings, these are not the sustained and complexly imagined torturings that characterise the experience of the Francis hero. Rather they are typical of the 'workaday' violence of the hard-boiled genre. Yet what must be set against this absence of torture is Vic's capacity for a form of mental masochism. She repeatedly beats herself with the emotions of guilt and responsibility, and these emotions give her the ability to physically push herself beyond sense and exhaustion: 'it was still much too cold for swimming . . . [w]ithin a few minutes my feet and ears were aching with cold, but I kept pushing myself until I felt a roaring in my head and the world turned black around me' (1992: 98).

There is no pleasure in Warshawski's masochism and, in contrast to the experience of the Francis hero, the capacity to endure does not reinforce her power. Rather the extremity of this psychological masochism leads inexorably towards self-annihilation and returns me to Kristeva's speculations regarding women's identificatory choices. Under the heading of 'I who want not to be', Kristeva contemplates the suicide of women haunted by 'the call of the mother' (Kristeva, 1974/1986: 156):

> With family and history at an impasse, this call troubles the word: it generates hallucinations, voices, 'madness'. After the superego, the ego founders and sinks. It is a fragile envelope, incapable of staving off the irruption of this conflict, of this love which had bound the little girl to her mother, and which then, like black lava, had lain in wait for her all along the path of her attempts to identify with the symbolic paternal order. Once the moorings of the word, the ego, the superego, begin to slip, life itself can't hang on: death quietly moves in. (Kristeva, 1974/1986: 156–7)

Must suicide be the fate of the woman who attempts to identify with both mother and father? The final Warshawski novel, *Tunnel Vision*, certainly suggests that women's status within the symbolic is contingent and imperilled. The daughter has been tolerated rather than admitted, and she will be expelled without compunction should her actions set in motion anything more profound than a localised disturbance of patriarchal power. *Tunnel Vision* sees Vic take on the combined forces of business and capital, the legal profession, the police, the patriarchal family unit and the United States' Senate. This is sacrilege – and, unsurprisingly, she is punished for her sins.

Warshawski's self-destructive tendencies dominate *Tunnel Vision*. She will not tolerate compromise, and remains ominously terrified of dependence (1994/5: 285, 367); and although the novel goes some way to justifying her paranoid fear of betrayal, she nonetheless works hard to destroy all the relationships that previously sustained her. By the end of *Guardian Angel* her relationship with Lotty is already damaged, following a violent assault on Lotty by criminals who mistook her for Vic. Although the final novel sees them restored to speaking terms, they no longer share the intimacy that characterised earlier novels. Initially Lotty's place is taken by Vic's lover, the black policeman Conrad Rawlings, but that relationship is gradually eroded by external forces. American society's hostility to interracial relationships drives a wedge between the lovers and their wider social circle, while their fundamentally dichotomous understandings of legality threaten to divide them as policeman and private eye (1994/1995: 105, 124). Finally they are divided by gender, as Warshawski's investigation into sexual abuse reveals the extent to which even apparently reconstructed men still refuse to believe in women's stories (1994/1995: 177).

The problems of *Tunnel Vision*, however, predominantly emerge from Vic's remorseless quest for 'truth', or, more precisely, her crusade on behalf of truth. She discovers fairly rapidly exactly what is wrong, but lacks patriarchally acceptable 'proof', and consequently evolves into a modern-day Cassandra, the woman whose truth is fated never to be believed. *Tunnel Vision* throws brutal light on to the gendered nature of truth. Male lawyers, policemen and doctors join forces in the deployment of the classical binary opposition between male rationality and female hysteria in their attempt to discredit female accounts of patriarchal abuse. Emily Messenger, sexually abused by her father, becomes the mad daughter in the bedroom, allegedly consumed with Oedipal desires for her father. Vic becomes the predatory 'feminist', putting disgusting ideas into the innocent daughter's head (1994/1995: 357, 393, 401). Throughout the novel, women are accused of emotional prejudice, while men rewrite history in the name of rationality, bringing the weight of their symbolic power to bear on the conspicuous partiality of justice. This is the context within which Vic persists in her headlong attempt to prove that it is she, and not the patriarchal order she opposes, who is the guardian of truth.

For Julia Kristeva, the 'truth' is that which is repressed within the symbolic paternal order of sign and time. That which is unspoken in patriarchal discourse forms a 'curious truth: outside time, with neither a before nor an after', which 'neither judges nor postulates, but refuses, displaces and breaks the symbolic order before it can re-establish itself' (1974/1986: 153). Within symbolic representation this 'truth' can only be imagined as woman, but even in the process of encapsulating her within such a representation, she ceases to function as the unrepresentable and the unspoken. To articulate the truth, as Emily Messenger discovers, is to risk its assimilation and incorporation into a hostile discourse, a discourse that denies truth's articulation even as it utters it. Spoken in the symbolic, the truth is no longer the 'truth'. Yet in spite of the impossibility of the truth being believed by the patriarchal symbolic, Vic persists in her quest to speak it. This is the truth of her mother's voice, and it has indeed lain in wait for her like 'black lava'. As Kristeva reminds us, the semiotic, that which exceeds symbolic representation, is not a site of comfort but a place of madness and psychosis, and while it has the power to disrupt the symbolic, it cannot offer a stable alternative to that which it displaces. By *Tunnel Vision* it becomes clear that Gabriella's legacy to Vic is the drive to disruption, to anarchism and terrorism, and not, as the earlier novels suggested, a sustaining extension of the pre-Oedipal bond.

In *Tunnel Vision,* we learn at last that it was Tony who nurtured and Gabriella who imposed the law:

> I longed for the sight of him at the counter, waiting to buy me an ice cream after school, or to listen to my tale of woe with a gentle smile my mother never wore. I longed for a comfort that life could not give me. (Paretsky, 1994/1995: 159)

> I was sick of pushing myself, but the old blue-collar work ethic wouldn't leave me alone. Or maybe it was just my dead mother's voice. Once when I was eight and had been in trouble at school I couldn't face going back the next day. In tears I

> pleaded a stomachache. My tender-hearted father wanted to tuck me in bed with a book and my teddy bear, but Gabriella dressed me by force . . . she told me only cowards ran from their problems, especially ones they'd created themselves. (Paretsky, 1994/1995: 73–4)

Paretsky has inverted the customary binary opposition: Vic's father nurtures and her mother punishes, and this new perspective on the 'revolutionary' mother effects a considerable change on the narrative. Vic is no longer the orphan in search of the lost mother, but rather the daughter struggling to win her all-too-present mother's approval, while the tasks that she must perform are exactly those which cut her off from the imaginary plenitude of dyadic unity. Vic comes close to achieving the Holy Grail of comfort with Lotty and Conrad, but on both occasions the revolutionary quest takes precedence over the intimacy of human bonds. In *Bitter Medicine*, Vic's duty was to act for the mother and avenge the death of the child, and once again in *Tunnel Vision* this becomes her task – only this time she must metaphorically kill her lover to protect her child:

> To dig a channel between us would be like cutting off a piece of my heart. But to abandon Emily to salvage my life with Conrad would mean cutting off a chunk of my soul. (Paretsky, 1994/1995: 357)

Gabriella's legacy means that the daughter's inheritance is motherhood. She becomes neither subject nor lover, but rather a revolutionary *ur*-mother at the service of a needy dependent community. And thus it is that by the end of *Tunnel Vision*, Vic has truly reached an impasse. As a revolutionary agent she cannot let herself rest and, as a transgressor of patriarchal laws, she is not allowed to rest. On both counts her fate is perpetual motion, and the end of the novel sees her for once unmotivated and unable to act. Told by a friend to take a holiday, she jokingly contemplates the Reichenbach falls, a singularly appropriate location for detectives seeking self-annihilation, and one that suggests that the contradictions of the feminist detective must ultimately end in death (1994/1995: 480).

But death is not the end of *Tunnel Vision*. Far from it. In a remarkable resurrection of the *deus ex machina*, the fairy godfather, Mr Contreras, effects the unexpected fantasy of a fairy-tale ending. In a utopian scene of transformation and reconciliation, everyone (with

the notable exception of Conrad Rawlings) gathers for the detective's fortieth birthday party. This conclusion makes the fantasy behind the detective genre's customary resolution painfully apparent. Detective fictions, as much as fairy tales, have traditionally been narratives of reassurance and reward. Marina Warner writes of the 'heroic optimism' that characterises the fairy-tale genre – the belief that somewhere along the line, at least temporarily, everything will be all right (Warner, 1994a: xvi). The essentially pessimistic trajectory of the final two Warshawski novels would seem to deny such a possibility, but ultimately Paretsky does not want to let go of the fantasy of feminist revision with which she began her detective series and, consequently, she caps the contradictions of her texts with a happy ending as bizarre as any invented by the brothers Grimm:

> What else can I say, except that good friends are a balm to a bruised spirit? And that Mitch – aided by Nathan – got into the cake and ate most of it. And that champagne flowed like water, and we danced until the pale moon sank. (Paretsky, 1994/1995: 483)

Perhaps Paretsky, like Warner, believes that '[t]he faculty of wonder, like curiosity, can make things happen; it is time for wishful thinking to have its due' (Warner, 1994a: 418). But, however attractive the idea, it remains at odds with the evidence of the Warshawski novels, which suggest that the reappropriation of the detective genre requires something more than wishful thinking. The tension between outsider and agency seems irresolvable and the 'hard-boiled' heterosexual female private investigator threatens to implode under the contradictions of her subject position. Could a lesbian policewoman possibly fare any better?

NOTES

1. I am grateful to a very perceptive group of students at the University of Glamorgan who first drew my attention to Warshawski's peculiar attachment to her red Magli pumps.
2. Barbara Wilson's aptly titled *Murder in the Collective* (1984/1994) is a typical example of the development of a 'co-operative' model of investigation within a lesbian feminist framework . Wilson's challenge to traditional detective methodologies is discussed in Chapter 7. See also Maggie Humm, *Border Traffic* (1991) and Paulina Palmer, *Contemporary Lesbian Writing*, (1993).
3. Warshawski's failure to sustain a viable relationship aligns her with the majority of contemporary heterosexual female private investigators. There are few exceptions to this rule, but perhaps one of the most notable is Val McDermid's Kate Brannigan. Brannigan's relationship with rock journalist Richard spans the entire series of novels, but in the early novels its stability was threatened by Richard's need to assert his masculinity. However, in

contrast to Warshawski, Brannigan succeeds in negotiating the crisis, with the result that *Star Struck* (1998) shows both partners comfortably occupying their own separate spheres of expertise.

4. Although precedent can be found in the classical tradition for the detective's encounter with familial tensions – for example, the often fraught family relations of Sayers's Lord Peter Wimsey – it is not until postwar reinscriptions of the genre that the hard-boiled upholder of the law comes to be given a patrilineage of his own.
5. Family and friends are key distancing devices in a novel that is otherwise modelled upon the traditional hard-boiled formula. The 'tough-talking' language clearly pays homage to Chandler, while the book's structure, from the opening scene in the detective's run-down office to the closing rescue of a male 'damsel in distress', similarly owes a debt to Marlowe's investigative process.
6. Examples might include Agnes Paciorek from *Killing Orders* and Malcolm Tregiere from *Bitter Medicine*, as well as her cousin Boom Boom Warshawski, the only one of her family who also qualified as a friend.
7. In contrast, her conception of legality seems to suffer from a terminal degree of relativism. While she has a right to privacy, anyone who pisses her off does not (Paretsky, 1994/1995: 260). That she is usually right in her extra-sensory perception of skeletons in the closet does not make her illegal actions any easier to justify, but it does emphasise the fact the law primarily works to protect patriarchy's dirty laundry, and if women are to challenge corrupt institutions, their most likely route to success will be from without rather than within the Law.

6

Passing/Out: The Paradoxical Possibilities of Detective Delafield

> You had to make a choice: you could be gay or a Los Angeles police officer. You could not be both. If you walked into a room full of police officers and they knew you were gay, they'd clear out. If you walked into a gay party and people knew you were a cop, they'd clear out. You were a part of both worlds and a member of neither. You were alone; you were isolated. (Mitch Grobeson, quoted in Buhrke, 1996: 32)

> To be against (opposed to) is also to be against (close up, in proximity to) or, in other words, up against. (Dollimore, 1991: 229)

'When it comes to lesbians . . . many people have trouble seeing what's in front of them,' claims Terry Castle in *The Apparitional Lesbian* (Castle, 1993: 2). Castle's book comprises an erudite and witty search for the traces of female homosexuality in modern culture, and her ghostly metaphor seems highly appropriate to describe the paradoxical position of Katherine V. Forrest's lesbian policewoman, Detective Kate Delafield. In her 'polemical introduction' to *The Apparitional Lesbian*, Castle claims that she wants to bring the lesbian out of the margins and admire her substantial centrality within twentieth-century culture, and it is with considerable pleasure that she records the uncovering not of scarcity, but plenitude – a veritable surfeit of lesbian signifiers waiting to be read. Much the same could be said of Forrest's novels. Not only does the lesbian detect, but whenever and wherever she detects, she uncovers or encounters the lesbian, and yet these lesbian multitudes remain, in social terms, invisible. Tucked safely into the closet or coralled into the margins, the lesbian landscape remains unmapped: invisible not only to the law, but initially also to the detective herself.

Society's inability to 'see' the lesbian is central to this chapter and to the trajectory of Forrest's crime fiction. Forrest has now produced seven Delafield novels, the first four of which form a fairly homogeneous group, charting a continual process of emotional and political development on the part of the detective. Kate Delafield first appeared in a 1984 novel of office politics entitled *Amateur City*. An isolated figure, grieving for her recently deceased lover Anne, the early Delafield combined procedural correctness with a subscription to the Stephen Gordon school of lesbian deportment. Over the course of the novel some respite from her loneliness is achieved in the arms of her key witness, Ellen O'Neil, but it is not until the second novel that her position as archetypal detective-outsider is questioned.

Murder at the Nightwood Bar (1987) is perhaps the best known of the Delafield novels. Here Kate's isolation is challenged as she begins to form bonds of community among the patrons of the eponymous Nightwood Bar, while exposing the ills of religious fundamentalism, child abuse and homophobia. Delafield's third outing takes place in *The Beverly Malibu* (1989), where the intrepid detective tackles the legacy of McCarthyism and is introduced to a new love interest in the shape of Aimee Grant. The final novel of this first, or 'passing', phase is *Murder by Tradition* (1991). With the combined support of Aimee and the Nightwood Bar regulars behind her, Kate feels strong enough to go out on a limb in the case of Teddie Crawford, a young gay man murdered in a violent, homophobic assault. Forging new alliances along the way, Delafield triumphs over the forces of institutional homophobia, and the distinctly utopian conclusion of this novel can be seen as a watershed in her fictional career.

A five-year gap separates *Murder by Tradition* from the novels of Delafield's second phase, *Liberty Square* (1996), *Apparition Alley* (1997) and *Sleeping Bones* (1999). This transition involves substantial changes in the narrative – not the least of which is the shedding of Kate's lumbering police partner, Ed Taylor. However, it is within the first phase of the Delafield novels that the paradox of lesbian visibility is most marked and unsettling. Although the spectral themes that characterise the early novels remain as traces in the three most recent books, the second phase seems more concerned with the ethics of coming out than the subversions of passing.[1]

The first four Delafield novels, then, offer one of crime fiction's most sustained engagements with the politics of sexuality. Throughout these novels there exists a complex dynamic of vision – of seeing and not seeing, or of misrecognition – that is profoundly connected to the process of naming that also concerns Terry Castle:

> The law has traditionally ignored female homosexuality – not out of indifference, I would argue, but out of morbid paranoia . . . Yet this seeming obliviousness should not deceive us. Behind such silence, one can often detect an anxiety too severe to allow for direct articulation. When members of the House of Lords decided in 1921, for example, not to amend the antihomosexual Criminal Law Amendment Act of 1885 to include acts of 'gross indecency' between women, it was not because they deemed the threat of lesbianism an inconsequential one – quite the contrary – but because they were afraid that by the very act of mentioning it, they might spread such unspeakable 'filthiness' even further. The result of such denial: the transformation of the lesbian into a sort of juridical phantasm. (Castle, 1993: 6)

To name the lesbian is to empower her, to concretise her amorphous, 'apparitional' identity. Yet, this strategy of denial has the capacity to backfire. The lesbian may be legal by default, but allowing the other into the patriarchal fold does not guarantee the absorption, conformity or silencing of that other. What the lesbian lacks in name, and in the tangibility of legal or criminal stigmatisation, she makes up for in mobility. If she cannot be named, how can she be known, and if she cannot be known, how can she be contained? Hence the appeal of Castle's spectral image. Ghosts can pass through walls – so can Detective Delafield. Her apparitional status carries her through barriers and boundaries closed to the out or 'tangible' lesbian.[2]

The dangerous game of proximity also has other theoretical resonances. In the dialectic of inside/out, can it be other than utopian to imagine that proximity will not lead to contamination? Can the outsider resist the perks of institutional power? Indeed, as her attack on the homophobic 'creep' in *Murder at the Nightwood Bar* reveals, even the saintly Delafield is not immune to the temptations of institutional violence (Forrest, 1987/1993: 92). A substantial amount of irony surrounds this unprecedented outburst of police brutality. Arriving at the Nightwood Bar to find an interestingly multi-ethnic group of thugs attempting to abduct one of the bar's regulars, Delafield takes charge and contains the situation. However, as one of the 'creeps' continues to hurl abuse, she succumbs to the temptation of excessive force, breaking the man's nose as '[a]ll control left her. Rage poured through her, engulfing the adrenalin, choking her. ' "You *slime*," she screamed into his ear.' (Forrest, 1987/1993: 92). It is possible to read this outburst of violence as partially self-directed, 'choking' Kate like the myriad frustrations of her closeted life. However, the resolution of the conflict nonetheless presents a satisfying series of subversions that challenge cultural and institutional norms. First, a woman assaults a man in defence of an oppressed minority, and, second, Delafield as a cop is saved from the potential repercussions of her loss of control by her victim's commitment to traditional gender roles. The preservation of his machismo will not permit him to acknowledge his defeat by a woman, and Delafield's 'transgression' in consequence escapes censure.

Yet Delafield's outburst is the exception rather than the rule and, with perhaps ungrounded optimism, most representations of the female police officer challenge the assumption that women will become complicit in strategies of oppression if they are allowed access to the benefits of the patriarchal order. TV detectives Cagney and Lacey, for example, in a move that could be seen as reinforcing stereotypes of female nurturing, but can more effectively be read as a continued effort to destabilise patriarchal norms, continue to champion the rights of 'others' from their relatively empowered positions. As Lorraine Gamman argues, Cagney and Lacey operate to diffuse and disperse homogenous power structures by breaking down the distinction between public and private and challenging the masculine 'gaze'. She suggests that the presence of women within the squad room displaces rather than inverts masculinised power relations:

> Cagney and Lacey don't invert power relations, claiming total mastery for themselves, but instead subtly displace such relations . . . Their presence alters the dynamics of the squad room, not only because they are different to men but because their 'difference' does not simply translate into 'otherness': Cagney and Lacey are not simply passive objects; they 'speak' female desire. (Gamman, 1988: 16)

Incorporation, then, does not necessarily result in the unquestioned adoption of institutional norms, and the lesbian policewoman cannot simply be categorised as either binary inversion or empowerment fantasy. Structures of power and 'otherness' are historically determined, subject to change and flux in accordance both with the demands of the dominant culture and the process of resistance to those demands. Citing Frantz Fanon's work on racial discrimination, Jonathan Dollimore insists that:

> [T]he demonizing of the other is, above all, a mercurial process of displacement and condensation, so fluid yet always with effects of a brutally material, actually violent kind. (Dollimore, 1991: 344)

And Delafield's relationship with and alienation from the structures of law that she also embodies remain in a condition of constant and complex renegotiation. She attains a considerable degree of agency, but this power is contingent and unstable, and, as the narrative develops, we witness neither its consolidation nor its collapse. Her 'passing' appears to be a state rather than a journey.

Delafield does undergo some form of transition in the course of these novels, but she does not move from the 'passing' of the closet to the 'out' of disclosure. So why, beyond the obvious appeal of the fashionable slash, 'passing/out'? Although this is not a linear progression, there *is* a tension between the closet and disclosure that plays a fundamental structuring role within the Delafield novels. Both categories are dissected, from the pain of passing, described by one character as 'all the humiliation I can swallow' (Forrest, 1987/1993: 101), to the instability of the category 'out': 'They think they've come out because they're at a lesbian bar. But they're scared like all of us' (1987/1993: 37). However, coming out is not the main trajectory of Forrest's narrative. The courtroom confrontation that concludes *Murder by Tradition* threatens to 'out' the detective, but this crisis is averted, and Kate's sexuality remains apparitional.[3] Yet the very fact that she came so close to the boundary of disclosure is indicative of the transition she has undergone from the archetypal 'objectivity' of the detective to the somewhat more subjective position of lesbian avenger – a position that remains paradoxically predicated on her continued disguise.[4] The notion of the detective's objectivity of course belongs in the realm of myth, but I do want to foreground the contrast between the Delafield who approaches *Amateur City* armed with the detective's traditional qualities of rationality and detachment, and the Delafield who (almost) 'comes out' to fight her corner in *Murder by Tradition*. Passing/out, then, suggests not a single, linear transition, but a sort of sexual conjuring trick: now you see it, now you don't.

This boundary-crossing dynamic is central to the structure of the Kate Delafield novels, all of which engage with a variety of contemporary debates in a more or less polemicised fashion. While *Amateur City*'s focus is on sexual politics, *Murder at the Nightwood Bar* moves on to tackle the politics of sexuality. *The Beverly Malibu* is concerned with the history of censorship and oppression, using the McCarthy witchhunts to debate the possibility of forgiveness. The need to come to terms with, and transcend, past events and hostilities underpins nearly all the Delafield novels. Both the characters under investigation and the detective must bury their dead. Significantly, this concern with the past continues to manifest itself in Delafield's second phase. Both *Liberty Square* and *Apparition Alley* feature murders committed to prevent the revelation of long-buried truths, and the exposure of these truths is symbolically linked with sexuality to create narratives in which coming out has the capacity to seriously threaten the status quo.[5] *Liberty Square* takes ex-Marine Delafield to a Vietnam Vets' reunion, while *Apparition Alley* uses the by-now familiar device of homophobic homicide, but brings the threat of 'otherness' closer to home by making the gay victim a cop. There is, however, both a certain irony and a reminder of the unstable and fluctuating nature of power relations in the extent to which this novel is haunted by the ghost of Ed Taylor, the archetypal symbol of bigotted policing.

Ed Taylor was the partner who accompanied Delafield through the first phase of her fictional career. An unlovely redneck bigot, Taylor has been described as existing solely to 'set off Kate's qualities with his defects, her perfection with his imperfections' (Décuré, 1992: 270). This is perhaps a little harsh: although by and large Taylor acts as an all-purpose embodiment of cultural norms (and his memory is invoked for this purpose throughout *Apparition Alley*), he is also sometimes used to playfully invert gendered expectations. Indeed, *Murder at the Nightwood Bar* would have been a considerably shorter novel had Kate abandoned her creed of procedural rationality and listened to Taylor's early, instinctive and correct identification of the murderers (1987/1993: 51). In a clear reversal of gender stereotypes, Taylor's 'feminine' instinct convinces him of the Quillins' guilt, while

Delafield's 'masculine' rationality deceives her. Nonetheless, in policework terms this is the exception that proves the rule. Taylor's attitudes are deplorable and his policework sloppy, so the reader soon perceives that this partnership does not conform to the traditional generic mould of equal-but-different elements pulling together within the happy police family.

However, it is worth noting that four years later, in *Murder by Tradition*, the boundaries have shifted, and the strategies of detection have undergone a substantial review. Taylor's instinct has fallen over the edge into irrationality and prejudice, while Kate has adopted a distinctly more subjective approach to investigation. Teddie Crawford's homosexuality is sensed with 'gut deep certainty' (1991/1993: 12), while the mystery of 'how-he-dunnit' is resolved through a bizarre passage of semi-spiritualist role play in which Kate acts as medium to the ghost of Teddy Crawford:

> *Let go of me!* Oh God this tiny kitchen . . . I'm trapped, trapped. *Wait, no . . . Take anything you want, just don't . . . Don't . . .*
>
> She slumped down onto the cold tile of the claustrophobic kitchen, her back against the wall, seeing him frantically thrash on the floor . . .
>
> She felt his fear. His terror at the ebbing of his life. With her own sense of sight blanked out she listened to the building as Teddie Crawford had last known it. (Forrest, 1991/1993: 91. Fifth elipsis mine)

The detective must, then, tread a narrow line between instinct and irrationality, but the implication for Kate's development seems clear. Her success as a 'lesbian avenger' is dependent not upon the deployment of compromised strategies of rationality, but upon her adoption of 'other', more subjective, modes of knowledge.[6]

There is no doubt, however, that the Delafield novels make gratifying reading on those days when you're feeling swamped by the ills of society. Sally Munt comments upon the multiple pleasures they offer to the reader, not least of which is revenge. '[P]atriarchs get gruesomely murdered in horrifically explicit ways which often border on parody' (Munt, 1994: 139), she observes, and indeed, the first four books in the series could be simply retitled for the convenience of the library browser: 'Justified Murder of a Sexist Pig', 'Welcome Punishment of a Child Abuser', 'Long Overdue Murder of a McCarthyite Bastard' and 'Regrettable Murder of a

Good Gay Guy – But Don't Worry the Perp's Going Down for Life'. These, then, are somewhat didactic novels, but their ostentatiously radical content has not been sufficient to ward off considerable reproach from a variety of feminist critics. Lesbian detection in general has been accused by Bonnie Zimmerman of abandoning the lesbian community, while the Delafield novels in particular have been subject to a series of interrelated criticisms. Nicole Décuré boldly announces that 'the radical element is absent in the Forrest novels' (1992: 268), while Sally Munt voices a more subtle criticism, suggesting that the radical possibilities of the series are frequently undermined by the demonisation of the killer. In a binary inversion, the criminal replaces the pervert as the abject other of social organisation:

> If Man is depicted as a rational agent imbued with an ethical code which he is free to transgress, then by choosing to do so he cannot cease to be human. The text constructs crime as being against nature, and the offender as unnatural. Criminals become commonsensically Other: labelling deviants as non-human in this way exonerates society. (Munt, 1994: 136)

It is a persuasive reading, and one which situates the novel firmly within the classical paradigm of the detective as upholder of bourgeois individualism, absolving society of its criminal complicity through the creation of a convenient criminal scapegoat. Yet I am not sure that even this demonisation of the criminal is a stable signifier within the Delafield novels. Looking back to *Amateur City*, Kate suggests that anyone might be capable of murder (1984/1987: 64) and this point is reiterated in *The Beverly Malibu* (1989/1993: 28). Most significant, however, is *Murder by Tradition*, where the whole narrative thrust seeks to deny the existence of a clear-cut distinction between society and its transgressors by figuring the murdering Kyle Jensen as the archetypal product of societal norms. In a fascinating combination of essentialist and constructionist theories of subjectivity, Jensen's defence lawyer, Kenneth Pritchard, presents a violently homophobic summary of the case:

> 'How could Kyle Jensen not know that Teddie Crawford was homosexual, the State thunders. Well, Mr Jensen was brought up in a normal, conservative household. His father fought and nearly died for this country in Korea. Mr Jensen has been

> brought up like most of us – taught that homosexuality is one of society's deepest taboos. I ask you to imagine yourself in his place. Here he is a stranger in Los Angeles, confronted by a man who embodies everything he has been taught to abhor . . .
>
> 'We are all products of our culture and upbringing. In the same situation, how much control would you have? If you were confronted by a coiled snake, aside from its threat to you, wouldn't you lash out at that snake from sheer, natural revulsion?' (Forrest, 1991/1993: 179)

In a series of paradoxes, Jensen's lawyer tries to build a case for justifiable homicide by creating a hierarchy of otherness. Pritchard suggests that the social taboo against murder be overlooked in the face of the greater threat to cultural stability represented by homosexuality. Jensen's revulsion from and violence towards the homosexual Teddie Crawford are constructed not as the abberrant acts of the individual demonised criminal, but as the 'normal' and 'natural' responses of a typical American citizen. In condemning Jensen, therefore, the court must at least implicitly be acknowledging that it is society and not its 'other' that is responsible for Teddie Crawford's death.

Stephen Knight has suggested that the thriller is 'a form that most have assumed to be inherently complicit with bourgeois culture' (Knight, 1990: 172), but it seems increasingly possible that the Delafield novels might present a subtle structural challenge to the conservative boundaries of this form. Knight's definition comes from an article in which he argues that the thriller genre is not 'completely tainted with conservatism' and 'crime fiction can be an instrument of political justice' (1990: 185, 186). Yet, having made this bold declaration, Knight proceeds to categorise Delafield, alongside Sara Paretsky's V. I. Warshawski, as a 'less polemicised' detective (1990: 184). Gillian Whitlock, however, sees far more potential in these texts, suggesting that not only do the Delafield novels present lesbian culture and sexuality as an 'unstable, shifting terrain' (Whitlock, 1994: 116), they also offer the reader 'the kind of discursive play and inconsistency which is foregrounded in experimental writing' (1994: 118). What then is the relationship of the Delafield novels to the conventions of the police-procedural genre?[7] Superficially, at least, the relationship would seem to be a close one: the novels exhibit enough conformist tendencies to have (briefly) attracted Grafton books, a mainstream publishing house. There is an appropriate emphasis on the dull and detailed minutiae of everyday policework, which detracts from the archetypal individualist conception of the 'Great Detective'. They also embody society's attempts both to normalise and justify ongoing structures of surveillance by moving towards what Winston and Mellerski have described as a 'utopian vision of co-operation between the police and society' (1992: 7).[8]

This structural proximity to the norm, combined with the development of clearly 'political' narratives, might seem to suggest that the subversive potential of these fictions is confined to their content. But Gillian Whitlock argues that this proximity to generic norms can be viewed in a different light:

> The four Delafield fictions to date suggest that the conventions of the procedural *enable* a complex and very contemporary mapping of the relationships between locations which formerly seemed mutually exclusive and in eternal opposition: the gay bar and the police station. (1994: 113)

By bringing opposing structures and subjectivities into an uncomfortably close proximity that always threatens some form of irruption or reaction, Forrest's novels can be seen to challenge traditional genre conventions.

I suggested earlier that Delafield stands outside the conventions of 'buddy' or team partnership, or the construct of a police family that Winston suggests transforms the detective from an individual to a 'corporate hero' (1992: 6).[9] Indeed, the resistance to this comfortable dynamic becomes increasingly disturbing as the novels progress and Taylor moves from the status of tolerable boor to that of irredeemable homophobe. An unbreachable gulf opens between Taylor and Delafield in *Murder by Tradition*, as Taylor not only fails to 'come good', but also frighteningly reveals that all along he has been subscribing to the 'asking for it' school of justifiable homicide (1991/1993: 27). Delafield, then, is betrayed by a key member of the 'family' – she cannot wholly belong to such an ideologically flawed institution – and her isolation is acknowledged to the extent that her position within the police force more closely resembles the role of the private eye (or 'Lady Dick' as she is called in *Amateur City* (1984/1987: 20)). Aside from bringing her into line with the majority of other lesbian detectives who prosecute their investigations from the margins, this categorisation defines her in formal terms as an isolated figure, battling against a hostile urban environment in which, ironically, not even the police can be trusted. This 'hard-boiled' picture is not inappropriate. There is constant emphasis within these novels on Delafield's need to check and control the actions of her 'sloppy' male colleagues.

Detective Delafield is, then, the product of a blending of genres. The lesbian private investigator has been contained within – or has invaded – the police procedural. The outsider has come *into* the cold. This formal development is significant and returns us to Knight's desire for a definition of the radical thriller. Forrest's novels suggest that radical detective fiction is precisely *not* that which most proudly flaunts its feminist credentials, but that which most closely approximates the generic norm, while yet fundamentally altering or destabilising it.[10]

If I wanted to look on the critical bright side, then, I might suggest that these texts interrogate and destabilise both sexual and textual norms, enabling boundaries of gender and genre to be subtly transgressed. But would such optimism be justified? After all, however liminal her existence, and however close to exposure she finally comes, Kate Delafield remains a closeted lesbian detective who survives in a hostile homophobic environment through 'passing'. What are the implications of this 'performance', both for Delafield and the order she subverts? Those around her fail to see, or actively choose not to see, that their fellow police officer is also the 'other', the target of their loathing and the source of their fear. The hostility of the police environment is made abundantly clear in *The Beverly Malibu*. Coming out embodies a threat not only to livelihood but to life itself:

> Last month Mitch Grobeson, a former sergeant at Pacific Division who had compiled a superb performance record, had filed the first-ever lawsuit, claiming extreme harassment because he was homosexual, claiming endangerment to his life in the performance of his job – that he had been persecuted and tormented into resigning . . . LAPD's queer-hating fraternity of macho cops would turn a gay officer's existence into a nightmare. (47)

Kate Delafield is persistently misrecognised by her colleagues: her lesbianism is the spectre that haunts her LAPD relationships and, like all good ghosts, it is transparent. In Margery Garber's terms, Delafield's sexuality is looked 'through rather than at'. 'Mistaken, misread, overlooked', Delafield is the cross-dressed detective (Garber, 1992/1993: 187). Garber's analysis of the primarily criminal manifestations of the transvestite in detective fiction suggest that 'when he or she is "found", or discovered, the mystery is solved' (1992/1993: 187), and it is equally the case that the discovery of Delafield's spectral sexuality would effect an abrupt closure upon her transgressive narrative.[11]

So effective is Kate's 'passing' that her physical (visual) assimilation into the body of the law is accompanied, at least in the early novels, by a parallel mental assimilation. A dangerous consequence, or cost, of the continued disguise involved in 'passing', the novels suggest, is the forgetting of one's mother tongue. This is in marked contrast to Joseph Hansen's Dave Brandstetter, who is not only singularly adept at reading the signifiers of repression, but also seems able to move in and out of the closet with ease. However, Brandstetter's capacity for 'tactical' passing is also indicative of the far greater freedom he enjoys as an independent investigator – a contrast that acts as a pertinent reminder of the institutional forces that Kate must negotiate. Nonetheless, the Kate of *Amateur City* is blinded by her disguise. She seems unable to see the lesbians around her and proves singularly inept at reading sexual signifiers. Gretchen Phillips, for example, evades Delafield's detection by the simple 'femme' disguise of a 'filmy lilac blouse' and a 'strand of tiny pearls' (Forrest, 1984/1987: 75). Delafield's assumptions regarding the boundaries and limitations of lesbian identity are repeatedly undercut by the subjects of her investigations. These relatively peripheral characters instigate a chain of sexual signification that extends far beyond the perspective of the individual detective. Discussing the contradictory positions that surface within the text, Gillian Whitlock argues that:

> These inconsistencies lead to a depiction of identities which are anything but essential or natural. Across the series of fictions a number of causes of lesbianism are expressed. Each needs to be read in terms of an unsettled field of identifications. (Whitlock, 1994: 115)

The texts, then, do not express lesbian identity, or lesbian desire, as something which can be simply or straightforwardly categorised. Indeed, in another of the series' many paradoxes we are presented with a central character who, while never doubting her lesbian identity, seems to have severe problems with deciphering and negotiating her patterns of desire. There is an element of disembodiment in *Amateur City*'s depiction of Kate Delafield, and this is paralleled by a strategy of narrative detachment, which obliges the reader to first approach Detective Delafield from without rather than from within. Although the novel gradually acquaints us with Delafield's processes of detection, her opinions on those around her, her sense of isolation and her grief for her lost lover, Anne, a more immediate site of narrative intimacy is offered through the character of key witness Ellen O'Neil, whose perspective dominates much of the novel.

Within *Amateur City*, then, Delafield seems often to be displaced from the position of desiring subject – a state which can in part be read in generic terms as an ironic displacement of the detective's authority. Here, as in the later *Murder at the Nightwood Bar*, there is a revisionary imperative evident in the construction of scenarios that complicate rather than replicate 'hard-boiled' narratives of desire. In the early Delafield novels the females who would love and leave Kate are not punished for their betrayal: rather the encounters are depicted as mutually beneficial. The detective attains (albeit provisionally) the object of her desire, and in return operates as a one-woman sexual counselling service, ensuring her lovers' safe return to the stability of their lesbian romances. Both for the desiring subject and for the object of that desire, sex no longer culminates in death nor threatens a destabilising loss of self.

However, there is another dimension to the configurations of desire that surround the lesbian detective. Within *Amateur City* a pattern emerges that does not conform to traditional (heterosexually inflected) psychoanalytic theories of sexuality. Rather it evokes the model of 'perverse desire' constructed by Teresa de Lauretis in her 1994 study *The Practice of Love*. An integral component of the perverse model is the concept of the lesbian fetish, which de Lauretis defines as 'something which signifies at once the absence of the object of desire (the female body) and the subject's wish for it' (1994: 22). De Lauretis is profoundly concerned with the structures of loss and displacement that underpin sexuality in general and lesbian sexuality in particular, and as part of the process of illustrating her complex theory of desire, she undertakes an analysis of the archetypal mannish lesbian, Radclyffe Hall's Stephen Gordon. The figure of the 'mythic mannish lesbian' is a spectre implicit within the sexual economy of Forrest's novels, and the significance of this lesbian cultural ghost begs examination.[12] Sally Munt has observed that '[t]he moment of closure and resolution in *Murder at the Nightwood Bar* is not the arrest of the murderer but the integration of one lonely dyke into her culture' (Munt, 1994: 135), and this comment highlights the extent to which Delafield's career is not only concerned with the breaking down of formulaic conceptions of the detective. Rather her narrative combines generic reconstruction with the reconfiguring of lesbian history and desire. Delafield's distance from the heterosexual matrix sets her in a profoundly different relation to the discourses of power that circulate within the detective novel, and Forrest's serial narrative begins with the conflation of the archetypal loner detective and the very specific model of lesbian identity that is the 'mythic mannish lesbian'. Delafield embodies this mythic figure. In *Amateur City* she is at once both the fetishised object of others' desire and the perverse subject whose desire is itself constructed upon a structure of fetishistic displacement. This duality complicates the concept of detective agency that might be seen to arise specifically from the body of the lesbian detective and thus reveals the tension between appropriation and innovation that underpins feminist narrative strategies.

The fetishistic objectification of Kate is immediately evident in *Amateur City*:

> Ellen relaxed. She had always been comfortable around people – especially women – like Stephie, like Kate Delafield, with authority in their voices, strength in their faces, deliberation in their gestures and manner. (Forrest, 1984/1987: 33)

De Lauretis illustrates this dynamic of desire with a quotation from Joan Nestle's *A Restricted Country*: 'I loved my lover for how she stood as well as for what she did' (quoted in de Lauretis, 1994: 228). The fetish can be attribute as well as object; it signals difference and desire, while precisely not signifying either the penis or the paternal phallus, the loss or presence of which has so long been constructed as the sole determinant at the centre of psychoanalytic configurations of desire. This refusal of the phallus is crucial, for while this easily confused penis substitute remains the privileged signifier in psychoanalytic discourse, lesbian desire is displaced beyond representation. It has nothing to do with the phallus/penis, and it cannot therefore be articulated within existing terms of reference. In de Lauretis's formulation, therefore, the lesbian fetish assumes a crucial function, becoming the mark, or signifier, of perverse desire. De Lauretis explains:

> [W]hat the lesbian desires in a woman . . . is indeed not a penis but a part or perhaps the whole of the female body, or something metonymically related to it, such as physical, intellectual, or emotional attributes, stance, attitude, appearance, self-presentation – and hence the importance of clothing, costume, performance, etc. in lesbian subcultures. She knows full well she is not a man, she does not have the paternal phallus (nor would her lover want it), but that does not preclude the signification of her desire: the fetish is at once what signifies her desire and what her lover desires in her. It is both an imaginary or fantasmatic 'object,' a cathected signifier, whose erotic meaning derives from its placement in a subjective fantasy scenario; and a symbolic object, whose meaning derives from a socio-historical context of cultural *and* subcultural discourses and representations. In short, then, the lesbian fetish is any object, any sign whatsoever, that marks the difference and the desire between the lovers. (de Lauretis, 1994: 228)

The fetish, then, is a marker of difference, but it is also a signifier of loss, and it is in this context that Delafield herself can be constructed as fetishistic. *Amateur City* is set shortly after the death of Kate's lover, Anne, and in narrative terms this loss functions as an originatory act of castration. Kate's violent grief acknowledges that nothing can replace the lost lover, but she nonetheless continues to act as a desiring subject, pursuing a variety of lovers, perhaps the most clearly fetishistic of which is the first, Ellen O'Neil. It is Ellen's partial resemblance to Anne that facilitates the attraction, enabling Kate to undertake a fetishistic reconstruction of the lost love relation:

> At the sight of Ellen O'Neil, Kate felt a twisting sensation, an excruciating pleasure-pain that became mostly pain. The same height – give or take half an inch. Hips only a little thinner, well-shaped breasts like Anne's . . . Lips a little fuller, nose straighter. Prettier. (Forrest, 1984/1987: 33, ellipsis mine)

> She glanced at her watch, decided to call Ellen O'Neil.
>
> Her scrupulous inner voice whispered, you don't need to. You can wait until tomorrow. You just want to call her because

> she is like Anne and you want to hear her voice . . . (1984/1987: 105)

Kate acknowledges that Ellen is not Anne. She recognises the unbridgeable gap opened up by loss and desire, and yet she desires those very parts of Ellen which resemble and hence signify the lost object, Anne.

De Lauretis's analysis of perverse desire also has wider implications for the Delafield novels. De Lauretis comments that she prefers 'to call the the signifier of perverse desire *a fetish* in order to avoid the unavoidable semantic complicity of phallus with penis' (1994: 231). This is a crucial distinction. However, I would like to work backwards from de Lauretis's formulation to reconsider a rather earlier analysis of female subjectivity, that is, Joan Riviere's 'Womanliness as Masquerade' which turns crucially on a notion of visibility, of performing femininity in order to disguise the possession of a culturally problematic 'masculine' authority. The construction of Delafield in fetishistic terms as the 'mythic mannish lesbian' might suggest by extension that she is a woman who to some degree possesses the phallus of masculine authority but, unlike the women of Riviere's analysis, displays no need to disguise this authority. Kate does not perform the masquerade: in an ironic inversion of the ghostly metaphor of intangibility, her possession of the phallus becomes as visible as her sexuality is obscured. Kate, then, is a woman who must ensure that her sexuality is not seen, but who can nonetheless display the marker of masculinity that is the phallus. What are the implications of this? Why is Kate's occupation of the site of masculine authority not read as a signifier of her transgressive sexuality? Perhaps it remains unintelligible because, as Terry Castle suggests, 'people have trouble seeing what's in front of them'. Society does not want to see the lesbian; so it simply looks *through* the evidence.

Once again we have arrived at a refusal to name the lesbian, as if to identify the source of cultural paranoia were to empower it. Interestingly, Riviere's short article on feminine masquerade makes frequent, if unelaborated, reference to men's fear of the 'hidden danger' that may lurk behind the mask of femininity, and she goes so far as to suggest that some men 'prefer a woman who herself has male attributes, for to them her claims on them are less' (Riviere, 1929/1986: 42). There is perhaps an element of reassurance in Delafield's proximity to the masculine paradigm. For the likes of

Ed Taylor, there is considerable comfort to be found in the fact that in terms of his familiar cultural constructions, which render femininity and authority wholly incompatible, this is precisely *not* a 'woman' in authority. It is Delafield's lack of womanliness which makes her authority possible, and, in her culturally sanctioned role as a police officer, it is her authority rather than her sexuality that is immediately read by those outside what might be termed the lesbian field of vision.[13]

So although homophobia *is* a key determinant in both contemporary American society and the Delafield novels, it co-exists with rather than displaces the forces of misogyny and sexism.[14] Woman remains the ultimate signifier of passivity, weakness and disgust, as Taylor makes abundantly clear when Kate asks him to explain his extreme hostility to gay men:

> 'What's to tell? They aren't men. They're faggots.' He raised a hand, waved it limply. 'Mincy little faggoty fake-men.'
>
> '. . . All those masculine-type guys are perverts. They use the faggoty men like some guys use sheep or a piece of liver.'
>
> '. . . Some people are freakish, but they're still men or women. Faggots, they want to be fucked, so they turn themselves into women. If you're a real man, then you aren't a woman.' (Forrest, 1991/1993: 67)

Taylor's phobia raises significant questions about the precarious construction of both 'normative' heterosexuality and masculinity. These are concerns that repeatedly resurface within *Murder by Tradition*. Both Kyle Jensen and his flatmate 'Burt' Dayton vehemently protest their heterosexuality (1991/1993: 35, 53, 59), eager to forstall any implication that two men in one flat might constitute *prima facie* evidence of homosexual desire, while the iconoclastic Shirley Johnson emphasises that masculinity demands a rigorous performance as much for other men as for women:

> Some instinct nudged Kate into a curiosity question. 'Why do you call him Burt Lancaster?'
>
> 'Walks around with that naked chest of his stickin out, thinks he's gonna be an actor, the dipshit. Struts like he's Bruce Willis. Kyle, he's a muscle-builder, so he struts too. You ask me, those two guys strut for each other.' (Forrest, 1991/1993: 55)

But whatever the anxieties that surround the maintenance of masculinity, what emerges most clearly from Taylor's bizarre sexual hierarchy is the stigma of femininity. It is not the 'faggot's' desire for another man that renders him disgusting, but his proximity to the feminine.

Across all the Delafield novels, then, gender and sexuality are presented as part of a complex and interrelated structure of prejudice, the implications of which are both evaded and manipulated by the characters. Given the strength of Taylor's revulsion from (and fear of) the 'perverse', it is perhaps not surprising that he would prefer to evade rather than confront the apparition of deviant sexuality. However, it is interesting to note the extent to which Delafield is able to manipulate the structures of prejudice that surround her. Although Delafield herself is frequently revealed as an inadequate reader of both her own and others' desire, it must equally be admitted that she excells at the art of recognising and exploiting others' misreadings of her. This is ably illustrated within *Amateur City* where she allows her silences to be interpreted as agreement by the racist Fred Grayson, a character who clearly reads Delafield as the visible phallus of patriarchal authority rather than the invisible fetish of perverse desire! Lulled into a false sense of security by Delafield's silence and by his own assumptions about the law, he later expresses his racist views in public, thus enabling Delafield to denounce him to his superiors, who, in turn, reveal attitudes scarcely superior to those of the obnoxious Grayson:

> 'I don't care what a man's personal opinions are so long as he keeps them out of his business life. So long as he's got the damn sense to keep private the things that should be private.' (Forrest, 1984/1987: 159)

But the damage has been done. Patriarchy's dirty linen has been aired in public, and once the boundary between the private and the public has been crossed, the law has no choice but to act, albeit reluctantly, in *defence* of the other.

Grayson, then, did not know what he was up against. Thinking he had identified proximity, he found opposition instead, illustrating a dynamic which is very much in the spirit of Jonathan Dollimore's propositions for 'Thinking the Perverse Dynamic': 'To be against (opposed to) is also to be against (close up, in proximity to) or, in other words, up against.' (Dollimore, 1991: 229). This is the site of cultural paranoia at which the fear of the other is exacerbated not only by the awful realisation of that other's sameness, but also through the recognition that similarity equates with undetectability.

Consequently, when Dollimore suggests that Oscar Wilde enacted 'one of the most disturbing of all forms of transgression, namely that whereby the outlaw turns up as inlaw' (1991: 15), he uttered a sentiment that would have been wholly endorsed by the culturally central bulk of Ed Taylor. ' 'Jesus', mutters Taylor on discovering yet another homosexual within the framework of the investigation, 'Half the world –' ' (Forrest, 1987/1993: 86). Taylor is exhibiting the classic symptoms of cultural paranoia. Perceiving that he cannot tell 'Stork from butter', he fears that he is surrounded, swamped by the invisible tide of homosexuality. The manifestations of Taylor's homophobia increase as the novels progress, and are perhaps indicative of his response to the changing world beyond the investigation. Increasingly, the homosexuals he encounters are out and proud, rather than discreetly closeted, and it is not entirely surprising that *Murder by Tradition* marks the end of his police career.[15] Standing in a sea of Teddie Crawford's blood, his anxieties exacerbated by the spectre of AIDS, he can scarcely bring himself to speak to the openly gay suspects. Indeed, his fear of contamination becomes so great that he effectively abandons the investigation, heading off into the sunset of the archetypal American Dream: a new life on the California frontier, growing avocados with his wife.

If proximity can displace the 'old' police structures, as symbolised by Taylor, does this process of revision confirm the radical potential within Forrest's fiction? Certainly the lesbian policewoman represents a fundamental social contradiction. She is a fine example of Dollimore's 'perverse dynamic', in which the very body that upholds the law is in fact the other – the pervert against whom the law is directed. And it is this paradox, embodying the conflict between out/right challenge and subversion through 'passing', that lies at the centre of *Murder by Tradition*. Delafield's spectral presence profoundly destabilises its patriarchal, heterosexual environment, but within a novel about a dead gay man and a closet lesbian cop, can we really speak of a triumph of transgression? The issue is further complicated by the private relational dynamics that accompany the public business of detection. As Nicole Décuré and others have noted, the radical nature of Delafield's subject position is not always matched by an equally radical sexual position. After a hard day making the streets safe for god-fearing homosexuals, Detective

Delafield likes nothing better than to return home to the comely charms of a good woman, who ideally will have been waiting around all day for this desirable consummation. Even Aimee Grant, whose butch charms are introduced in *The Beverly Malibu*, seems to have little long-term impact on Delafield's 1950s conception of relational norms. Aimee's bedroom assertiveness initially destabilises the detective's authority. Kate finds her 'sexual defenselessness' to be 'beyond comprehension' (1989/1993: 134) and is forced to confess that she too associates the role of femme with passivity and weakness (1989/1993: 142–3). Yet this revaluation of cultural and relational norms is short-lived, and *Murder by Tradition* finds Aimee safely relegated to the wifely role. No longer seeming to threaten the detective's composure, she scarcely leaves the marital bed all novel and is constantly described either in terms of sensual heaviness (1991/1993: 186, 69) or of childlike innocence (1991/1993: 69, 101, 113), which is set against the brisk efficiency and adult preoccupation of Kate.

Yet irrespective of its conservative configuration, romance is an important structural element within the novels. Kate struggles to negotiate her grief over her previous lover Anne's horrific death and, having completed the work of mourning, is 'granted' love anew. However, in the provision of a stable relationship, Forrest seems to have foundered on a familiar generic rock – the same rock that has troubled writers from the 'golden age' on. If the detective is to be the archetypal loner, then lovers must remain a disposable, or a strictly domestic, commodity. Other recent feminist fictions, such as those of Barbara Wilson, have been able to refigure the lover through a reconceptualisation of the detective's relationship to her community, but the 'out' lesbian negotiating new emotional and relational structures makes an unlikely candidate for the police academy.[16]

Nonetheless, Delafield's sexual exploits are not wholly without transgressive potential. Kate Delafield, supercop, upright upholder of procedural conformity, is also Kate Delafield, maverick, transgressor of just about every rule in the book concerning sex with witnesses. Before she settled down with Aimee, a book never passed without her giving grievous bodily pleasure to a lucky lesbian witness; but within a patriarchal, homophobic society that recognises neither female desire nor lesbian existence, these transgressions cannot exist, and Delafield's sexual incursions across the boundaries of procedural propriety become instead challenges to generic norms. Inspector Morse, after all, has only to look at a woman for her to be murdered, commit suicide, or become a homicidal maniac. Within the Delafield stories, by contrast, the 'transgressive' act is transformed. Throughout the novels, lesbian sexuality is figured as a replenishing, life-giving force that can be set against the patriarchal death drive.[17] In her precarious position as the passing lesbian, Detective Delafield embodies a vulnerability that prevents her actions from becoming an abuse of power. Rather, the detective's sexual encounters are presented as an exchange of power, whereby the woman *outside* replenishes the failing strength of the woman *inside*. The woman outside the closet gives Delafield the strength to return to her 'undercover assignment' as an infiltrator at the heart of the patriarchal state.

Delafield, then, is the enemy within: not only a ghost, but a spy. The spy after all represents the archetypal incidence of the other who is also the same: the enemy (or pervert) within who cannot be distinguished from the 'true' nation or righteous heterosexual. So does Delafield act to fulfil the worst nightmares of the moral majority, infiltrating society, disseminating propaganda, and working to promote the interests of her own 'Lesbian Nation'? The Delafield novels certainly represent a challenge to the myth of the American family, even if they cannot in the end disperse the founding myth of the American Dream. The 'rainbow coalition' that forms in the final scenes of *Tradition* could be seen to reiterate the fantasy of a brave new world in which America – the idealised land of opportunity – is restored to its prelapsarian state through the fictional reassurance of the detective genre. But irrespective of the affirmation of the wider American Dream, there can be no doubt that the American way of life and its much-vaunted family values receive their most comprehensive and clearly articulated challenge in *Murder by Tradition*.

In their final outing together, detectives Delafield and Taylor investigate the brutal murder of Teddie Crawford, a young, very obviously gay, man. The culprit is fairly swiftly identified as the archetypal all-American boy, Kyle Jensen, whose defence is one of 'justifiable' homicide: murder is a 'natural' reaction to being propositioned by a man. Not surprisingly, the authorities adopt a somewhat perfunctory attitude towards this particular crime, and it is left to Delafield to effectively go-it-alone and bring the perpetrator to justice. In a dramatic courtroom confrontation, the prejudices of American society are put on trial, resulting in a utopian fantasy of posthumous vindication for the unfortunate gay corpse. This is the classic fantasy of the detective genre, a fantasy of agency: in the words of Linda Foster, counsel for the prosecution, 'You have the power to change something' (1991/1993: 183). It is also, however, a classic fantasy of lesbian fiction, which is frequently permeated by utopian ideals. In the second part of *Murder by Tradition*, Forrest is not only challenging the prejudices of the detective genre, she is also undermining the canonical plot of western literary tradition. Quoting Eve Sedgwick's contention that '[l]iterature canonizes the subject of male homosociality' while in return, 'male homosociality canonizes the work of literature' (Sedgwick, quoted in Castle, 1993: 70), Castle argues that lesbian fiction is precisely that which struggles to displace or rearticulate the triangulated structures of male homosocial desire, of which the patriarchal family is the exemplary paradigm. Here, within the fundamental building block of the American Dream, fathers and sons manipulate a market economy in which the objects of exchange are women: the daughters and wives who facilitate the continuance of patrilineal tradition and the homosocial privileges of father and son.

Yet in order to displace the structures through which male bonding will always inevitably supersede relationships with and between women, lesbian fiction must inevitably assume, in Castle's words, 'a profoundly attenuated relationship with what we think of, stereotypically, as narrative verisimilitude' (1993: 88). Castle's comments, concluding a discussion of Sylvia Townsend Warner's somewhat elusive fiction, seem equally applicable to the semi-didactic fantasy that ends the Delafield fictions:

> Precisely because it is motivated by a yearning for that which is, in a cultural sense, implausible – the subversion of male homosocial desire – lesbian fiction characteristically exhibits, even as it masquerades as 'realistic' in surface detail, a strongly fantastical, allegorical, or utopian tendency. (Castle, 1993: 88)

The multiple female bondings that form and disperse within the courtroom situation – moments of connection between Delafield and Foster, the female jurors and the female witnesses – are presided over by the figure of Judge Alicia Hawkins. Although the courtroom remains a site of patriarchal influence, that influence is dispersed as women literally 'take over the asylum'. The masquerade of realism is evident in Forrest's procedural correctness and her careful depiction of form and ritual; but the final section of *Murder by Tradition* is, in fact, a truly fantastical game of 'what if?' If women ruled the courtroom, never mind the world, look what might be achieved!

This fantastical dimension, which aligns *Murder by Tradition* as much with the narrative patterns of lesbian utopia as with the structures of the crime novel, is fundamental to the undermining of the heterosexual imperative within the text. However, Forrest's fiction is more complex, and more immediately political, than this scenario might suggest, and what interests me about *Murder by Tradition* is not the novel's somewhat saccharine happy ending, but the route by which this ending is achieved. Female personnel undoubtedly facilitate the prosecution of justice, but it is the courtroom struggle for semantic control, the tension between being named and self-definition, and the speaking of the inarticulable subtext of social organisation that renders this novel a 'triumph of transgression'.[18]

As Jonathan Dollimore suggests:

> The perverse dynamic challenges not by collapsing order but through a reordering less tolerable, more disturbing, than chaos. Its difference is never the absolutely unfamiliar, but the reordering of the already known, a disclosure of a radical interconnectedness which *is* the social, but which present cultures can rarely afford to acknowledge and must instead disavow. (Dollimore, 1991: 229–30)

The disavowal of this interconnectedness has been evident in the homophobic irruptions of Ed Taylor and Kyle Jensen (particularly when there is any suggestion that they might be homosexual). This fear returns me to the earlier quotation from Dollimore which defines the most disturbing form of transgression as that 'whereby the outlaw turns up as inlaw'. Dollimore's sentence concludes with the assertion that 'the other as proximate proves more disturbing than the other as absolute difference' (1991: 15). The ultimate fear of the dominant culture is that the other might turn out to be the same. Nothing is more disturbing than the inability to recognise the other, and it is this anxiety that Delafield exploits in order to win support for the character of the dead man. If society cannot trust the incorporated other, then might it not find the clearly defined spectacle of the stigmatised other an altogether more welcome sight? By defining Teddie Crawford as obviously other, the prosecution render him visible, and safe. In a fitting paradox, justice is achieved by making Teddy's sexuality as tangible as Delafield's is obscured.[19]

The concerns of this chapter, then, have been predominantly paradoxical; but in spite of, or perhaps precisely because of, these paradoxes, I'd like to suggest that Stephen Knight revise his categorisation of the Delafield novels. These are 'radical thrillers' in that they represent a constant renegotiation of the boundaries of law and disorder, through the appropriately paradoxical assertion that the restoration of order can simultaneously represent a challenge to that order. In the investigation of crimes motivated by racism, sexism and homophobia, making the law work outside its dominant white, heterosexual, male framework of interests may both disrupt expectations and successfully avert the threat of chaos. This conclusion suggests that lesbian detective fiction is less about maintaining the law than about reinscribing, or even *deceiving*, the law. In an ironically legal form of blackmail, Detective Delafield forces the law to contradict its founding prejudices and work in favour of women, lesbians and gay men, even when it doesn't want to.

NOTES

1. This transition is indicative of the beginnings of change in the Los Angeles Police Department (LAPD) itself. In 1993 former sergeant Mitch Grobeson won a landmark harassment case against the LAPD, after which some restraints were set upon the virulent homophobia of the service. The most recent Delafield novel, *Sleeping Bones*, acknowledges the influence of Grobeson's victory on Delafield's narrative in a dedication that recognises his 'pioneering activism that has changed the face of law enforcement in this country'. Nonetheless, Forrest continues to depict the LAPD as an uncomfortable and potentially threatening environment for lesbian and gay officers, and *Sleeping Bones* is marked by Kate's ongoing anxiety over the open secret of her sexuality (1999: 43).
2. This ability to transcend boundaries is not confined to the homosexual infiltration of heterosexual power structures. In her dual identity as lesbian and cop, the apparitional Delafield also gains access to areas closed to the heterosexual world. This is most clearly evident in the second Delafield novel, *Murder at the Nightwood Bar*, where Kate is able to cross the barrier of distrust that separates the lesbian bar from homophobic law enforcement.
3. This intangible condition might best be regarded not as the confinement of the closet, but rather as a potentially enabling omnipresence. As Terry Castle argues:

   > [T]he metaphor meant to derealize lesbian desire in fact did just the opposite. Indeed, strictly for repressive purposes, one could hardly think of a *worse* metaphor. For embedded in the ghostly figure, as even its first proponents seemed to realize, was inevitably a notion of reembodiment: of uncanny return to the flesh . . . To become an apparition was also to become endlessly capable of 'appearing.' (Castle, 1993: 63)
4. I am grateful to Kate Chedgzoy for compounding the ironies of this scenario by observing that 'lesbian visibility' is a key aim of the Lesbian Avengers direct-action group!
5. This change of political strategy emerges from the 'rainbow coalition' conclusion of *Murder by Tradition*. Whereas the earlier novels clearly suggest that exposure would destroy the lesbian detective, the later novels imply that such exposure would not only be survivable, but that unilateral action on the part of a community of outsiders *might* have sufficient force to effect change.
6. This distinction is further complicated by the generic tradition of 'gut-feeling'. This hard-

boiled version of feminine intuition, which has salvaged many a failing plot, remains a staple of contemporary buddy fictions, such as the *Lethal Weapon* film series. Here, a conventional 'by-the-book' policeman is teamed with an inspirational psychopath, presumably to suggest the need for balance in all things. However, the prevalence of gendered binary thinking within mainstream homosocial narratives reiterates society's fear of the homosexual. It is significant that the character endowed with the 'feminine' quality of intuition is also the one most prone to macho displays of performative violence, while the rationalist is allowed the 'softer' dimension of a family life. The casting of a black actor, Danny Glover, as the caring family man significantly denotes America's ongoing cultural anxieties regarding black masculinity, but in terms of homosocial desire, care has been taken to endow each character with qualities that balance out the gender-stereotype equation and steer the narrative safely clear of the spectre of homosexuality. To have one feminine trait may be regarded as forgivable, to have two would look distinctly provocative!

7. It was not until the 1950s that the police procedural emerged as a significant category within crime fiction, and its appearance at this point can in part be attributed to changing social realities in the aftermath of the Second World War (Knight, 1980: 169). One of the procedural's earliest and most successful practitioners was Ed McBain, whose enormously influential 87th Precinct novels did much to establish the conventions of the form. These fictions are characterised by a rigorous adherence to procedure, accompanied by a focus on the relational dynamics of the squad-room police 'family'. Forrest's fictions are something of a genre hybrid, combining McBain's template of meticulous detail with a focus on an individual detective more typical of private investigator narratives. However, there are notable similarities between the character of McBain's central detective, the exemplary Steve Carella, and the upstanding Detective Delafield. Both are models of integrity and tolerance, capable of breaking down the boundaries dividing cop from community, and both find comfort in the arms of more or less mute, devoted and sensual women.
8. It should be noted, however, that this vision does not go wholly unchallenged. *The Beverly Malibu* contains an unresolved debate concerning social surveillance that culminates in the re-humanising defence of the previously demonised killer by a witness who refuses to swallow the panacea of co-operation (1989/1993: 175–83).
9. The police family is a remarkably powerful generic marker, visible in almost all fictional, filmic and televisual manifestations of the procedural. Delafield can and does feel part of this 'corporate family'. It is her job, she's good at it, and the family respects her for her ability. But this is a corporate family, and its rules are different to those of the family of choice. In fact, the police family defines as transgressive that which defines the lesbian family of choice. It is interesting, therefore, that both families are subject to change in *Murder by Tradition*. The corporate family rejects Taylor in favour of Kate, while the lesbian family opens out and welcomes the heterosexual Linda Foster.
10. Examples abound of the arguably less successful didactic school of 'radical' detection. Two prime suspects, one from either side of the Atlantic, are Maggie Kelly's *Burning Issues* (1995), which cannot resist the temptation of lecturing (at length) to its captive audience, and Mary Morrell's *Final Session* (1991), which combines narrative didacticism with a radical context so pc as to be painful. A lesbian Chicana policewoman teams up with an analyst abused in childhood to uncover a murderer more roundly condemned for her abuse of analyst-patient trust than her homicidal tendencies.
11. Garber regards cross-dressing as an index of 'category crisis', by which she means:

    > a failure of definitional distinction, a borderline that becomes permeable, that permits of border crossings from one (apparently distinct) category to another: black/white, Jew/Christian, noble/bourgeois, master/servant, master/slave. The binarism male/female, one apparent ground of distinction (in contemporary eyes, at least) between "this" and "that," "him" and "me," is itself put in question or under erasure in transvestism, and a transvestite figure, or a transvestite mode, will always function as a sign of overdetermination – a mechanism of displacement from one blurred boundary to another. (Garber, 1992/1993: 16)

12. De Lauretis builds on the title of Esther Newton's 1984 essay 'The Mythic Mannish Lesbian: Radclyffe Hall and the New Woman' (*Signs* 9.4: Summer 1984), and I too have appropriated Newton's admirably succinct phrase.
13. Those within the 'lesbian field of vision' construct a very different and, for Delafield, more disturbing reading:

> *Where does my integrity begin and end? What if someone asks pointblank if I'm a lesbian?*
> *They won't ask.* She was looking into the faces of the women at the bar. *They don't need to.*
> She felt stripped of her gray gabardine pants and jacket, her conservative cloak of invisibility in the conventional world . . .
> Their direct, perceptive glances penetrated her like an X-ray. (Forrest, 1987/1993: 19, ellipsis mine)

14. This point is borne out by interviews conducted with lesbians and gay men working in the American criminal justice system between 1993 and 1995. 'The biggest thing has been to establish myself as a woman, not as a lesbian' reports one woman (Buhrke, 1996: 50), while another comments, 'I think the real issue for me was being a woman' (1996: 56). As the editor, Robin A. Buhrke, observes in his introduction: 'Most positions of power in police departments continue to be dominated by heterosexual, White men . . . Integrating women into policing has been routinely opposed and resisted' (1996: 16).
15. This sense of change is not confined to the visibility of the homosexual community. Change is also evident within mainstream gender relations. While the female office workers of *Amateur City* accepted sexual harassment as a prerequisite of promotion, the professional women of *Murder by Tradition* have independence and integrity. Admittedly Linda Foster's gender confines her to the bottom of the prosecutors' ladder, but set against this discrimination is the quiet authority of Judge Alicia Hawkins, the unflappable professionalism of 'blood spatter' expert Charlotte Mead and the confident clarity of female witnesses such as Stacey Conlin (1991/1993: 122). Throughout the novel alliances are formed across class, race, gender and sexuality, and these alliances give rise to the novel's optimistic conclusion: if enough dissidents and 'outsiders' infiltrate patriarchal structures of oppression, then these seemingly monolithic structures can be forced to change.
16. This may be changing. In Laurie R. King's *A Grave Talent* Inspector Kate Martinelli is very publically forced out of her closet. Prior to this exposure, however, she had shared a number of concerns with her predecessor Kate Delafield, not least of which was her belief in the need to pass, not just as heterosexual, but also as 'one of the boys'. Kate feels a need to efface both her gender and her sexuality from the workplace (1993/1996: 83). King's second novel, *To Play the Fool*, complicates and develops the triangular relationship between detective, police family and lover. Martinelli has not only been brought out of the closet, she has also been obliged to negotiate the changing demands of a relationship permanently scarred by its contact with the detective's work.
17. This parallel is made most explicit in *Murder by Tradition*. Murder scene and bedroom blur into one as Kate attempts to erase the horror of Teddie Crawford's death through the inverted 'violence' of lovemaking:

    > For a long moment she breathed in a woman smell that seemed to go beyond woman to creation itself. Then she claimed the woman, sucking into her, and stroked and drank the satiny wet, dimly aware of thighs shuddering against her face, of thrashing on the bed, of muffled cries, of stillness, of soft moaning.
    > She raised herself. Aimee's supine body lay in strips of moonlight from the vertical blinds. An image of another body, slashed, splashed with blood, filled her vision. (Forrest, 1991/1993: 71–2)

    Although the text continues to make explicit the life-giving properties of the sexual act, in this particular instance the association seems somewhat uncomfortable. This may be because of the novel's emphasis on the particularly sexual quality of stabbing as a method of murder, or because of the frequent attempts made by Kate to visualise the blood-soaked thrashings of Teddie Crawford's last moments in order to resolve the case.
18. This subtext might be seen as the Kristevan concept of 'underlying causality' (Kristeva, 1974/1986: 153).
19. Although the irony remains that it was precisely this visibility that got Crawford killed in the first place.

Part III

Shifting Paradigms

Shifting Paradigms: Introduction

> Nothing exercises such power over the imagination as the nature of sexual relationships, and the pornographer has it in his power to become a terrorist of the imagination, a sexual guerilla whose purpose is to overturn our most basic notions of these relations, to reinstitute sexuality as a primary mode of being rather than a specialised area of vacation from being and to show that the everyday meetings in the marriage bed are parodies of their own pretensions, that the freest unions may contain the seeds of the worst exploitation. (Carter, 1979: 21–2)

> There is not one of us who, given an eternal incognito, a thumbprint nowhere set against our souls, would not commit rape, murder and all abominations. (Barnes, 1936/1963: 128)

At the end of Part II, my discussion of Katherine V. Forrest suggested that lesbian detective fiction might constitute a viable site for a radical challenge to reactionary and repressive social forces. However, it must be acknowledged that the political challenge embodied by Delafield's proximity to the law is contained within a largely conventional deployment of the police-procedural form. Admittedly Forrest goes beyond the traditional ending or closure of the detective narrative. The trial of Kyle Jensen foregrounds an aspect of the *process* of law that has traditionally been elided by detective narrative.[1] It is more concerned with empirical proof and punishment than metaphysical truth and investigation. The formula is stretched and destabilised through the 'other's' infiltration of the law, but such key structural pillars as the integrity of the detective and the provision of closure remain intact. Yet Forrest's fiction constitutes the thin edge of what has become a very substantial wedge. In Part III I will consider the substance of that wedge as it is constituted through the massive popular success of the lesbian investigator and through the rise of the serial killer narrative, a generic variant that reinstates the epistemological complexity of the criminal.

In his brief account of the development of the crime novel 'From Private Eye to Police Procedural', Peter Messent is largely pessimistic about the genre's potential for radical reappropriation. However, he does make some notable exceptions:

> The genre is one which, especially in recent years, has been developed in many different directions, and the representation of the relationship between the individual detective and the existing social order *can* be used (as both lesbian detective fiction, and that by members of ethnic and racial minority groups, illustrate) to challenge dominant values and stereotypes. The more effective the nature of that challenge, I would suggest, though, the further the writer must depart from the basic generic model. (Messent, 1997: 17)

Messent identifies the central paradox of Part III: only by evading the genre can the genre be subverted. Deconstruction must precede reconstruction; if, indeed, it is possible to construct a mode of crime fiction that does not depend upon the problematic structures of the 'basic generic model'. In the fictions examined here, the paradigm of detection is being pushed to its limit. It has already been extended to include and explain such anomalies as the female investigator and the gay detective, but now it reaches a point of crisis, and it is arguable whether some of the fictions discussed in this section actually belong within the category of crime fiction.[2]

The genre has reached an impasse: it has so far departed from its original paradigms that it scarcely knows itself. The texts at the 'cutting edge' of crime have moved into a border zone of indeterminacy, and raise questions as to whether 'crime fiction' can continue to exist as a viable critical and cultural category.[3] Kuhn's study of scientific development recognises the complexity of this moment:

> The transition from a paradigm in crisis to a new one from which a new tradition of normal science can emerge is far from a cumulative process, one achieved by an articulation or extension of the old paradigm. Rather it is a reconstruction of the field from new fundamentals, a reconstruction that changes some of the field's most elementary theoretical generalizations as well as many of its paradigm methods and applications. During the transition period there will be a large but never complete overlap between the problems that can be solved by the old and by the new paradigm. But there will also be a decisive difference in the modes of solution. When the transition is complete, the profession will have changed its view of the field, its methods and its goals. (Kuhn, 1962/1970: 84–5)

While the fictions examined in Part III do not suggest that a 'scientific revolution' has already occurred, they clearly indicate that contemporary crime fiction is faced with a clash 'between incompatible modes of community life' (Kuhn, 1962/1970: 94). Part III documents a paradigm shift in process, and attempts to suggest some of the problems and achievements of those texts which refuse to abide by the rules of 'normal science'. The formula of crime is experiencing seismic structural changes, some of which this section will chart, but whether a 'new paradigm of detection' is actually possible or desirable is beyond the scope of this book to decide!

In Part III, then, the focus is on mutation, instability and the disruption of formula. Chapter 7, 'Out of Order: Lesbian Detection and Textual Pleasure' considers the capacity of the lesbian detective to disrupt and destabilise literary and political reading practices. I argue that the decomposition of the formula is achieved not only at the level of production, but also at that of consumption. Lesbian crime fiction is characteristically multiple: its version of the crime story is parodic, didactic and erotic – and there can be no guarantee that these fictions are read in order to establish 'whodunnit'. Lesbian crime fiction thus provides a basis for reading *away from* the ending, and suggests practices which destabilise our conception of the pleasure of the generic text.

This is not, however, the only mode through which lesbian detection disfigures the genre. These novels also present a profoundly disturbing reworking of the violence inherent in crime fiction, and it is the 'matter' of violence that forms a connection with the equally disruptive but profoundly different forces of Chapter 8. 'Consuming the Boundaries of Crime' is concerned with serial killers: multiple murderers whose patterns of crime and motivation bear scant resemblance to the chains of cause and effect familiar from earlier manifestations of the genre. The serial killer's transgression also lies in his or her centrality. This is an adversary rather than a criminal, a complex figure with the capacity to marginalise, or even destroy, the detective. The main focus of this chapter falls upon Thomas Harris's *Hannibal*, a novel that, like the lesbian detective fictions of the previous chapter, pushes so hard at the boundaries of genre that those boundaries collapse, leaving the reader bereft of the familiar signposts through which genre is traditionally interpreted and understood.

In critical terms, one name paradoxically unites and divides these chapters: the Marquis de Sade. Although Sade and his writings are not themselves a concern of this book, his formulations of power, desire and excess have prompted considerable cultural commentary. Sade as symbol creates a singularly appropriate lens through which to view the violent contradictions of the crime genre. Angela Carter, whose essay *The Sadeian Woman* informs Chapter 8, uses Sade to refract a feminist dilemma: he becomes the spur for an acute analysis of gender and patriarchy. By contrast, Roland Barthes, whose thinking underpins Chapter 7, is interested in Sade as a signifier of excess, multiplicity and a mobile, performative pleasure that can never be definitively located. Carter, too, is attracted by the potential Sade offers for woman to evade the category of feminine passivity, but ultimately she sees the Sadeian 'performance' as controlled and authorised by patriarchal structures. Consequently, any freedom offered to women by this paradigm will be constrained and contained by the law of the father.

Both Carter and Barthes engage with Sade in order to encounter and reconceptualise the fundamental question of pleasure, and implicit within Part III is the question, what do readers want? Why do they continue to read fictions that can no longer be seen to fulfil their original function of reassurance? What pleasure can possibly be found in the serial killer's dismemberment of the corpse, or in lesbian crime fiction's assault on the body of the detective? What, indeed, do we understand by the pleasure of the text, and what function does it play in the maintenance or disruption of symbolic structures? I return to these questions in Chapter 9, which is an ending, if not a conclusion, and which contemplates some of the inferences that might be drawn from both the life and the death of the detective.

NOTES

1. Discussing the roots of the genre, Dennis Porter observes that:

   > Of the three ritual practices of the law, which are investigation, trial and punishment . . . the nineteenth-century detective story usually retains only the first. Thus it reflects the reformed legal system of its time to the extent that it, too, reversed a previous state of affairs by making the investigation public and hiding punishment and execution. (Porter, 1981: 123)

   This transition also concerns Stephen Knight (1980), who charts the shift from the eighteenth century *Newgate Calendar*'s concern with the fate of criminals, to the nineteenth- and twentieth-centuries crime novels' concern with their capture.
2. Although their status is uncertain, all the texts discussed in Part III have been marketed as crime fiction.
3. I distinguish here between crime fiction which is in some sense innovative, and that which might be termed 'degenerate'. At the forefront of the genre (the 'normal science' of Part II) crime fiction has always retained its relevance and bankability through a chameleon-like adaptation to its environment, and through its dialectical relationship with the texts that preceded it. However, crime fiction is also possessed of a rump: a mode of fiction that endlessly replicates the tried and tested formulas of either classical or hard-boiled detection (and more recently of feminist detection). This is genre at its most conservative – a nostalgic, reactionary reworking of the structure and stereotypes of detective narrative.

7

Out of Order: Lesbian Detection and Textual Pleasure

> Text of pleasure: the text that contents, fills, grants euphoria; the text that comes from culture and does not break with it, is linked to a *comfortable* practice of reading. Text of bliss: the text that imposes a state of loss, the text that discomforts (perhaps to the point of a certain boredom), unsettles the reader's historical, cultural, psychological assumptions, the consistency of his tastes, values, memories, brings to a crisis his relation with language.
>
> Now the subject who keeps the two texts in his field and in his hands the reins of pleasure and bliss is an anachronic subject, for he simultaneously and contradictorily participates in the profound hedonism of all culture . . . and in the destruction of that culture: he enjoys the consistency of his selfhood (that is his pleasure) and seeks its loss (that is his bliss). He is a subject split twice over, doubly perverse. (Roland Barthes, 1973/1990: 14)

> Somehow I was in the driver's seat, with no idea of where I wanted to go. I took a deep breath and looked around. (Mary Wings, 1997: 54)

This chapter begins with a series of questions and queries that are neither new, nor likely to be resolved, but which nonetheless can be profitably readdressed. First, though, a statistic: in the last fifteen years the number of professional lesbian detectives on the literary marketplace has more than tripled from 14 in 1986 to 43 in 1995 (Walton and Jones, 1999: 41–2). How are we to account for the phenomenal success of lesbian detective fiction? What is the appeal of the formula to writers and readers? Who is the lesbian detective and what are the pleasures she affords to the reader? Who consumes these fictions and why?

Some answers have already been offered in the work of Sally Munt, Maggie Humm and Paulina Palmer. Palmer takes the most positive stance, arguing that lesbian detection 'has by no means lost the political vigour which characterised the genre in its early stages' and suggesting that the survival of the form will be guaranteed by its ability 'to successfully interrelate sexual politics with entertainment' (1997: 108). Munt is less certain of the formula's cohesion, and in *Murder by the Book?* she poses a series of pertinent questions about the suitability of the genre for lesbian appropriation. Acknowledging that the figure of the detective has always embodied a paradox – 'he is at once a representative of society and a critique of it' (1994: 120) – Munt argues that this duality represents an unstable basis for the foundation of a radical literature:

> Popular lesbian-feminist crime novels have tended to produce a particular version of this antithesis. Manifestly they are opposed to patriarchy; implicitly, however, they depend on many aspects of the mainstream genre, such as an overriding Manichean morality of good versus evil, notions of unified subjectivity, innateness, natural justice and tidy textual closures. (Munt, 1994: 120)

Maggie Humm, however, reads this contradiction as enabling. By choosing to work with 'material that is indifferent to, and often actively hostile to, women' (1991: 189), the writer of feminist crime fiction crosses a border. She acknowledges the limitations of the genre, while forcing a reconsideration of the boundaries that have traditionally defined it. 'When writing detective fiction', argues Humm, 'feminist writers go to a great deal of trouble and some awkwardness to show that the forms of knowledge of traditional detective narratives do not best solve the crime' (1991: 189).

From these critical interventions we might, then, conclude that lesbian detective fiction is entertaining but awkward, politically motivated – but not quite radical enough – and stands outside the mainstream while yet being compromised by it. The reservations revealed by these comments are only part of the problem of accounting for the popularity of the genre. In an article entitled 'Death and the Mainstream: Lesbian Detective Fiction and the Killing of the Coming-out Story', Anna Wilson approaches the question from a different angle. Arguing that the rise of the lesbian detective marks a crucial paradigm shift in the meaning of 'lesbian' as a cultural sign, she suggests that the satisfactions once afforded by the coming-out narrative are now provided by the lesbian detective's fantasy of agency (1996: 271). For Wilson, this transition is riven with contradictions and represents an evasion of the political specificity that previously characterised lesbian fictions:

> The death or absence of the significant other(s) enables the lesbian detective to be not only solitary but also, specifically, a nonlover. This is not to say that lesbian detectives are celibate, but, rather, that their identity is not constructed, as is that of an earlier lesbian hero, by experience of self in sexual relation . . . The lesbian detective novel has not gently edged out the coming-out story but, instead, has murdered it in the person of the loved other . . . The dead lover is the sign both of the death of the coming-out story and of the lesbian's new move into engagement, her passage across the ghetto boundaries into the mainstream. (Wilson, 1996: 260)[1]

From Wilson's criticisms, as from the reservations of Sally Munt, it quickly becomes clear that the lesbian detective is somehow not quite coming up to scratch. She is subject to a plethora of expectations emerging from both the template of the detective genre and the politics of feminism and, perhaps not surprisingly, she fails to satisfy them all, not least because she is herself undergoing a process of evolution. Anna Wilson's assertion of a movement towards the mainstream is not misplaced: in the words of Val McDermid's Lindsay Gordon, '[i]f I was ever radical, it's ancient history now' (1996/1998: 143). In 1991 Maggie Humm described lesbian detection as 'a literature of social outsiders'. Only three years later, contributing to a volume tellingly subtitled 'lesbian culture from margin to mainstream', Barbara Wilson observed that 'if one pushes hard enough at the outside edge, the boundaries change, and what was once outside is now inside' (Gibbs, 1994: 228). Wilson, who was herself an exemplary producer of the 'outsider' fiction of the 1980s, pertinently asks:

> [W]hat happens when a genre which once defined itself as new and in opposition to established forms becomes its own establishment, when writers and readers who were once drawn to the form precisely because there was something new about it now turn to it because it is familiar. (Gibbs, 1994: 219–20)

But how familiar is this form? Have the comforts of genre won out over the edge of politics? Or might lesbian detection still maintain the capacity to disrupt and destabilise both our literary and our political reading practices? And is it this disruption that constitutes the pleasure of the lesbian text?

In order to advance some explanation for the popularity of the genre and for the persistence among lesbian writers of this appropriative mode of writing, we need to consider both the formula of lesbian detection – the component parts that set it apart from mainstream genre narrative – and the reading pleasures that may be derived from these constituents. Lesbian detective fiction is undoubtedly characterised by a major investment in material that seems little to do with detection and a lot to do with life, love and politics – so much so that these fictions often bear scant resemblance to the genre which ostensibly defines and contains them. Some of the most successful writers in the field have adopted a position of postmodern self-consciousness in their approach to the genre, undermining generic conventions to the point where genre status becomes almost meaningless. Others treat the formal conventions of detection as a vehicle for the development of relationships, and for the exploration of sexuality and sexual practice. Alternatively the genre makes an excellent soapbox, and many of the contemporary crop of lesbian feminist fictions can be heard making vociferous appeals to the reader's socio-political conscience.

In bulk, then, lesbian detection might be judged by its conformity to a hypothetical and not entirely serious 'Scale of Queer Credibility'. Some of the less assured examples seem to overcompensate for the conservative ballast of generic form by an equal and opposite dead weight of political correctness. But even in the clumsy loudness of overt didacticism, a significant queerness can be detected. Although, as Judith Butler has observed, the concept of queer is itself a 'site of collective contestation' (1993: 228), queer notions of performativity, displacement and the disruption of the heterosexual matrix undoubtedly suit the lesbian detective novel. Moe Meyer offers a helpful definition:

> What 'queer' signals is an ontological challenge that displaces bourgeois notions of the Self as unique, abiding, and continuous while substituting instead a concept of the Self as performative, improvisational, discontinuous, and processually constituted by repetitive and stylized acts. (Meyer, 1994: 2–3)[2]

And what could be more repetitive and stylised than genre fiction? Lesbian detection, like its mainstream counterpart, has increasingly moved away from certainty and fixity, both in terms of narrative resolution and the figure of the detective. It is no longer possible to assume that any contemporary crime fiction will offer the secure, ratiocinative solutions that we associate with earlier manifestations of the genre, and (on an optimistic day) we might argue that feminist and lesbian crime fiction's refusal of androcentric bourgeois methodologies was instrumental in bringing about this change. But what does lesbian detection insert into the void left by the absence of investigative closure and narrative certainty? Discussing the pleasures of Sadeian literature Roland Barthes hypothesises that much of the appeal of this writing lies in the juxtaposition of 'antipathetic codes'. Through these textual 'collisions', language is 'redistributed':

> Two edges are created: an obedient, conformist, plagiarizing edge (the language is to be copied in its canonical state, as it has been established by schooling, good usage, literature, culture), and *another edge*, mobile, blank (ready to assume any contours), which is never anything but the site of its effect: the place where the death of language is glimpsed. These two edges, *the compromise they bring about*, are necessary. Neither culture nor its destruction is erotic; it is the seam between them, the fault, the flaw, which becomes so. (Barthes, 1973/1990: 6–7)

What then does lesbian detection bring to confront the rawness of ruptured convention? What constitutes the 'edge' of these texts?

In short, there are four elements – the parodic, the didactic, the erotic and the apocalyptic – that constitute the ingredients inserted into the body of the genre to open up a signifying space through which the familiar text of pleasure might be translated into the unfamiliar and destabilising text of bliss. It is important to acknowledge, however, that Barthes's categories are not wholly discrete. The 'comfortable' text of pleasure and the 'unsettling' text of bliss are subject to historical uncertainty and the vagaries of the reader's reception. With each new encounter the text is reconstituted and renewed, and inevitably some degree of uncertainty is a product of the reading process. To illustrate this point Barthes refers to the 'diluted tmesis' that inheres even within classical narrative forms.[3] Although this mode of narration encourages an urgent, linear, teleological mode of consumption that would seem to negate the possibility of a blissful crisis of language, readers nonetheless *cut* the text to their own specification. They skip, they skim (and I would contend they linger), as appropriate to their own satisfaction (Barthes, 1973/1990: 10–11).

Lesbian detective fiction can be seen at the level of both its production and consumption to enact and encourage a tmetic process. In the first instance, the compound of genre narrative is subject to the insertion of other matter, thereby disrupting formulaic expectations and creating Barthesian 'seams' or 'flaws' in the structure of the text. Second, however, the finished product of lesbian detection becomes itself the subject of tmetic reading: the author cannot know whether the text will be consumed for its criminal, erotic, didactic or parodic matter. Neither will that which has been cut remain stable. Thus in both its writing and its reading the tmetic text of lesbian detection encourages the decomposition of formula. This generic 'decay' exposes the reader to the possibility of loss encoded in a destruction of narrative expectations, and ensures that the space of popular fiction attains at least the potential for bliss.[4]

Given the inherent misogyny of the formula that is being appropriated, it is almost impossible for the lesbian text not to adopt at least one of the disruptive strategies outlined above. Katherine V. Forrest's Kate Delafield novels, for example, also operate on the level of lesbian romance, inserting transgressive desire and its explicit fulfilment into the law-abiding text of the police procedural:

> Her mouth came to Aimee's breasts, captured a nipple. Tantalized by the faint salt taste she sucked each nipple in turn, she moved her fingers strongly in the creamy wet, greedy for more of the ecstatic gasps. She would gorge on this feast of a woman, feed herself till she burst. (Forrest, 1991/1993: 71)

Kate Delafield began her serial narrative as the archetypal isolated loner, but as the novels progress she finds, first, a community of women at the Nightwood Bar (a movement away from isolation that challenges Anna Wilson's characterisation of the lesbian detective as outside or opposed to the 'lesbian nation'), and second, a new and ongoing relationship with Aimee Grant. However, as I suggested in Chapter 6, the lesbian relationship itself is not automatically a transgressive one. Unlike many other writers in the genre, Forrest offers little in the way of sexual experimentation; but even within the relatively conservative sexual landscape of Forrest's novels, the erotic retains the potential to dislocate narrative convention. Kate's tendency to indulge in sex with suspects represents a potentially serious transgression, a 'procedural irregularity' that threatens the detective's security at the same time as it challenges the structures of the law. Significantly, however, Kate is never betrayed by these women, nor is her investigation jeopardised. Rather she is replenished and renewed by sexual contact, returning refreshed to the hostile, homophobic environment of the LAPD.[5]

Unlike their hard-boiled precursors, dyke detectives are seldom left wholly alone. While the erotic content of the novels may vary, the presence of (or search for) a relationship is one of the few genre constants it is easy to identify. This is in sharp contrast to the heterosexual female private eye (as well as to the earlier male paradigm), whose investigations most often proceed at the cost of her intimate relationships – a prime example of which is provided by Paretsky's V. I. Warshawski, who is literally torn apart by the contradictory demands of female agency and heterosexual desire.[6] In lesbian detection, however, the erotic has been an integral component. But how does this erotic dimension interact with the second of my categories or 'edges' – the didactic?

On one level it must be acknowledged that the erotic itself is didactic. When what is being depicted has for centuries been invisible or prohibited, the very fact of textual inscription is potentially radical. Alan Sinfield expresses serious concerns about the security of the gains achieved by les/bi/gay people over the last two decades, observing that a 'rabidly homophobic' minority has proved itself capable of causing 'damage quite disproportionate to its size' (1998: 196):

> This phobic minority . . . maintains a bridgehead for attitudes that, among people generally, may be dormant but still available. For ideology is always conflicted and contradictory, and composed of residual and emergent, as well as dominant elements; people may hold amiable libertarian attitudes while harbouring also ancient anxieties. They may give little thought

> to same-sex relations from one month to the next, but then be roused into traditional prejudices by hostile media treatment of a provocative instance. (Sinfield, 1998: 196–7)

Sinfield's concerns are shared by Eve Sedgwick, who describes the ongoing repression of lesbian and gay lives in the American mainstream. Sedgwick describes the 'complicity of parents, of teachers, of clergy, even of the mental health professions in invalidating and wounding kids who show gender-dissonant tastes, behaviour, body language' (1993/1994: 2). In such a context, the presence of a validated desiring lesbian body within the framework of a popular genre cannot be other than radical.

But is the erotic always unproblematic? Obviously not. Lesbian eroticism comprises diverse and conflictual agendas – multiple desires and subjectivities that even supposedly feminist platforms have been reluctant to acknowledge. An example of these tensions is provided by the debate surrounding lesbian sadomasochism. Lynda Hart's study of lesbian s/m provides a detailed account of the attempt by the American feminist organisation NOW (National Organization for Women) to disassociate itself from the stigma of masculinity, with which lesbian s/m was seen to be irrevocably tainted (1998: 43). Hart defines sadomasochists as 'a group within the lesbian subculture who not only play openly with power but who also assert their absolute right to do so' (1998: 47), an agenda potentially at odds with the identity politics and 'woman-centredness' that dominated feminist discourse in the 1970s. To insert the erotic lesbian body into the appropriated space of the crime narrative in consequence becomes a political statement, both in terms of the 'external' discourse of crime and the 'internal' discourse of feminism. Surveying the history of the battle, Hart observes that 'the fact that vocal opposition to lesbian s/m has come from within lesbian-feminist communities signals the contest for habitation of a sign whose borders can presumably be controlled' (1998: 47). The stakes are high and they crucially serve to further destabilise the construct of the detective, whose relationship to detective agency is complicated by the gendered implications of that agency. In a genre predominantly controlled by the narrative voice of the detective-protagonist, who has the textual capacity to validate or invalidate the subjects of her investigation, the pleasures enjoyed by the detective herself will have repercussions far beyond the bedroom.

When the lesbian detects, therefore, a great deal is at stake, and in the formative years of the subgenre, lesbian identity was as much a subject of investigation as the specific event of the crime. The didacticism of these investigations was frequently loud, leaving novels on the verge of becoming public-information pamphlets. But the textual tensions emerging from such narrative indeterminacy put another significant dent in the comfortable integrity of the crime genre. Kate Allen's *Tell Me What You Like* (1993) explores the politics of the erotic and is in many respects typical of the didactic novel's oscillation between narrative progression and scene of explication. The novel focuses on a policewoman tempted by the forbidden pleasures of lesbian sadomasochism, and makes an explicit comparison between structures of social and sexual power:

> You don't think that being a cop is all about power? You don't have any qualms about working in a system that is still incredibly oppressive to women, not just as criminals but as victims, and on the force as well? (Allen, 1993: 34)

But it's not just as a policewoman that Officer Alison Kane gets read the riot act. Once out of uniform she is subject to a heavy dose of political correction at what might best be described as an s/m coffee morning: 'I paid my dues as a flannel-shirt dyke', cries lipstick lesbian Diane, 'and I now have gotten to the point where I feel that I have the right to create my own sexual image without sticking to dyke standard rules' (1993: 40).

Allen's novel progresses from Officer Kane's discomfort, through her education and reappraisal, to an acknowledgement of her desires, and her involvement in a role-playing s/m relationship. In contrast, when Barbara Wilson's detective Pam Nilsen comes face to face with s/m in *The Dog Collar Murders*, she maintains a greater degree of detachment from the debates surrounding her. Nonetheless, the educational pattern persists as Pam moves from a position of anxiety and antipathy towards s/m practices to an acknowledgement of her own arousal by the erotic images of pornography. In both novels the hierarchies of the lesbian community are themselves laid bare. The s/m dyke is presented as the outsider – an outlaw challenging the stifling conformity of a 'vanilla' lesbian relationship-focused norm.[7] Throughout the novel, the various characters argue over who has maximum marginality. Who is truly transgressive, and who is simply representing 'established notions of sex' (Wilson, 1989/1994: 27)? The boundary-crossing potential of s/m is set against both anti-pornography and anti-s/m positions,[8] and the complexity of the debate threatens to swamp the unfortunate reader, but thankfully (and conveniently) a lesbian academic is standing by, ready to encapsulate the issues and clarify any points you might have missed (1989/1994: 40–1, 187–8)!

You would be forgiven for forgetting that somewhere in the midst of all this, a murder has taken place, and our intrepid sleuth Pam Nilsen is on the track of the killer. Wilson's novels are unashamedly didactic in their desire to mobilise feminist debate, but they remain among the most successful in this category because they also contain the element of parody. This is most evident in her later Cassandra Reilly novels, but the deflationary impulse is also present in the Pam Nilsen mysteries, saving us from what Sally Munt has described as 'death by political correction':

> 'I'm really looking forward to hearing Loie Marsh speak,' said Debi. 'She's been one of my heroes for years.'
>
> 'Me too,' said Sarah. 'I remember when I read *The Silenced Heart*. It just blew me away. It expressed so many things about men and living in a male world that I had just taken for granted.'
>
> 'They don't write books like that anymore,' agreed Debi. 'Really groundbreaking books like that.'
>
> I hadn't read it, just like I had never managed to read *The Female Eunuch, Future Shock* and Carlos Castenada. No good reason – I just happened to be reading something else at the time and then the historical moment passed. (1989/1994: 16–17)

Just as the boundary between the erotic and the didactic has been blurred, so, increasingly, is the line between didacticism and parody.

Barbara Wilson's growing desire to deconstruct feminist absolutes receives its most thorough airing in her first Cassandra Reilly mystery, *Gaudí Afternoon*. This text is not merely deflationary or uncertain, it is unashamedly and gloriously parodic. Sally Munt has observed that:

> Lesbian and feminist writers interfacing with masculine genres tend to estrange through using parody, which accentuates the reader's sense of superior distance. Parody addresses a highly knowing audience, through the use of style; it is closely connected to pastiche, its sceptical, deflationary intention highlighting the presence of ambiguity in its target. (Munt, 1994: 77)

Although claiming to be a detective novel, *Gaudí Afternoon* is less concerned with the solving of a crime than with the detection of the enigma that is sexuality and desire. In a cast comprising cross-dressers, lesbians, homosexuals, transvestites and transsexuals, the detective is, appropriately, a translator (Wilson, 1990/1991: 74). The text offers a multiplicity of narrative levels, nothing is ever quite what it seems, and our desire for resolution is constantly undercut and displaced by disruption.

This instability is achieved through a number of textual strategies. Characters are repeatedly misread in terms of gender and sexuality, confusing both narrator and reader alike. The novel is set in Barcelona, and when Cassandra arrives in the city it is as if all familiar points of gender reference have been removed. Names and appearances prove unreliable signifiers of identity. The transsexual Frankie looks like a woman, behaves like a woman, but has left behind her the biological legacy of fatherhood. Lesbian mother Ben looks and behaves like a man, while yet clinging to essentialist notions of her 'biological role' as a mother (1990/1991: 64). The conflict between these warring parents provides both narrative impetus (helpless, feminine Frankie hires Cassandra to find errant husband Ben), and the underlying didactic purpose: the novel debates the meanings of motherhood and the family through an analysis of essentialist and constructionist models of identity:

> In what did her masculinity reside then? Her voice was low, but I'd thought that came from smoking. She had breasts and hips and the gestures and movements of a woman. She was more feminine than I or many of my women friends. It wasn't only surgery that had changed her sex, or hormones, it was a conscious choice to embrace femaleness, whatever femaleness is. (Wilson, 1990/1991: 82)

The novel persistently refuses to assign gender fixity to anyone, including the detective. The perception of Cassandra by those she meets is fundamentally shaped not by Cassandra herself, but by her context. Searching the barrio for Frankie with her ultra-feminine friend, Carmen, Cassandra is read variously as a transsexual and as a man, before being dismissed and 'explained' as an 'American' (1990/1991: 73). Shortly afterwards, in the company of Ben, her gender is reassigned: 'I was back to womanhood, but only because the world thinks in dyads and Ben was more of a man than me' (1990/1991: 103).

The parodic, meanwhile, takes equally diverse forms within the novel. Wilson is acutely aware of genre conventions, opening the novel with what *appears* to be the *femme fatale*'s traditional and deceptive call for the detective's help. But this is not the only generic trait that the novel parodies. Built into the structure of Cassandra's search for the endlessly displaced, but never endangered, child Delilah (offspring of Ben and Frankie) is an example of her work as a translator.[9] Throughout the novel the reader is given excerpts from *La Grande y su hija* (*The Big One and Her Daughter*), a gloriously hyperbolic parody of magic realism. Another disruptive edge is introduced into the detective narrative, and a parallel quest established to piece together the mystery of this fragmented text. This story within a story also acts as an ironic counterpoint to the main narrative's concern with gender identities. *The Big One and Her Daughter* exposes the destructive patterns of compulsory heterosexuality, encoded in and regulated through what Judith Butler would describe as 'hyperbolic versions of "man" and "woman"' (1993: 237). The mystery of this text, meanwhile, is a search for nothing less than the Holy Grail of patriarchal power. What is the secret source of power contained within Raoul's black bag? An answer seems to be forthcoming, but of course proves as evasive as the phallus it mocks. Cassandra's translation is stolen on the final page of the novel, a final poetic displacement within the novel's repeated refusal of certainty.

Finally, coming full circle, *Gaudí Afternoon* also presents a parody of the erotic impulse in lesbian crime fiction, through which our expectations of erotic transgression are themselves deconstructed:

> I went into the big old-fashioned bathroom and locked the door. Carefully I took off my black jeans and Japanese shirt and wrapped myself in a towel so as not to get too cold. I took what I needed out of my cosmetic case and perched on the side of the tub in front of the full-length mirror. I didn't do it this way very often but that added to the excitement. I had a few goosebumps and I was perspiring lightly. The fantasy was very strong.
>
> Slowly, very slowly, I raised the scissors to my crown and started snipping. (Wilson, 1990/1991: 37–8)

Parody, then, is crucial to the success of these novels. In a definition which could almost have been written with lesbian detection in mind, Linda Hutcheon defines parody as 'an intertextual manipulation of multiple conventions' and 'an extended repetition with critical difference' (quoted in Meyer, 1994: 9). Such a conception opens up a significant challenge to the claim that lesbian detection is simply the grafting of a superficial radicalism on to a fundamentally conservative formula. Moe Meyer argues that 'parody becomes the process whereby the marginalized and disenfranchised advance their own interests by entering alternative signifying codes into discourse by attaching them to existing structures of signification' (1994: 11). In these terms, to reappropriate the genre cannot be other than to parody it. Or, to go a stage further, to insert the lesbian into hard-boiled detective fiction is always and inevitably to construct a parody – irrespective of the tone or intent of the text. Given that hard-boiled detection is premised upon a set of profoundly anti-feminist gender ideologies, the introduction of feminist didacticism and lesbian eroticism will inevitably 'queer the pitch'.[10] The erotic charge of dyke detection might thus be read as a parodic raising of the dead, in which the abruptly discharged bodies of the *femme fatale* and the woman-as-other return to haunt the form from which they were so brutally excluded. Now the roles are reversed – or even conflated. If the detective is not in the happy position of enjoying the living body of the *femme fatale*, it is usually because she is herself that demon woman.

Which brings me back to the question that frames this discussion: wherein lies the pleasure of these texts? Can the substitution of erotic certainty for narrative certainty really be said to have translated these fictions from the comfortable text of pleasure to the unpredictable text of bliss? Might not the fantasy of reciprocated desire represent as much of a conservative closure as detection's archetypal fantasy of resolution?

The answers to these questions depend upon both the construction and the context of lesbian desire. There is a parallel to be drawn between the patterns of s/m role play and the parodic performativity of the lesbian crime genre. Lesbian detection in fact presents the ultimate in passive role-playing fantasies. In a vicarious version of the s/m dynamic, the reader explores the power of both detective and killer. The reader submits to the power of the narrative, trusting the text to provide the desired combination of pain and pleasure, risk and resolution. The reader is thus exposed and vulnerable, capable of being wounded by textual inscriptions that go beyond or work against the familiar script. Yet the relationship remains consensual. All the reader has to do is close the book. The concept of trust is fundamental to the contract of genre and, to a certain extent, all detective fictions work upon this model. The reader identifies primarily with the (usually detective) protagonist, and trusts that whatever physical and emotional hardships are thrown in the path of this character, ultimately they will be overcome. But contemporary lesbian crime fiction has increasingly come to interrogate this trust and with it the complacency of the reader who seeks pleasure in a displaced narrative of vicarious violence. Consequently, it is not simply in its deployment of overt eroticism that lesbian crime fiction disorders the pleasurable text; rather it discomforts through its continued, but qualitatively different, investment in the generic staple of violence.

These novels have a fascinating and shocking tendency towards apocalypse. Many have quite remarkably violent endings, and the detective is far from exempt from the fall-out. Obviously the physical abuse of the detective has a long and illustrious history, but there seems to be something extra here, an excess that complicates the appropriation of genre, and resists what Barthes describes as a '*comfortable* practice of reading' (1973/1990: 14). On the one hand this can be read as part of the wider trend in detective fiction towards an acknowledgement of the realities of violence. People who are repeatedly hit on the head are more likely to suffer brain damage than to get up and apprehend the perpetrator. And in terms specifically of lesbian detection, the subgenre's concern with the depiction of the detective's relationships demands a recognition of the ongoing effects of violence, both physical and mental. Laurie R. King's Kate Martinelli novels provide a good example of this. The first novel in the series concludes with the serious wounding of Kate's partner, Lee, an event that not only brings the detective forcibly out of the closet, but also physically and emotionally rewrites the landscape of their relationship – a destabilising impact that is still being negotiated three books later.

So, violence is real, nasty and has long-term consequences. But is that it? I'm not sure that it is, and I think that its excessive inscription, particularly on the body of the detective, bears witness to a sadistic impulse within lesbian crime fiction. In using the word 'sadistic' I am not suggesting that the increasingly battered appearance of the lesbian detective necessarily indicates an increasing desire for the pleasures of sadomasochism among lesbian readers.[11] Rather I am invoking Barthes's concept of Sadeian multiplicity, which emerges from the abuse of the detective's body. Paraphrasing Barthes, Harold Beaver observes:

> Everyone can be either sodomizer or sodomized, agent or patient, subject or object since pleasure is possible anywhere, with victims as well as masters. This art is revolutionary, Barthes argued, not as a myth of virility but as a new language of signs. The sadistic novel is rhapsodical, picaresque, defiant of logical, natural, organic order; resisting conclusion; alternating erotic scene and explication in an infinite, self-generating series. (Beaver, 1981: 118)

The bodily disfiguration or disablement of the detective opens up this dynamic because it destabilises the patterns of agency otherwise established by the narrative. This disabling is integral to the tendency of lesbian detection to avoid closure and certainty, as it opens a point of dissolution at the very moment of resolution. In other words, just as the plot prepares to fall into some degree of order, the detective's agency is fundamentally undermined, roles are reversed and agent becomes patient. The flow of power switches and the locus of pleasure shifts from vicarious control to vicarious submission.

This dynamic is effectively, and contrastingly, illustrated by two writers: Mary Wings and Stella Duffy. In Duffy's novel *Beneath the Blonde* (1997), the third to feature detective Saz Martin (and what might we make of those initials?), the concern with appearance, role and identity typical of novels such as *Gaudí Afternoon* is still very much in evidence. The title *Beneath the Blonde* immediately directs the reader to a surface/depth dichotomy, particularly in relation to female identity.[12] However, the novel itself begins not with a consideration of what is beneath the blonde (incidentally a mousy-brown bob), but rather of what is beneath the detective's tough exterior. Saz Martin's vulnerability is laid bare with the unexpected and shocking exposure of her burn-scarred body. The previous novel, *Wavewalker* (1996), concluded with Saz's translation from agent to patient following a truly apocalyptic dénouement, and the problematic of the wounded hero crosses over into *Beneath the Blonde*. Duffy's decision to burn her detective merits closer examination. Burn scars are slow to heal and leave an indelible mark. Following her exposure to the fire, and to the failure of her investigation, Saz must literally and metaphorically grow a new skin. Saz's lover, Molly, a doctor, is in contrast empowered by the destruction of the detective. Molly gets both to pull her lover back into the private, erotic sphere and become the agent within this sphere, caring for the damaged detective. Yet by the beginning of *Beneath the Blonde* Saz needs again to become an agent, and it is interesting to note the extent to which the patterns of agency and dependence within this third novel replicate and amplify those established within the second. While controversially increasing the scope of her agency by choosing to kill the killer, Saz is wounded again, both physically and emotionally (her relationship with 'the blonde' is revealed as meaningless). After the bloodbath of another apocalyptic ending, Saz is once more returned as patient to the erotic agency of Molly:

> Two nights later, weary, dirty and jet-lagged, Saz fell off the plane and into Molly's arms. Home again to wash, to have her dressing changed, to sit by the fire and drink hot soup with fresh bread and be scolded and loved and warmed and held gently while she cried away the telling of everything that happened in that house. Almost everything that had happened. (Duffy, 1997: 249)

Yet Duffy is not prepared to let her readers become complacent, even within a dynamic of apocalypse and salvation. Her recent novel, *Fresh Flesh* (1999), concludes with the detective being subject to a horrifically violent beating that represents the absolute destruction of detective agency. Ironically, this beating is not even specifically aimed at Saz. She is simply the displaced object of 'mindless violence': the rage of a character driven to irrationality by the past lies and present truths that Saz, as detective, believes she must reveal (1999: 278–9). After the beating, Saz drifts in and out of consciousness, and the novel begins to threaten the reader's security through indeterminacy. Saz makes no decisions or judgements, she does not analyse, but she knows, through her body, that something is profoundly wrong (1999: 281, 285). Saz loses control of her agency not simply at the level of captivity, but at the most basic corporeal level. She can control neither her mind nor her body (281, 282). Eventually her delirium takes her into a dream of Molly – a dream that re-enacts the reassuring transition from agent to patient familiar from previous novels. But this time the security is illusory:

> Then Saz's body was awake and screaming out again. Last scream, real scream, first time out of her mouth with actual noise in so many hours and raw and angry and primal and fierce and no Molly to make it better. (Duffy, 1999: 286)

This is the reader's final insight into Saz's interiority. From this point the focus shifts to the characters around her, and to the realisation that in the fluctuating dynamic between agent and patient, not even Molly, the doctor, will be able to assume authority, agency and control. Indeed, her only power becomes that of *lying* to comfort the patient (1999: 296). Expressly and ominously the reader is told that 'Molly wasn't going to get a chance to cope' with the 'bloody mess of her girlfriend' (293) and the novel concludes with the simple statement: 'when Molly looked back at her girlfriend, Saz's eyes were closed' (297).

As a point of closure this refuses all conventional comforts and satisfactions. We do not *know* what has happened to the detective. We do not know the dimensions of the damage wrought by this particular textual apocalypse. Yet in terms of the novel's bliss – the crisis created in the pleasurable generic contract between reader and text – whether Saz is dead or alive at the end of the novel is almost immaterial. What matters is that her agency has been not just temporarily but traumatically undermined. As have the reader's expectations. The erotics of risk have been ruptured and the Sadeian boundary between pleasure and pain has been pushed to the limit that is death. Without a fundamental reinscription of the terms of agency, Saz cannot be restored. Although the woman might survive, the detective is dead.

Duffy thus confronts the complacency of genre with a devastating refusal of comfort. In contrasting style, but with similar effect, the American Mary Wings forces the reader to confront some uncomfortable questions regarding female power and subjectivity. Throughout her series of Emma Victor novels, Wings has used parody to question patriarchal power and its impact on women.[13] She is a practised appropriator of the hard-boiled form who comically approximates and undermines the language of her predecessors:

> I let a silence fall and took a long look into the shadowy world I was about to enter. A world away from slimy divorce cases. A step into a world of parasites who fed off public figures, fungi

> who lived fast, rodents who lived to die in a reckless volley of gunfire. (Wings, 1997: 17)

But it is also Wings who most clearly exposes the additional 'edge' of bliss embodied in the Sadeian power dynamic. Consider the monumental contradictions and remarkable generic destabilisation contained within the short opening line of *She Came to the Castro*: 'I'm sorry about the gun, Mom' (Wings, 1997: xvii). This one brief statement encapsulates both the detective's power and its negation. Wings offers the child's submission to parental authority at the same time as the gun is being cited as the defining characteristic of a new independence. Or, in gender terms, we might read this as an apology for the betrayal of the maternal that resides in the acquisition of the phallic gun. Either way, Wings crams into this incredibly succinct opening a vertically layered mass of contradictory signification. Here, in a nutshell, lie both the problem and the pleasure of lesbian detective fiction.

So where does this leave the consumer of these fictions? Lesbian detection begins by empowering the disempowered. It confers a degree of agency upon the outsider, who challenges the status quo through a variety of erotic, didactic and parodic interventions – but why then must the lesbian agent be cut down to size? Perhaps to facilitate identification. If, as Anna Wilson has argued, this is the logical successor of the coming-out novel, then flawed vulnerability is surely a more secure site for reader identification than superhuman strength. But the success of lesbian detection is not simply down to an audience of hungry lesbians, desperate to find a recognisable self-image writ large upon the page (although this is always welcome). After all, as Clare Whatling has observed in *Screen Dreams*, the lesbian consumer is perfectly capable of constructing her own fantasy by rewriting the mainstream narrative of heterosexual desire (1997: 5). It would seem, then, that something else is going on. Lesbian detection has also succeeded because it represents the highest or furthest point of the genre's possibility. More than any other appropriation or development of the formula, it has followed narrative possibilities to their extreme. Traditional detective fiction has always contained the potential for Sadeian multiplicity. Be it Agatha Christie or Raymond Chandler, there are so many possible solutions – anyone could have committed the crime, any character contains the potential to be sodomiser or sodomised, agent or patient, murderer or victim – but historically crime fiction has retreated from this potentiality, offering a fixed solution and at least a relative restoration of the status quo. Not so the lesbian detective novel. Like the heterosexual feminist crime novel it performatively undermines the masculine hegemony that was once embodied in the figure of the detective. Similarly, it resists the concept of a straightforward conclusion and the restoration of the status quo, but it also moves beyond this paradigm in its refusal of compulsory heterosexuality. The Sadeian novel alternates 'erotic scene and explication in an infinite, self-generating series' and, for as long as lesbian desire remains in excess of symbolic representation, its erotic scene will continue to evade the limits of textual closure. In the words of Monique Wittig: 'Lesbian is the only concept . . . which is beyond the categories of sex (woman and man), because the designated subject (lesbian) is *not* a woman, either economically, or politically, or ideologically. For what makes a woman is a specific social relation to a man' (1992: 20).[14]

So where does an examination of the parodic, didactic, erotic and apocalyptic impulses of lesbian detection leave us? Within the terms of the didactic and the erotic, the regulation and constraints built into the concept of popular genres paradoxically facilitate a short cut to fantasies of agency. They open a space of transgressive desire that is nonetheless underpinned by a safety net of narrative certainty. As with all detective narratives, the agent ventures where the reader fears to tread, but, equally, the reader identifies where the genre fears to tread, pursuing the novel not (as its early theorists would have had it) for the abstractions of the detective puzzle, but for its characters, its romance, its sex, its comedy and, above all, for its textual inscription of the female body.

Finally, however, this fiction satisfies because it endorses multiplicity. The layered complexity of the lesbian detective text facilitates a reading that is both sequential and vertical. Barthes describes the subject who simultaneously holds both the text of pleasure and the text of bliss as an 'anachronic' subject – a subject out of time and out of order, a disruptive reading subject created by the collision between the comfortable edge of traditional genre narrative and the sadistic edge of uncertainty. Pursuing his analogy of the textual 'edge' Barthes asks, '[i]s not the most erotic portion of a body *where the garment gapes*?' (1973/1990: 9), and it is in a paraphrase of this question that we might decode the enigma of lesbian detection's success. Is not the most erotic portion of a text *where the genre gapes*?

NOTES

1. While lesbian detection does indeed have its fair share of dead lovers, Wilson's contention that the detective is a 'nonlover' seems wilfully contrary. The dead lover often acts within these fictions as a motor propelling the search for a new lover, and – as I argued in Chapter 6 – the erotic can perform a vital regenerative function for the detective. Maggie Humm reinforces the structural significance of the sexual in her analysis of Mary Wing's *She Came Too Late*:

   > The description of lesbian love-making and their rhythms of interpenetration are a vivid formulation of the story's theme in a physically feminist structure. Lesbian love-making is a simile of Emma's social transgression and a more useful code for her to acquire than the powerful and sexual antagonism of most detective hieroglyphics. (Humm, 1990: 244)

2. Eve Sedgwick offers a further definition of 'queer' that complements Meyer's emphasis on the performative. For Sedgwick, one of the most crucial aspects of queer is its significatory excess:

   > That's one of the things that 'queer' can refer to: the open mesh of possibilities, gaps, overlaps, dissonances and resonances, lapses and excesses of meaning when the constituent elements of anyone's gender, of anyone's sexuality aren't made (or *can't be* made) to signify monolithically. (Sedgwick, 1993/1994: 8)

3. From the Greek *Tmesis* – cutting: 'The separation of the elements of a compound word by the imposition of another word or words' (*OED*).
4. Dennis Porter also observes that detective narrative reveals aspects of Barthes's '*texte de plaisir*' (1981: 54), and offers a substantial account of the importance of suspense and digression in the construction of detective textual pleasure. I am, however, confused by his assertion that Barthes consigns detective stories to a 'despised third category' of textuality: the '*texte de désir*':

   > According to Barthes, the reader of a detective novel tends to behave like a schoolboy at a burlesque show; he is so aroused in his desire to see the female sex organ that he is tempted to rush the stage in order to help the stripper strip faster. (Porter, 1981: 53)

   Admittedly Barthes asserts that '[n]o significance (no bliss) can occur, I am convinced, in a mass culture . . . for the model of this culture is petit bourgeois' (1973/1990: 38), but the plurality of Barthes's *own* text, which itself invites a multiplicity of interpretations, countermands in practice such an uncomfortably fixed assertion. In Richard Miller's English translation the text of desire is the 'victorious rival' of the text of pleasure, a category reserved for 'so-called "erotic"' books which focus wholly on the *expectation* of the erotic scene and end in 'disappointment, deflation' (1973/1990: 58). Whether this model fits the generic template of crime is debatable. Can the unveiling of the murderer be as great an anti-climax as the textual inscription of the f/act of copulation? Barthes's pronouncements are evasive. His own text of pleasure is also a text of bliss – the categories are unstable and held in place only for the duration of each reading – and it would seem presumptive to foreclose the interpretative possibilities exposed by his perverse polemic.
5. The erotic trajectory of the Forrest novels is discussed at length in Chapter 6, where I argue that the fourth novel in the series represents a watershed, after which Kate's relationship to both her job and the closet undergoes a series of subtle changes. What does not change, however, is her almost vampiric need for the sustenance provided by the lesbian body – a sustenance she draws upon whenever and wherever she finds it. Having dragged herself away from a delicious suspect in the most recent novel *Sleeping Bones* (1999), she satisfies herself instead by once again *consuming* Aimee: 'with Aimee's shivering thighs against her face, she drank and drank her fill' (1999: 199).
6. This tension is discussed in Chapter 5.
7. The origins and implications of the term 'vanilla' are explored at length by Lynda Hart (1998: 220–2). In the context of this chapter, however, I use the term to describe one half of a sexual binary opposition emerging from 'an historical moment of impasse' in the 1980s:

   > [W]hat came to be known as 'vanilla' sex was established in opposition to a range of other alternative sexualities – including commercial sex workers, sadomasochism, transvestism, transsexualism, transgenderism, pedophilia, bisexualism, and 'homosexuality' in general. (Hart, 1998: 38)

8. To give just two examples:

'S/M is about power, that's true, but it's about the flow of power. Power in heterosexual relations is frozen and static, with one side always dominant and one side always submissive. S/M is about movement and the exchange of energy.' (Wilson, 1989/1994: 28)

'Why don't you talk about the pain and humiliation, Nicky? . . . About women with scars from razor blades all over their breasts, about women who've had internal hemorrhaging from being fist-fucked. About women who have to eat shit and drink urine. Don't just talk about power and trust; talk about broken arms and whip marks and burns from hot wax.' (Wilson, 1989/1994: 29)

9. Delilah might be seen as the novel's 'Maltese Falcon' – a precious object for which all the characters search, but which turns out to be not quite what the detective had expected.
10. The basis of this misogyny is succinctly described by Ann Wilson:

    Despite appearing to be immune to the contagion of the world, [the hard-boiled detective] is vulnerable underneath and capable of falling in love with a pretty girl – who often turns out to be treacherous, a femme fatale, an agent of evil. The attractive woman is duplicitous, her physical beauty working a deadly web in concert with her depraved spirit. This scheme of gender relations gives hard-boiled fiction a decidedly male, even misogynistic, quality. (Wilson, 1995: 148–9)
11. Although it is difficult to see how readers of hard-boiled crime fiction could avoid indulging in the pleasures of both sadism and masochism, given that the generic form is structured around the flow of power, and incorporates both the active infliction and the passive endurance of pain.
12. The title also comprises an erotic dimension, offering an admirably succinct description of where the detective would like to be.
13. Wings also builds a structural critique into her deployment of the detective narrative. As Maggie Humm argues in her analysis of the first Emma Victor novel, *She Came Too Late*: '[t]he solution to the detective problem . . . is not found in the detailed empiricism of detective science, but rather lies in Emma's ability to identify with other sexual outsiders' (1991: 194).
14. Wittig extends her point to contend that '"woman" has meaning only in heterosexual systems of thought and heterosexual economic systems. Lesbians are not women' (1992: 32). Her assertion suggests that lesbian detection will inevitably disrupt the 'straight mind', but it simultaneously suggests the impossibility of the heterosexual female private eye. It is precisely because a lesbian is not a woman – that is, she is outside the heterosexual matrix – that she can occupy the space of the hard-boiled detective and assume a subjectivity defined in opposition to the feminine.

8

Consuming the Boundaries of Crime: Serial Killing and the Taste for Violence

> On close inspection, all literature is probably a version of the apocalypse that seems to me rooted, no matter what its socio-historical conditions might be, on the fragile border (borderline cases) where identities (subject/object, etc.) do not exist or only barely so – double, fuzzy, heterogeneous, animal, metamorphosed, altered, abject. (Kristeva, 1982: 207)

> The voice of reason, always subversive, must issue from a monster. (Carter, 1979: 82)

In the previous chapter I suggested that lesbian detection takes both the body and the concept of the detective to the brink of destruction. Within this subgenre, the embodiment and the behaviour of the detective exceeds the rules of the form. The lesbian investigator destabilises both the classical respect for law and order, and the foundational misogyny of hard-boiled narration. Modern crime fiction was founded on the repression of unruly criminality and the suppression of excessive femininity, and through its containment of these twin terrors it established itself as the supreme generic form of the twentieth century. The formula offered a reliable narrative mode for exerting control over unprecedented socio-political change, but in her challenge to the structures of law and patriarchal authority, and in her embodiment of the spectre of feminine desire, the lesbian detective reinscribes precisely what the formula had so long sought to erase. By the logic of crime fiction, such transgressions must render the detective criminal. The detective is split – she is simultaneously both agent and other, rupture and resolution – and in this multiplicity she embodies the crisis of the genre.

Stephen Knight has argued that it is the presence of 'an investigating agent' that gives cohesion to the concept of modern crime fiction. Although stories concerned with the control of crime preceded the appearance of the detective hero, it was the emergence of this 'specially skilled' individual that consolidated an ideological pattern particularly suited to the values of bourgeois culture (1980: 8, 39). If, then, it was the appearance of the detective that instituted the formula, it is equally his or her disappearance that above all suggests the fragmentation and dispersal of the form. Lesbian detective fiction contributes to this conceptual dissolution, but the lesbian is not alone in her challenge to the reassuring individualism of detective agency. The dyke detective's transgression is paralleled by another subgenre that carries the potential to deconstruct detective authority: the serial-killer narrative.

This version of the genre is not in itself transgressive. Indeed, as Harry Ziegler has suggested, it can also invite the expression of a 'reactionary modernism'. Taking the work of Patricia Cornwell as his example, Ziegler argues that the Kay Scarpetta novels detach crime from its socio-political context and present it as 'the expression of individual pathology' (Ziegler: 2). Serial killers are born and not made. Ziegler is also concerned by Cornwell's relocation of the female private investigator. As a Chief Medical Examiner, Scarpetta operates within the corporate structure of crime management. She accepts, supports and collaborates with the patriarchal status quo, advocating women's right to a place within the hierarchy of power (Ziegler: 4).[1] The detective agent's retreat to the shelter of institutional authority, and his or her assumption of new weaponry in the form of science and technology, is indicative of a perceived intensification of the criminal threat, which can only be countered by a more vigorous prosecution of the letter of the law. But although institutional support would appear to be integral to the pursuit of serial killers, Cornwell is perhaps atypical in her construction of a detective who remains firmly detached from the killer's pathology. Cornwell's Scarpetta novels suggest an absolute belief in the essential and evil otherness of the killer, whereas, for writers such as Val McDermid and Thomas Harris, such moral clarity is impossible to maintain.

The serial-killer narrative is also a formula which facilitates a decentred and destabilising approach to the detective hero. More often than Cornwall would perhaps like to admit, these fictions present a narrative of proximity – a discourse in which the other proves uncomfortably similar to the bourgeois individual self. The formula incorporates a series of structural developments that ultimately push the detective ever closer to the very criminality he or she seeks to contain. The serial killer is also a super-killer, and the presence of this force creates a shift of focus through which the thought processes or handiwork of the killer comes centre stage and assumes a far greater epistemological complexity.[2]

Serial killers are different. They seldom emerge from the classical environment of a tidily contained group of suspects; rather they are defined by their exclusion from the community. Or, if they belong somewhere, their habitat is usually significantly removed from the 'community' of their victims.[3] These are outsiders, then, but powerful, evasive outsiders, and it will take new methodologies of detection to define and contain them. The capture of the serial killer consequently demands a collective effort, and the formula favours the presence of an agent working within the structures of law and order. This is not a job for the individual alone, not least because science and technology have become newly significant in the search for the mobile and resourceful mass murderer, whose random acts evade legibility. Consequently, like the police procedural before them, many of these fictions operate through modes of composite detection, making the detective one of a group working to counter a traumatic threat to social stability. However, the integrity of the group seldom replicates the co-operative patterns of squad-room narratives. Rather, these are multiple forces pulling in different directions, suggesting disorder at the heart of the investigative machine. Yet within these fictions a place remains for the inspired individual, the exceptional investigator gifted not only with the 20/20 vision of science, but also with the insight of intuition. The key detective, however, will seldom be the leader of the group, and this detective's insight – his or her advanced capacity to read the situation and the mind of the killer – will be marginalised by institutional complacency. Narrative tension is generated through this compromising of detective agency, and it is predominantly through gender that the agent is disabled.

The pathologist Dr Kay Scarpetta reads bodies with uncanny accuracy, finding traces of guilt writ large upon the corpse. Yet Scarpetta's almost superhuman agency is frequently undermined by gender antagonism, as even these otherwise conservative fictions cannot ignore the problems facing a woman operating within the patriarchal symbolic. FBI trainee Clarice Starling, key investigator within Thomas Harris's *The Silence of the Lambs,* meets similar resistance, but from rather further down the pecking order. The machinery of the FBI provides her with the information she requires to study the victims of serial killer Jame Gumb, while her gender gives her the insight to correctly read the bodies of those victims. However, her ability to act on her knowledge is blocked by the fact that she is an unwelcome woman in what is still very much a man's world. Her misguided belief that the FBI is a meritocracy and her refusal to play the role of submissive female lead her in to conflict with her superiors and, by the time of her second appearance in *Hannibal,* she has been rendered marginal, her agency undermined by the unremitting misogyny of the patriarchal institutions of the law. Serial-killer fictions repeatedly reveal that these structures have not changed. Police women and FBI agents, pathologists and doctors – all must behave as 'good girls' to survive within the system, and all must ultimately learn that there is no reward for the good girl. Although the evolving criminal threat demands new modes of thinking and new approaches to detection, the law itself remains resistant to, and fearful of, change.

Although the detective as brilliant outsider has been incorporated into the police panopticon, the purpose of this incorporation is as likely to be containment as empowerment. British author Val McDermid provides a powerful example of the ongoing force of patriarchy within investigative structures in her award-winning novel *The Mermaids Singing* (1995). McDermid's work offers a complex analysis of patterns of gender and exclusion within the composite detective structure of the serial-killer hunt. Detective Inspector Carol Ashton is that rare thing, a promoted woman, but her authority is repeatedly undermined by her colleague, Tom Cross. Cross is the embodiment of a patriarchal old guard, and his lack of vision is symbolised by his refusal even to acknowledge that the serial murders are related. The tensions within the police environment are intensified and complicated when a psychological profiler, Dr Tony Hill, is brought in to aid the investigation, and it is he, rather than Carol Ashton, who will occupy the space of feminised other within the narrative.[4] In the public arena of the workplace, his 'soft' science is set against the hard masculine edge of old-fashioned policing, and this contrast is reinforced in the private arena by the trauma of his impotence. Thus disabled and 'othered', Tony Hill comes to occupy a role that is closer to the 'female victim-hero' of horror fiction than the detective agent of crime (Clover, 1992: 4). This repositioning is significant in terms of both gender and genre. The remorseless capacity to return, which characterises both the serial killer and the slasher-killer of horror narratives, is indicative of a significant generic proximity. Crime fiction that explores the cultural terror of the serial killer's excess also represents that excess, and in so doing dissolves the boundary between detection and horror. But this generic proximity is not confined to the graphic depiction of the killer's violence.

Priscilla Walton and Manina Jones have observed that the serial-killer narrative frequently constitutes an uncomfortable space for a woman. Aside from the fact that the majority of serial killers are men, and the majority of their victims are women, the genre encodes specific terrors for the female, or feminised, investigator. Walton and Jones argue that:

> [T]he serial killer film's use of a psychopathic monster creates a hybrid between the police procedural and the horror genres, one in which female characters are often ambiguously placed as retributive agents and eroticized victims of violence. The repeated association of the female agent with the investigation of serial killings and stalkings might also be read as a disturbing negotiation of female fears and male fantasies. It certainly makes the permeability of the roles of victim and investigator central to narrative interest. (Walton and Jones, 1999: 233)

The amalgamation of hero and victim suggested here has profound implications for the concept of the detective agent.[5] In her analysis of gender in the modern horror movie, Carol Clover argues that gender is a product of narrative function:

> Sex, in this universe, proceeds from gender, not the other way around. A figure does not cry and cower because she is a woman; she is a woman because she cries and cowers. And a figure is not a psychokiller because he is a man; he is a man because he is a psychokiller. (Clover, 1992: 13)

Within the gender categories of the genre, then, Tony Hill is a feminised figure, and his potential vulnerability is exacerbated by the fact that in *The Mermaids Singing*, the serial killer's victims are men. When Tony himself is captured by this killer, he evolves into the 'final girl' of the slasher film: a character notable for her gender ambiguity, her muted sexuality and her destructive agency (Clover, 1992: 39–53).

Clover argues that in the battle between the 'feminine male' killer and the 'masculine female' final girl there is a struggle for 'sexual selfhood' (1992: 62, 50), and this scenario is singularly appropriate for the impotent Tony's climactic meeting with the killer, who for weeks has been stimulating him with telephone sex. Their violent encounter has the potential to replicate the chain of association central to the horror movie: to kill is to be the hero, to be masculine, to abolish uncertainty and to effect closure. In Clover's words: 'the moment at which the Final Girl is effectively phallicized is the moment that the plot halts and horror ceases. Day breaks, and the community returns to its normal order' (1992: 50). However, McDermid complicates the pattern she has adopted and challenges the horror movie's unquestioned association of masculine agency with stability.

Tony Hill's position as hero-victim is particularly fraught. He cannot fight physically, so he must save himself through the use of 'feminine' skills of persuasion and the offer of his body. He offers to fuck for his life. He feigns desire in order to kill, and this semblance of desire paradoxically both reasserts his jeopardised masculinity and renders him profoundly other. He saves himself through killing, but there is still a generic distinction to be made, and in crime fiction the act of killing carries very different cultural freight from its role in horror narrative. To kill in a horror movie is an act of self-assertion. To kill in crime fiction is to encounter the other:

> Then that kiss. The whore's kiss, the killer's kiss, the lover's kiss, the saviour's kiss, all rolled into one. A kiss from the mouth that had been seducing him for weeks, the mouth whose words had given him hope for his future, only to leave him stranded in this place. He had spent his working life worming his way into the heads of those who kill, only to end up one of them, thanks to a Judas kiss. (McDermid, 1995: 387)

Tony is reconstituted as male through the act of killing, but he has also become the other – the killer he had sought. Serial-killer narratives thus problematise detective agency through their emphasis on the extent to which the specialist hunters of police, FBI and psychological profiling are also 'serial killers'. The detective identifies the killer through proximity and similarity rather than from a comfortable analytic or moral distance. Where once the detective outsider was a figure uncontaminated by the actions or values of the community under investigation, now he or she is simply a socialised killer. 'Do you know how you caught me?' asks Hannibal Lecter, turning the tables on his interrogator, Will Graham, in *Red Dragon*. The answer is one that both Graham and Tony Hill know all too well, but which Lecter nonetheless repeats with relish: 'The reason you caught me is that WE'RE JUST ALIKE' (Harris, 1981/1993: 69).

In its repeated emphasis on murder as an enactment of sexual gratification, the serial-killer narrative confronts our most basic and horrific taboos. It confronts both our desire for violence and our most violent desires, foregrounding the uncomfortable proximity between hunter and killer, while also destabilising the bond between reader and detective. Taken to its extreme, this proximity offers the killer rather than the detective as the point of identification, and nowhere is this dynamic more evident than in the case of Dr Hannibal Lecter – serial killing's most celebrated exemplar and the modern bogeyman *par excellence*.[6]

'ON MURDER, CONSIDERED AS ONE OF THE FINE ARTS': THE DREADFUL PLEASURE OF *HANNIBAL*

Hannibal Lecter's underground incarceration in *Red Dragon* and *The Silence of the Lambs* makes him a singularly appropriate symbol of society's 'underlying causality' – 'the social contradictions a given society can provisionally subdue in order to constitute itself as such' (Kristeva, 1974/1986: 153).[7] He embodies the drives and desires that shape but cannot be admitted to consciousness. However, in *Hannibal*, Thomas Harris's long-awaited return to Lecter, the monster of the contemporary psyche is not below but above ground. He is free to roam like a latter-day Satan, tempting those around him with the sins of greed and self-aggrandisement before condemning them to death. The Lecter of *Hannibal* is a mesmeric, Miltonic figure – a man with immense powers of suggestion, who sees the worst in humanity and exploits it ruthlessly. He is also, disturbingly, a fantasy figure with the effortlessly magical ability to make problems (usually synonymous with people) disappear. In a moment of black comedy, for example, his pathology is presented as semi-philanthropic:

> 'They sound a hundred percent better with the new viola player,' she breathed into Pazzi's ear. This excellent *viola da*

> *gamba* player had been brought in to replace an infuriatingly inept one . . . who had gone oddly missing some weeks before. (Harris, 1999: 178)

As a ruthless arbiter of taste, Lecter would think nothing of eating an inadequate viola player for the greater good of the orchestra.

But what does Lecter's freedom and his ongoing pursuit of aesthetic pleasure tell us about the state of the contemporary detective novel? Is *Hannibal* a morality play on the subject of greed, a modern gothic novel owing a substantial debt to *Frankenstein*, a contemporary reinvention of the bogeyman, a love story, a horror story, or an FBI procedural? It is, undoubtedly, a serial-killer narrative, but establishing exactly who is hunting whom, and who is ultimately responsible for the novel's fairly phenomenal body count, is a rather less clear-cut process.

Hannibal builds on the symbols and concerns of the previous two 'Lecter' novels and represents the apotheosis of a slowly developing serial narrative. In *Red Dragon* Lecter was a marginal figure – a bogeyman haunting the past of investigator Will Graham – a figure used to scare children and rookie investigators. Lecter is glimpsed only twice, but it is enough to establish his urbane monstrosity as a cautionary tale and, crucially, a mystery. Lecter is a phenomenon for which there is no adequate explanation. Asked why Lecter killed nine people before his capture, Will Graham can only reply:

> 'He did it because he liked it. Still does. Dr Lecter is not crazy, in any common way we think of being crazy. He did some hideous things because he enjoyed them. But he can function perfectly when he wants to.' (Harris, 1981/1993: 54)

In *The Silence of the Lambs* Lecter's role is more central. It is his probing questioning that gives the reader insight into the detective, FBI trainee Clarice Starling. His reading of her body tells the story of her impoverished past and establishes the roots of the repressed anxieties that drive her ambition (Harris, 1989/1991: 21–2). It is Lecter's eventual escape, facilitated by the self-serving greed of a complacent establishment, that helps the novel resist the detective genre's hallmarks of closure and reassurance. His escape suggests that evil can never be wholly contained, and will always be out there awaiting its opportunity. His freedom also consolidates his role as a contemporary bogeyman: like the slasher-killer he is capable of endless returns. In an insightful analysis of the first two Lecter novels, Barry Taylor argues that the novels comprise two distinct modes of narration. The foregrounded narrative involves the pursuit and capture of an active serial killer: in *Red Dragon*, Francis Dolarhyde and, in *The Silence of the Lambs*, Jame Gumb. This 'classical' account is accompanied in both books by a 'more diffusely structured narrative' centred around Lecter which aims 'to destroy the very distinctions and oppositions which found the "classical" models of explanation upon which the narrative capture of the other killers depends' (Taylor, 1994: 219). Taylor expands on this point to illustrate how Lecter's narrative undermines the generic reliance on closure:

> Lecter is narrated in present-tense passages which offer no explanatory or recuperative story of origin and causes . . . Lecter in the present tense is not a reviewed, placed and known subject, but a (fatal) object, some thing that happens (keeps happening) in an unrecuperable serial presentness. (Taylor, 1994: 220)

Lecter's escape also had the effect of creating an unprecedented audience demand for the return (rather than the capture) of the killer, which Harris eventually satisfied with *Hannibal* (1999).[8] As its title unequivocally suggests, this novel is unquestionably about the Doctor. It brings Lecter from margins to centre stage, and gives the reader unprecedented insight into his psyche, suggesting that he, too, has needs, desires and vulnerabilities. Lecter is not the infinite resource of pure evil suggested by the earlier fictions. But the reader's greater access to his motivation does not straightforwardly translate into a more easily accountable narrative. Seeing into Lecter does not wholly explain him, nor does it make him any less of a danger. Knowing why the bogeyman is going to eat you does not make him any less hungry; the appetite remains, and Harris continues to use the destabilising device of fluctuating tenses to assert the omnipresence of Lecter's threat. The shocking immediacy of the present tense consequently acts to brings the bogeyman into focus:

> 'Thank you,' Dr Lecter said, and swung the leather sap against the base of the surgeon's skull, just a flip of the wrist, really, and caught him around the chest as he sagged. It is always surprising to watch Dr Lecter lift a body; size for size he is as strong as an ant. (Harris, 1999: 366)

Hannibal also reminds us that Lecter is beyond categories: '[h]is ego, like his intelligence quota, and the degree of his rationality, is not measurable by conventional means' (1999: 136), and it is here that his ongoing capacity to terrify is consolidated. Lecter is at best a hybrid and, at worst, another species altogether:

> [T]here is no consensus in the psychiatric community that Dr Lecter should be termed a man. He has long been regarded by his professional peers in psychiatry . . . as something entirely Other. For convenience they term him 'monster.' (Harris, 1999: 136–7)

However good the detective, however impressive his or her powers of deduction and containment, it is still a case of man against monster. This is not the disenfranchised other who will eventually succumb to the phallic power of the symbolic order, but rather a superheroic other. How can the detective defeat that which is beyond comprehension and which occupies a wholly different temporal and moral order? And if the detective is an increasingly disenfranchised female agent, struggling against institutional sexism and stupidity, why would she want to defeat this fascinating symbol of gratified desire? The conflict at the centre of *Hannibal* could be described as a battle for the soul of Clarice Starling, but such a description would underestimate Starling's role in the struggle. Long-haunted by the ghost of her dead father, Starling now finds herself betrayed by her adopted 'father' – the institutional patriarch of the FBI. She is drawn to Lecter as another surrogate father, but also as a mother, a force of truth – sometimes kind, sometimes painful – who will facilitate her rebirth after her sacrifice by the FBI. Once again Harris mobilises two narratives of detection – the classical search for the killer and the ongoing 'happening' of Lecter – but this time the boundaries between them have blurred. Lecter is the object of the classical pursuit as well as the subject of his own agenda, and it is Lecter who will ultimately triumph. There will be no resolution of the classical narrative, rather it will be subsumed and absorbed into the unknown that is the 'unrecuperable serial presentness' of Lecter's alternative narrative.

Hannibal also mobilises an unsettling discourse of moral retribution. Lecter's Satan is very much the fallen angel of Milton's ideal, and there is an element of Old Testament justice in many of his summary executions. His acts of murder and cannibalism are complicated by their contextualisation: these are also acts of vengeance, of justice, of self-defence and, most disturbingly, of love.[9] But perhaps the most unsettling aspect of Lecter in generic terms is the extent to which he reveals the corruption of the symbolic order and those who uphold it. Lecter becomes a symbol of Mammon that exposes the weakness of a society founded on marketplace values and hypermasculine competition. Those supposedly representing the interests of law and righteousness see him only in terms of Mason Verger's vast reward or their own career advancement. He is a prize to be captured – the Holy Grail of killers – and those who succumb to the temptations of the false god of symbolic reward are duly punished by death. Among those pursuing Lecter only Clarice Starling is excluded from the big-game hunt. She is to be the unwitting tethered goat that lures the monster from its lair. But she would not have joined the game anyway: for, while Starling is not without the ambition to catch Lecter, she does not subscribe to the myth of the bogeyman. She believes Lecter to be a man, not a monster, who should be punished according to the dictates of the law. As a dutiful daughter, her ironically humanitarian aim is save him from the tortures of corrupted masculinity and offer him up for due punishment by the true father of American justice.

Starling is an ambiguously coded figure in her relationship to the institutional father of the FBI. Three times interservice combat pistol champion, she is described by Lecter as a 'warrior' (1999: 32). However, it is not the force of the phallic gun that Starling uses to hunt the bogeyman: rather it is a process of demythification. Through her low-key investigation Starling consciously demystifies Lecter, pursuing him through his humanising tastes rather than his dehumanising terrors. Even cannibals have to shop, and it is this rather more mundane mode of consumption that leads Starling, the domestic hunter, to her prey.

I suggested above that those who succumb to the temptations of greed are ultimately punished by death, and that the pursuit of Lecter does more to expose the corruption of his pursuers than to consolidate Lecter's own reputation for evil. The 'villain' of the novel is Mason Verger, whose 'legitimate' pathology acts as the text's clearest indication that those Lecter punishes have brought their fate upon themselves.[10] Verger is a shameless and remorseless paedophile who, while under the influence of drugs, cut off his own face at Lecter's suggestion. Now, faceless and paralysed, he hides behind a mask of piety, alternately plotting revenge on Lecter and amusing himself through the psychological abuse of children.

The children of the poor are brought to Verger's mansion as fodder, and their tears are decanted into his martinis. He has become, in effect, a monstrous version of the death's-head moth which acted as a symbol of destructive becoming in *The Silence of the Lambs*: he is 'a thing that lives on tears' (1989/1991: 102–3). Mason's power lies in his wealth, and that wealth, a family fortune made in meatpacking, is based on cannibalistic exploitation of both workers and animals alike (1999: 52, 102–3). Money talks in this novel, and it will buy almost everything – from the tears of a child to a seat in congress. The biblical flourishes are deceptive: little more than a surface embellishment beneath which *Hannibal* is a Darwinian novel, presenting nature 'red in tooth and claw'.[11] It is eat or be eaten, and the barbaric abattoirs that fund Verger's search for revenge are singularly appropriate to the book's interrogation of the boundaries dividing hunter and killer, killer and victim, fresh flesh and dead meat.

In the 'speculative finale' to *The Sadeian Woman*, Angela Carter explores the distinction between flesh and meat. Flesh, she observes, is imbued with connotations of humanity, while meat is 'dead, inert, animal and intended for consumption' (1979: 137). Typically this distinction is bounded by the species barrier, but, Carter argues, in the erotic landscape of the Sadeian libertine, flesh becomes meat and sex mutates into butchery:

> Sade explores the inhuman sexual possibilities of meat; it is a mistake to think that the substance of which his actors are made is flesh. There is nothing alive or sensual about them. Sade is a great puritan and will disinfect of sensuality anything he can lay his hands on; therefore he writes about sexual relations in terms of butchery and meat. (Carter, 1979: 138)

This, suggests Carter, is nothing less than erotic cannibalism, 'the most elementary act of exploitation, that of turning the other directly into a comestible' (1979: 140), and her paraphrase of Sadeian ethics has infinite resonances for the power play that permeates *Hannibal*:

> The strong abuse, exploit and meatify the weak, says Sade. They must and will devour their natural prey. The primal condition of man cannot be modified in any way; it is, eat or be eaten. (Carter, 1979: 140)

'Eat or be eaten' in short epitomises the dilemma facing the detective Clarice Starling. She begins the novel not as an agent but as a victim. However, the cause of her vulnerability is not the monster/predator Lecter, but rather her own institutional 'father', the FBI. Starling has come to embody the problem of the 'good girl', and has fallen into the narrative vacuum reserved for the dutiful daughter. Having done everything that Daddy asked of her, she is nonetheless offered up as a sacrifice to the gods of popular opinion:

> 'In the matter of the late Mrs Drumgo with her MAC 10 and her meth lab, shot to death while holding her baby: Judiciary Oversight wants a meat sacrifice. Fresh, bleating meat. And so do the media. DEA has to throw them some meat. ATF has to throw them some meat. And we have to throw them some. But in our case, they just might be satisfied with poultry. Krendler thinks we can give them Clarice Starling and they'll leave us alone.'[12] (Harris, 1999: 24)

In the red-blooded machismo of the FBI, Starling is nothing more than 'poultry' – a cheap, expendable alternative to 'real' meat. She is also expendable because of her disobedience: Daddy will not mourn her loss because her 'smart mouth' has displeased him, and because she has refused him access to her body (1999: 24, 264–5). Clarice thus begins the novel looking less like a detective than an uncomfortable amalgamation of Sade's two heroines: the passive, virtuous and doomed Justine and her sister, the patriarchal accomplice and pro-active survivor, Juliette.

Starling is both passive victim and monstrous agent. The novel opens with a catastrophic confrontation between two women who have transcended the social construct of femininity, but who will nevertheless be redefined according to its rules. The drug-dealer Evelda Drumgo almost succeeds in escaping the FBI through the devious deployment of femininity as a decoy, hiding her gun behind her baby in its sling. Once dead, however, she will be reinscribed by the media as the maternal ideal. In contrast, Starling, the officer of the law who sees through deceptive femininity and kills the false mother, will be recoded as deviant: the *femme fatale* or 'death angel' (1999: 19, 95).

Thus begins the betrayal of Clarice Starling by the father she trusted. She is thrust across the species barrier from flesh to meat, from good girl to monstrous woman, and in the process begins what might be described as a 'becoming other' that will be central to the narrative. She has learnt that 'a free woman in an unfree society will be a monster' (Carter, 1979: 27), and she has also learnt that freedom is an illusion within the patriarchal symbolic order. Her role as detective, her agency, was 'a liberation without enlightenment' and thus 'an instrument for the oppression of others, both women and men' (Carter, 1979: 89). Disenfranchised and disgraced, the female detective must become newly acquainted with the extent of her otherness. Having thought that she could belong, that she could overcome the problems of her class and gender through her demonstrable competence, Starling is remorselessly thrust back into the place of 'cornpone country pussy' (Harris, 1999: 265). She sought subjectivity, but her admission into the symbolic order turned out to be illusory, and she must consequently begin a process of relocation and reconstruction.

But what can Starling become? Is there a narrative beyond the ending for the *femme fatale* who evades the customary sentence of death? Starling's monstrous otherness was predicated on her rejection of femininity, not only through her role as a state-authorised killer, but also in her withheld sexuality. Starling is an attractive woman who will not let herself be owned, and it is significant that her vicious nemesis Richard Krendler imagines her future stripped not only of her agency but also her sexuality. He will not let her be either subject or object and defuses her threat by translating her from whore into hag:

> Krendler had the most active fantasy life his imagination would permit. Now, for his pleasure, he pictured Starling as old, tripping over those tits, those trim legs turned blue-veined and lumpy, trudging up and down the stairs carrying laundry, turning her face away from the stains on the sheets, working for her board at a bed-and-breakfast owned by a couple of god-damned hairy old dykes. (Harris, 1999: 339)

The fear and loathing of women exhibited by Krendler acts synecdochically to invoke the wider structures of both FBI and American society, and it is only on the margins that Starling finds the politeness, courtesy and kindness symbolic of an alternative mode of being. She is supported throughout by her room-mate and fellow agent, Ardelia Mapp, who seems better equipped than Starling to survive (and subvert?) the FBI. Mapp, it is suggested, draws strength and sustenance from a long family line of African-American women (1999: 27, 396).[13] Starling, the orphan, has only fragmentary memories and an institutional upbringing to fall back upon. To be cast from the FBI is thus to be bereft of what little family she had. Starling's situation looks hopeless. Within the FBI she has become dead meat and, if the plan to use her as bait for Lecter succeeds, she is destined for human consumption.

The 'meatification' of Starling is further emphasised by her unwitting role as bait. But Starling is not as vulnerable as her enemies imagine, and both she and Lecter are aided in their survival by Verger and Krendler's lack of psychological insight. It is the misguided gender assumptions of the villains that will, ironically, be their undoing. Verger, Krendler and the tame psychologist Dr Doemling are unable to believe that Lecter could be attracted by anything other than Starling's vulnerability:

> 'Dr Doemling, does he want to fuck her or kill her, or eat her, or what?' Mason asked, exhausting the possibilities he could see.
>
> 'Probably all three,' Dr Doemling said. 'I wouldn't want to predict the order in which he wants to perform those acts . . . his object is her degradation, her suffering and her death. He has responded to her twice: when she was insulted with semen in her face and when she was torn apart in the newspapers after she shot those people. He comes in the guise of a mentor, but it's the *distress* that excites him. (Harris, 1999: 276–7)

This scene serves to reinforce the extent to which Lecter is incomprehensible and ungraspable. Verger cannot conceive of desires outside his own understanding of pleasure, which is rooted entirely in dominance, exploitation and manipulation. Only the insightful but untrained Barney reads the situation correctly: it is Starling's power and not her weakness that appeals to Hannibal Lecter. He is attracted not by her status as meat, but by her potential as flesh. He recognises qualities within her to which the others – blinded by their deep-rooted sexism and lack of perception – are oblivious. In the logic of Lecter's otherness, his attraction to Starling's power thus becomes possibly his *only* act of cannibalism. In contemplating the consumption of Starling, he prepares to eat another predator, rather than his customary unthreatening prey.

Over the course of the novel, Lecter not only describes Starling as a warrior, but also draws a picture of her as a griffon: a mythical hybrid creature with the beak and wings of an eagle and the body of a lion. She is, he claims, 'the honey in the lion' – a sweet destruction – a predator who is good enough to eat (1999: 184, 356). It is a compliment as much as a threat. This emphasis on Starling's hybridity is important, and the question remains: now that her functional identity has been destroyed, and she has been ostracised by her 'family', what will she become?

In the first instance she becomes a stranger to herself. As the novel progresses, Starling experiences an increasing sense of alienation, and this distancing satisfies rather than disturbs her. When she makes her decision to rescue Lecter from Verger, 'she knew she was not quite herself, and she was glad' (1999: 398). A second epiphany occurs when she shoots the corrupt lawman Mogli. Having shot through the badge that once meant so much to her, she speaks 'in a voice she did not know' (1999: 421). It is after this epiphany that Starling is herself shot, and must in turn be rescued by Lecter. Her becoming by choice is now overlaid by the more controlled rebirthing orchestrated by Lecter, and Harris's novel enters its most enigmatic and gothic phase. Through drugs and hypnosis, Starling is finally severed from her old symbolic construction of self. 'She was awake and not awake', and significantly, 'she did not bother with her reflection in the mirror, so far was she from herself' (440). Lecter has taken Starling back from the symbolic into the ideal dyadic unity of mother and child. She no longer has a sense of herself as a social being, and during this period she evinces no interest in the affairs of the wider world (442). Rather she inhabits the primal drives of desire and anger, letting Lecter give her pleasure and sensory nurturance through food, clothes and music, while his analysis of her childhood forces her to confront her long-repressed anger at her original father's 'betrayal' of her through death. Throughout this process the reader is uncertain whether they are witnessing the activities of Doctor Freud or Doctor Frankenstein,[14] and it is equally uncertain whether the outcome of this creative process will be hysteric, hybrid, or the 'marriage of true minds'.[15]

However, in being 'rescued' by Lecter and in undergoing a lengthy analysis at his hands, has not Starling simply swapped one father for another? Her transgressive consumption of Richard Krendler is contained within the authority of the father. She is acting on Doctor's orders; her cannibalism is what Carter would term a 'conforming destruction', another instance of female freedom 'policed by the faceless authority beyond the nursery, outside the mirror' (Carter,

1979: 131). On the surface it would seem that Starling remains trapped within the impossible double-bind of patriarchy. The good girl can expect only the chilly comforts of virtue and the reward of death, while the bad girl, who might seem to have more freedom, is in fact in possession of only one route to satisfaction: the Sadeian one. The bad girl is rewarded for her tacit acknowledgement that Daddy knows best with the opportunity to experience pleasure – on Daddy's terms. She is permitted to experience the rarified development of her taste in the company of the master libertine: a role for which Hannibal Lecter would appear to be providentially well equipped.

This does not bode well for Starling as woman or detective. As Carter observes, the Sadeian woman 'subverts only her own socially conditioned role in the world of god, the king and the law. She does not subvert her society' (1979: 133). Detective agency has been deconstructed, but the formula remains one within which the transgressive woman is contained and controlled. However, Harris's novel is more evasive than this initial reading might suggest. It demands an attention to language and symbol and mobilises through its imagery an alternative narrative possibility.

It is no accident that the first sighting of Lecter in *Hannibal* sees him standing beside Donatello's bronze statue of Judith and Holofernes. It is probably the very statue that Marina Warner describes in *No Go the Bogeyman*:

> Despite Judith's canonical status as a Christian heroine, one of the Worthies – even a precursor of the virgin Mary – she was seen as an anomalous woman: in the famous discussion about the placing of Michelangelo's *David* in Florence, one citizen wanted *David* to replace Donatello's *Judith* outside the Signoria as the symbol of the city's freedom because 'it is not right that a woman should kill a man'. With Judith and Holofernes, the sexes reverse their genders: he is soft, luxurious, sensual; she is hard, warrior-like, virile. (Warner, 1998/2000: 51)

There is a conspicuous parallel between Judith and Starling the 'warrior'/'death angel'. In a patriarchal society the dutiful daughter will always be usurped by the idealised son, but the daughter is nonetheless capable of discomforting and destabilising that authority, and, in *Hannibal*, the daughter's ultimate power lies in her unexpected appetite for pleasure.

Starling begins her subversion, however, through *mimicry*. This is not simply the Foucauldian strategy of appropriating the master's discourse and turning it back against him, but rather mimicry of the type conceived by Luce Irigaray. Irigaray argues that mimicry is the first phase of the 'articulation of the female sex in discourse', a deliberate re-enactment of the feminine role that in its very self-consciousness destabilises and problematises the role that it performs:

> One must assume the feminine role deliberately. Which means already to convert a form of subordination into an affirmation, and thus to begin to thwart it. Whereas a direct feminine challenge to this condition means demanding to speak as a (masculine) 'subject' . . .
>
> To play with mimesis is thus, for a woman, to try to recover the place of her exploitation by discourse, without allowing herself to be simply reduced to it. It means to resubmit herself . . . in particular to ideas about herself, that are elaborated in/by a masculine logic, but so as to make 'visible,' by an act of playful repetition, what was supposed to remain invisible: the cover-up of a possible operation of the feminine in language . . . if women are such good mimics, it is because they are not simply resorbed in this function. *They also remain elsewhere*. (Irigaray, 1985: 76)

While I do not think that Harris's novel approaches the 'operation of the feminine in language', it does confront the impasse both addressed by Irigaray and implicit in the 'problem' of the female detective. Starling's attempt to speak as a (masculine) 'subject' has met with conspicuous failure, and her rebirthing in Lecter's care gives her the opportunity to adopt instead a mimetic approach to the problem of female subjectivity. Significantly, mimetic femininity is also a site of multiplicity – *'They also remain elsewhere'* – and this refusal of fixity renders far more uncertain Starling's occupation of the place so carefully set out for her by Lecter.

But what is it that Lecter actually wants from Clarice Starling? What is the place he has set out for her? Again, this is not wholly clear. While it is obvious that Lecter does not, as Verger imagines, want to fuck, kill and eat Starling for sensory gratification alone, it remains entirely possible that he wishes to take her life to create a conceptual space which might henceforth be occupied by Mischa, the sister whose death is offered as a possible explanation of Lecter's pathology. *Hannibal* provides the reader with a great deal of new information about the Doctor, but this information serves largely to construct a series of paradoxes. Lecter's whole being is contradictory. He is an outlaw and criminal dedicated to the preservation of the values of 'civilised' society. Building on this premise, the novel continues to complicate, without ever actually explicating. Although Lecter's rationality defies quantification, he nonetheless 'suffers from reminiscences', a condition of the hysteric, according to Julia Kristeva (1979/1986: 192). The traumatic memory of his sister's death – eaten by renegade soldiers at the end of the Second World War – resurfaces throughout the novel as a counterpoint to his otherwise flawless self-control. A further paradox is contained in the information that Lecter 'believes in chaos' (1999: 90). This statement from Barney receives no elaboration, and the reader is left to speculate as to what the precise, hyperorganised Lecter's relationship to chaos could be. Certainly Lecter struggles to relate time and space. Mischa is dead, but he imagines the possibility of creating a space for her: the construction in the present of an inhabitable vacuum that might be filled from the past rather than the future. In this impossible desire he seems to yearn for an alternative temporality – a cyclical, regenerative time, or a 'monumental' time, 'all-encompassing and infinite like imaginary space', a time 'which has so little to do with linear time (which passes) that the very word "temporality" hardly fits' (Kristeva, 1979/1986: 191). But, as alternative modes of temporal being, the temporalities imagined by Kristeva represent a space of otherness associated with women that Lecter is not willing to embrace. Rather, Lecter attempts to disrupt time through the remorseless breaking of taboos, as if by tearing apart the rules of the symbolic order he will somehow gain access to a different mode of temporal and spatial signification, within which lost objects can be restored.

Lecter is terrified of the maternal imaginary. He wants Mischa back, but not at the cost of his own maternal reabsorption, and in his oscillation between a yearning for the semiotic and an absolute investment in the symbolic – which he simultaneously seeks to disrupt and destroy – lies the substance of his madness. He fears the underlying causality that he also represents. Watching the film of Stephen Hawking's *A Brief History of Time*, with its focus on an ever-expanding universe, Lecter hopes rather that linear time might be reversed: he hopes 'for entropy to mend itself, for Mischa, eaten, to be whole again' (1999: 363). This is Lecter's attempt to preserve structure at the same time as he defeats time, an impossible reordering of disorder that represents a craving for an even greater systemic coherence than that provided by the patriarchal symbolic. Lecter's relation to chaos must thus be seen as a Sadeian one. His pleasure lies not in the experience but in the orchestration of chaos. He is the puppet-master whose greatest pleasure lies in participating in a spectacle: the coming together of a superbly organised and executed erotic scene. He is, in Angela Carter's elegant phrase, 'a choreographer of life and death' or, to put it more bluntly, a control freak (1979: 113). He 'wants a place for everything and everything in its place in the regimented pursuit of pleasure' (1979: 145), and one of the key items that must be placed and enjoyed is, of course, Clarice Starling. But Starling's occupation of this place is fundamentally altered through mimicry. She enacts the scene that Lecter has devised, and then she asks for more – not only in the literal sense of requesting a second portion of Richard Krendler's sautéd brains, but also discursively in her decision to analyse the analyst.

Lecter sets Starling a series of tests that she must pass in order to survive, but, in the final pages of the novel, she evolves into an analytic Scheherazade, adopting and adapting the master's voice to her own ends. Starling transmutes a narrative of self-preservation into a paradoxical story of love. She departs from the script, replacing linearity with multiplicity, and destabilises Lecter the libertine:

> 'Let me ask you this, Dr Lecter. If a prime place in the world is required for Mischa . . . what's the matter with *your* place? It's well occupied and I know you would never deny her. She and I could be like sisters. And if, as you say, there's room in me for my father, why is there not room in you for Mischa?'
>
> Dr Lecter seemed pleased, whether with the idea, or with Starling's resource is impossible to say. Perhaps he felt a vague concern that he had built better than he knew. (Harris, 1999: 476–7)

Lecter's words somewhat ominously invoke the *Frankenstein* story, and the uncertainty suggested here is augmented in the final chapter:

> Their relationship has a great deal to do with the penetration of Clarice Starling, which she avidly welcomes and encourages. It has much to do with the envelopment of Hannibal Lecter, far beyond the bounds of his experience. It is possible that Clarice Starling could frighten him. (Harris, 1999: 483)

Starling thus fulfils the threat encoded in the statue of Judith. When the dinner is over, she turns the tables on Lecter's Holofernes. However, in contrast to Christian tradition, she does not kill him; rather she nurtures him, offering her breast in recompense for his unarticulated anger against the lost Mischa (1999: 477). Although the drop of Château Yquem that she lays upon her breast is set there with 'her trigger finger', hostilities have been suspended. Starling gives Lecter the gift of her breast, and asks nothing in return. In so doing she refuses the place of the Sadeian woman and reinscribes their relationship in terms of pleasure rather than power. The Starling who was reduced to meat in the opening of the novel is, through her own desires, resurrected as flesh.

I have argued a case for Starling's renewed agency within her relationship with Lecter, but the scope of this agency is uncertain. It is certainly not agency within the terms of the patriarchal symbolic, as neither Starling nor Lecter can be said to occupy that space. In stepping outside the structures of law and order, in entering and sustaining their dyadic space, they take, like the lesbian detective before them, a step towards the destruction of detective fiction's *raison d'être*. *Hannibal* is a novel that renders detection impossible. While the whole world looks for Lecter (who due to plastic surgery no longer resembles himself), Starling tracks him through his tastes, and through the traces of his bodily desires (1999: 225). Her pursuit of Lecter's body makes her newly aware of her own body and her own desires, and she turns to the 'delicious perversion' of *couture* magazines to satisfy her own taste for style (1999: 226). Starling thus seeks to inhabit the body rather than the mind of the killer. She feels rather than thinks like Lecter, and this approach to detection sets the scene for her eventual betrayal of the detective story's ethos. The abstract moral conceptions of the symbolic order have been remorselessly revealed as tarnished and corrupt, and Starling abandons them for the corporeal pleasures of a semiotic rebirthing within a fairy-tale world of taste and style. Fantasy has supplanted realism, and bodily desires have replaced rational demands.

Where, though, does this leave the reader? The rationale of detection has been deconstructed. The detective has got into bed with the killer and departed the symbolic for an ideal dyadic union, abandoning the narrative without capture, conclusion or resolution. Lecter and Starling continue to occupy an 'unrecuperable serial presentness', and the reader is left gawping on the sidelines, uncertain what to make of what she or he has just read. The reader becomes an uncomfortable spectator of the primal scene, the ultimate voyeur in a book obsessed with voyeurism (1999: 482).[16] Just as Stella Duffy's *Fresh Flesh* pushed readers away from the detective's consciousness, so Harris pushes readers away from his monstrous couple and out into the night, to contemplate exactly what it was they wanted when they asked for a sequel to *The Silence of the Lambs*. *Hannibal* represents a deeply ambivalent response to the success of the earlier novel and the cult of its anti-hero. Harris drip-feeds death and mutilation throughout the novel, promising an ultimate feast, but, instead of an apocalypse of violence, the novel's conclusion confounds expectations and destabilises the genre with its profoundly uncomfortable feast of love. *Hannibal* ultimately refuses to satisfy the 'elemental ugliness' in the 'faces of the crowd' (1999: 128), and gives us Cinderella when we had both expected and desired Bluebeard.

NOTES

1. I am grateful to Harry Ziegler for permission to quote from his unpublished article.
2. The renewed epistemological complexity of the killer can take a number of forms. In *The Mermaids Singing*, for example, Val McDermid uses a technique of split focalisation. The reader is given insight into the mind of the criminal in parallel with the detective's attempts to second-guess and interpret that mind. Patricia Cornwell's pathology fictions, however, often present a narrative in which the killer is wholly absent, and in this case the killer's complexity is written upon the bodies of the victims, which come to represent, intentionally or unintentionally, the artistic expression of the killer's psyche. The concept of the victim as a message from killer to detective-hunter is most fully developed in the Hannibal Lecter fictions of Thomas Harris, and will be discussed later in this chapter.
3. Lynda Hart quotes a useful account of the 'typical' serial killer's profile:

   > All known cases of serial killers are males . . . Serial killers commit subsequent murder(s) and they are relationship-less (victim and attacker are strangers) . . . killings are frequently committed in different or widespread geographic locations and not for any material gain, but a compulsive act for gratification based on fantasies. (Stephen Egger, 1984, quoted in Hart, 1994: 136)

4. Implicit within the introduction of the psychological profiler is the belief, typical of earlier crime fictions, that the police are not wholly trustworthy. They cannot be relied upon to provide posthumous justice for the victim. Carol observes, for example, that Cross's attitude to the murders 'served his prejudices rather than the community' (1995: 10). However, the profiler also represents a different methodological dimension – a new mode of reading the crime. As Tony Hill observes, 'Dead men do tell tales, and the ones they tell profilers are not the same as the ones they tell police officers' (1995/1996: 11).
5. It is interesting to note that the female horror protagonist who welds together the 'functions of suffering victim and avenging hero' began to emerge during the mid-1970s, the period which also saw the gestation of the first female private investigators (Clover, 1992: 17).
6. Lecter is also a figure who plays on the most traditional of classical detective constructions. He is a doctor, a symbol of security, but, as was the case in the fictions of Agatha Christie, this security is illusory. The analyst in whom you confide your deepest fears is actually the source of those fears, the bogeyman who is coming to gobble you up.
7. The location of the FBI's Behavioral Science section – 'half-buried in the earth' (1989/1991: 1) – acts as a pertinent reminder of the detective's need to occupy the same territory as the killer.
8. The enormous demand for a sequel to *The Silence of the Lambs* was in part fuelled by the Oscar-winning success of Jonathan Demme's film version, but in the case of both film and book it

was the character of Lecter that prompted a fascination based on both attraction and repulsion. Barry Taylor suggests that Lecter is 'an ethical abomination with whom one is manoeuvred into identification' (1994: 220), and his popularity is indicative of a shift in audience allegiance from the detective to the transgressive and violent agency of the outlaw. However, Lecter also stands in a tradition of 'melodramatic villains' whose presence on page or stage is celebrated and anticipated at the same time as it is feared and loathed (Robert McCrum, *The Observer*, 6 June 1999).

9. It is important to note a degree of narrative disingenuity in the accounts of Lecter's attacks. We are ironically informed that 'he has killed hardly anybody . . . during his residence in Florence' (1999: 136). Lecter's best behaviour is still an abomination that transgresses the fundamental taboos of human society.
10. Examples of 'just-desserts' such as that provided by Mason Verger can, of course, be counter-balanced by examples of Lecter's gratuitous violence. His attack on a presumably blameless nurse, first cited in *The Silence of the Lambs*, is typical (1989/1991: 11). No explanation or justification is ever offered for Lecter's decision to eat her tongue.
11. An alternative mode of survival is offered by the wise nurse Barney, who exists symbiotically through compromise rather than consumption. He creates structures of mutual dependence that ensure his security, while remaining at all times respectful of the carnivores around him.
12. The Sadeian paradigm is exemplified by Krendler whose desire to destroy Starling is almost indistinguishable from his desire to fuck her: 'Mixed hungers crossed his face; it was Krendler's nature both to appreciate Starling's leg and look for the hamstring' (1999: 44).
13. Starling also finds kindness and respect among low-ranking officers, other women within the service and in the Medical Examiner's office, where she encounters the body of one of Lecter's victims (1999: 304–10). This acts in part to mobilise a discourse that sees the urban as the dehumanising base of a corrupt white male power. Harris reveals very ambivalent attitudes towards 'civilisation', relishing its tastes and textures at the same time as he depicts the barbarity of its foundations (1999: 111). I am grateful to Andy Smith for drawing my attention to the extent to which all three Lecter novels associate high culture with excessive violence. Implicit in this connection is the reminder that culture is dependent upon consumption.
14. Mary Shelley's *Frankenstein* suggests that men should be wary of assuming powers of creation, as they will have little control over what might emerge. The child, or monster, might well turn out to be both more intelligent and more articulate than its creator. *Hannibal* is steeped in the gothic tradition: from the presence of Agents 'Burke' and 'Hare' at the initial catastrophic shooting, to Lecter's decision to resolve Starling's father fixation by confronting her with his exhumed corpse.
15. In her description of the transgressive life of Sade's Juliette, Carter describes the relationship between the brigand chief, Brisatesta, and his sister, Clairwil: 'they now devote themselves to domesticity, brigandage and orgiastic recreations in their mountain fastness. A marriage of true minds, they are a model Sadeian couple' (Carter, 1979: 96).
16. The trope of voyeurism is evident from the opening pages, where Starling is surreptitiously ogled by the other agents in the FBI surveillance van. Verger is another voyeur, whose vast wealth has given him the capacity to see everything from his bed, and whose ambition is to watch the spectacle of Hannibal Lecter being consumed by pigs. Lecter is also a voyeur, visually consuming Starling as she runs through the forest (1999: 281), capturing an image of her to run endlessly in his mind. Above all, however, the book suggests that culture is voyeuristic, its painting and statues exposing death and desire to the public gaze. The torture exhibit makes this explicit – and here Lecter goes simply to watch the crowd as they take pleasure in the spectacle of human misery (1999: 128).

9

Postscript: The Death of the Detective?

'Now, if merely to be present at a murder fastens on a man the character of an accomplice; if barely to be a spectator involves us in one common guilt with the perpetrator, it follows of necessity, that, in these murders of the ampitheatre, the hand which inflicts the fatal blow is not more deeply imbrued in blood than his who passively looks on; neither can he be clear of blood who has countenanced its shedding; nor that man seem other than a participator in murder, who gives his applause to the murderer, and calls for prizes on his behalf.' (de Quincey, 1854: 3)

The text's principal characteristic and the one that distinguishes it from other signifying practices, is precisely that it introduces, through binding and through vital and symbolic differentiation, heterogeneous rupture and rejection: jouissance and death. This would seem to be 'arts''s function as a signifying practice: under the pleasing exterior of a very socially acceptable differentiation, art reintroduces into society fundamental rejection, which is matter in the process of splitting. (Kristeva, 1974/1984: 180)

The text is (should be) that uninhibited person who shows his behind to the *Political Father*. (Barthes, 1973/1990: 53)

A free woman in an unfree society will be a monster. (Carter, 1979: 27)

The detective is dead – and it looks like the woman did it. No surprises there. In a devious ploy designed to defeat even the most analytic of minds, she pulled off this coup first by becoming the detective, and then by destroying herself in a suicidal act of deconstruction. Alternatively, it might be a more familiar story: woman/detective/scapegoat merged into one and sacrificed to deflect attention from the greater crimes of patriarchy. The cross-dressed detective was getting too close for comfort. She was asking for it – and she got it, sentenced to death for crimes against the heterosexual matrix. Whichever way you look at it, the detective is not the man he was when this book began, and 'his' genre is in crisis.

Crime fiction no longer occupies a stable position in relation to contemporary cultural desires. Where once it sought to allay the anxieties of its readership, it now seems designed only to satisfy their appetites. Crime fiction has become the pre-eminent genre of the consumer age. It is bigger, better, and comes with 25 per cent extra free. That excess is largely comprised of variously dismembered, decomposed, displayed and eroticised bodies. Contemporary crime fiction is unflinching in its confrontation of the corporeal, and its readership, myself included, is remorseless in its consumption of that excess. Crime fiction has become a literature of self-assertion, endlessly pressuring its boundaries to satisfy audience demand, and to prove its own strength. This is the formula that knows no fear and walks a tightrope over crisis: the point at which the pleasure of the text becomes the abject horror of 'death infecting life' (Kristeva, 1982: 4).

Crime fiction depends upon an illusion: it categorically states that death can be confronted and explained. But such a premise is impossible. It assumes that the corpse, 'the ultimate in abjection' and 'a border that has encroached upon everything', will know – and stay in – its place (Kristeva, 1982: 4, 3). Kristeva articulates the problem in her definition of abjection:

> It is thus not lack of cleanliness or health that causes abjection but what disturbs identity, system, order. What does not respect borders, positions, rules. The in-between, the ambiguous, the composite. (Kristeva, 1982: 4)

Nonetheless, crime fiction is a literature designed to contain, and celebrate 'mastery' over the abject, and it attempts this through identity, system and order. Literature 'represents the ultimate coding of our crises, of our most intimate and most serious apocalypses'

(Kristeva, 1982: 208). It invites its readership to confront the unthinkable: death, the corpse, the transgressive body. Its existence as a genre depends upon its repeated testing of the conceivable, of what is imaginable and what unthinkable within any given society. Kristeva asks whether 'literature may also involve not an ultimate resistance to but an unveiling of the abject' (208). It shows us what to fear – it takes us to abjection – and then it reassures us that we, the reader and the detective, can thrust the abject away. But what if the abject cannot be identified? The abject both attracts and repels; it hovers on the boundary between self and other, being both integral and abhorrent. Its containment demands borders – a process of categorisation. Recognising the abject depends upon knowing and defining the other, and the act of self-assertion embodied in crime fiction is thus dependent upon the continued presence of that which has been rejected. Crime fiction needs that which is 'permanently thrust aside in order to live' (Kristeva, 1982: 3). Societies are built upon the repression of their 'underlying causality', and within crime fiction, each act of self-assertion, each new account of the integrity and strength of the detective, is dependent upon a process of endlessly reconfiguring and reconfronting the monstrous – a codification and expulsion of the abject.

In the original paradigm of detection, the monstrous was woman – or, more specifically, the feminine. The lesbian, the gay man, the racial other, the criminal: all could be, and were, in some sense 'feminised' and defined in deviant opposition to the legitimate authority of patriarchal masculinity. These monstrous others occupy the sign of 'woman', and the paradigm shift, or crisis, of contemporary crime emerges from the return of this fundamental repressed. 'Woman' has returned not only as the other, but as the self of the detective, and has exploded this self with her contradictory and multiple desires – with her refusal to adhere to the patriarchal codes of rationality, explicability and order. From Angela Carter's analysis of Sade comes a powerfully suggestive formulation of this return:

> [Sade] believed it would only be through the medium of sexual violence that women might heal themselves of their socially inflicted scars, in a praxis of destruction and sacrilege. (Carter, 1979: 26)

It is this notion of a 'praxis of destruction and sacrilege' that seems best to exemplify the state of crime fiction at the beginning of the twenty-first century. What began as a mode of restoring order – a series of fictional fantasies that envisaged agency and order even in the midst of chaos – has evolved into a narrative mode that embraces exactly that which it initially sought to exclude. This attempt to contain the other through incorporation and inclusion has led, however, to dilution. In embracing the criminal and the desiring female body the borders that once defined the genre have dissolved, and with nothing left outside, identity implodes.[1]

In the formulation presented by Angela Carter, the Marquis de Sade had a singularly eloquent, if ultimately limited, vision of female emancipation. His idea, she suggests, was that women should 'fuck as actively as they are able, so that powered by their enormous and hitherto untapped sexual energy they will then be able to fuck their way into history, and in doing so, change it' (1979: 27).[2] It is an enticing spectacle, and also a succinct account of the challenge posed by women's transition from victim, to *femme fatale*, to detective agent. The monsters of earlier crime fiction have indeed fucked their way into the narrative of detection, and they have done so through an explicit articulation of desire. The generic temple of conservatism has been overthrown by sacrilege, the fundamental blasphemy of female homosexuality. It is the lesbian detective who has pushed the genre to its limits, and who has finally destabilised a formula that otherwise seemed capable of absorbing all. Precisely because, in Wittig's formulation, the lesbian is *not* a woman, she has undermined the structures of detective rationality. She has thrown a spanner in the works of the 'logical sausage-machine'.[3]

But 'sacrilege and destruction' come at a cost, and that cost would seem to be a new 'paradigm of violence': a perpetual threat encoded within what were once the comforts of genre. I suggested in the introduction that crime fiction could be read as a secular religion, a mode of textuality designed to comfort and reassure. This notion emerges from Julia Kristeva's suggestion that literature is a space of becoming – a site for the destruction, dismemberment, reassembly and renegotiation of subjectivities. Literature holds together at the same time that it tears apart. It is a site of constant struggle, an encounter with the abject:

> For abjection, when all is said and done, is the other facet of religious, moral, and ideological codes on which rest the sleep of individuals and the breathing spells of societies. Such codes are abjection's purification and repression. But the return of their

> repressed make up our 'apocalypse,' and that is why we cannot escape the dramatic convulsions of religious crises. (Kristeva, 1982: 209)

The violent convulsions of crime fiction at the end of the twentieth century indicate the inescapability of the abject. The 'paradigm of violence' is a reassertion of ambiguity, uncertainty and multiplicity that tears apart the structures of the form, and foregrounds the impossibility of effectively policing the boundary between self and non-self, the 'I' and its others. These violent irruptions stem ultimately from the other who has fucked his or her way into history – the 'woman' whose refusal of monstrousness has left the genre without its fundamental sacrifice or its 'constitutive outside'. The return of the repressed encoded in the transformations of twentieth-century crime has thus given rise not to an excess of the monstrous, but to a lack thereof, and the religious crisis of crime fiction most accurately represents a search for new monsters to replace the bogeywoman upon whom the genre had depended. It is thus difficult to discern whether the detective is in the grip of death throes or birth pangs. But what is certain is that the life of the detective, and the order 'he' represents, will ultimately depend upon the genre's capacity to regenerate and reposition the essential body of the other.

NOTES

1. Lynda Hart observes that communities operate on a principle of displacement 'in which *some* figure must occupy the constitutive outside (what Lacan calls the "intimate exterior" or *extimate*) in order to sustain the fictive identity of another' (1998: 44).
2. Carter, however, has severe doubts as to whether doing things Sade's way will ever fundamentally alter anything – let alone the patriarchal status quo. Nonetheless, the image acts here as a vibrant illustration of transgressive desire's capacity to destabilise fictional paradigms.
3. See my introduction.

Bibliography

This bibliography extends beyond those writers specifically analysed in the preceding chapters to include a selection of key texts which have substantially influenced both the development of the genre, and the arguments of this book.

Allen, Kate (1993), *Tell Me What You Like*, Vermont: New Victoria Publishers.
Allingham, Margery (1929/1950), *The Crime at Black Dudley*, Harmondsworth: Penguin.
—— (1937/1940), *The Case of the Late Pig*, Harmondsworth: Penguin.
—— (1937/1948), *Dancers in Mourning*, Harmondsworth: Penguin.
—— (1938/1987), *The Fashion in Shrouds*, Harmondsworth: Penguin.
—— (1941/1954), *Traitor's Purse*, Harmondsworth: Penguin.
Chandler, Raymond (1939/1948), *The Big Sleep*, Harmondsworth: Penguin.
—— (1940/1949), *Farewell, My Lovely*, Harmondsworth: Penguin.
—— (1943/1951), *The High Window*, Harmondsworth: Penguin.
—— (1944/1952), *The Lady in the Lake*, Harmondsworth: Penguin.
—— (1949/1955), *The Little Sister*, Harmondsworth: Penguin.
—— (1950/1964), *Pearls are a Nuisance*, Harmondsworth: Penguin.
—— (1953/1959), *The Long Good-Bye*, Harmondsworth: Penguin.
—— (1958/1961), *Playback*, Harmondsworth: Penguin.
—— (1950/1964), 'The Simple Art of Murder', in Chandler (1950/1964).
Christie, Agatha (1920/1954), *The Mysterious Affair at Styles*, London: Pan.
—— (1923/1988), *Murder on the Links*, London: HarperCollins.
—— (1926/1957), *The Murder of Roger Ackroyd*, London: Fontana.
—— (1929/1958), *Partners in Crime*, London: Fontana.
—— (1934/1993), *Murder on the Orient Express*, London: HarperCollins.
—— (1935), *Cards on the Table*, London: Collins.
—— (1936/1962), *Murder in Mesopotamia*, London: Fontana.

—— (1936/1993), *The ABC Murders*, London: HarperCollins.
—— (1937/1994), *Dumb Witness*, London: HarperCollins.
—— (1938/1993), *Appointment with Death*, London: HarperCollins.
—— (1940/1993), *One, Two, Buckle My Shoe*, London: HarperCollins.
—— (1941/1962), *N or M?*, London: Fontana.
—— (1942/1994), *The Body in the Library*, London: HarperCollins.
Collins, Wilkie (1860/1980), *The Woman in White*, Oxford: Oxford University Press.
—— (1868/1982), *The Moonstone*, Oxford: Oxford University Press.
—— (1875/1992), *The Law and the Lady*, Oxford: Oxford University Press.
Cornwall, Patricia (1990/1992), *Postmortem*, London: Warner Books.
Doyle, Sir Arthur Conan (1887/1993), *A Study in Scarlet*, Oxford: Oxford University Press.
Duffy, Stella (1994), *Calendar Girl*, London: Serpent's Tale.
—— (1996), *Wavewalker*, London: Serpent's Tale.
—— (1997), *Beneath the Blonde*, London: Serpent's Tale.
—— (1999), *Fresh Flesh*, London: Serpent's Tale.
Ellroy, James (1987/1993), *The Black Dahlia*, London: Arrow.
Fleming, Ian (1953/1988), *Casino Royale*, London: Coronet Books.
Forrest, Katherine V. (1984/1987), *Amateur City*, London: Pandora.
—— (1987/1993), *Murder at the Nightwood Bar*, London: Grafton.
—— (1989/1993), *The Beverly Malibu*, London: Grafton.
—— (1991/1993), *Murder by Tradition*, London: Grafton.
—— (1996/1997), *Liberty Square*, New York: Berkley Publishing Group.
—— (1997), *Apparition Alley*, New York: Berkley Publishing Group.
—— (1999), *Sleeping Bones*, New York: Berkley Publishing Group.
Francis, Dick (1962/1976), *Dead Cert*, London: Pan.
—— (1965/1967), *Odds Against*, London: Pan.
—— (1967/1969), *Blood Sport*, London: Pan.
—— (1970/1972), *Rat Race*, London: Pan.
—— (1979/1981), *Whip Hand*, London: Pan.
—— (1995), *Come to Grief*, London: Michael Joseph.
Grafton, Sue (1987/1988), *'A' is for Alibi*, London: Pan
Hammett, Dashiell (1982), *The Four Great Novels*, London: Picador.
Hansen, Joseph (1970/1980), *Fadeout*, New York: Owl Books.
—— (1973/1996), *Death Claims*, Harpenden: No Exit Press.
—— (1975/1981), *Troublemaker*, New York: Owl Books.
—— (1978/1998), *The Man Everybody Was Afraid Of*, Harpenden: No Exit Press.
—— (1979/1980), *Skinflick*, London: Faber and Faber.
—— (1982), *Gravedigger*, London: Peter Owen.
—— (1984), *Nightwork*, London: Peter Owen.
—— (1986/1987), *The Little Dog Laughed*, New York: Owl Books.
—— (1987), *Early Graves*, New York: The Mysterious Press.
—— (1988), *Obedience*, New York: The Mysterious Press.
—— (1990/1991), *The Boy Who Was Buried This Morning*, New York: Plume.
—— (1991/1993), *A Country of Old Men*, Harpenden: No Exit Press.
Harris, Thomas (1981/1993), *Red Dragon*, London: Arrow Books.
—— (1989/1991), *The Silence of the Lambs*, London: Mandarin.
—— (1999), *Hannibal*, London: William Heinemann.

James, Bill (1987/1994), *Halo Parade*, London: Pan.
Kelly, Maggie (1995), *Burning Issues*, London: Onlywomen Press.
King, Laurie R. (1993/1996), *A Grave Talent*, London: HarperCollins.
—— (1995/1996), *To Play the Fool*, London: HarperCollins.
—— (1996/1997), *With Child*, London: HarperCollins.
—— (2000), *Night Work*, London: HarperCollins.
McBain, Ed (1956/1963), *Cop Hater*, Harmondsworth: Penguin.
—— (1958/1963), *Killer's Choice*, Harmondsworth: Penguin.
—— (1960/1966), *The Heckler*, Harmondsworth: Penguin.
McDermid, Val (1995/1996), *The Mermaids Singing*, London: HarperCollins.
—— (1996/1998), *Booked for Murder*, London: The Women's Press.
—— (1997/1998), *The Wire in the Blood*, London: HarperCollins.
—— (1998), *Star Struck*, London: HarperCollins.
Morrell, Mary (1991/1993), *Final Session*, London: The Women's Press.
Muller, Marcia (1977/1993), *Edwin of the Iron Shoes*, London: The Women's Press.
Paretsky, Sara (1982/1987), *Indemnity Only*, Harmondsworth: Penguin.
—— (1984/1987), *Deadlock*, Harmondsworth: Penguin.
—— (1985/1987), *Killing Orders*, Harmondsworth: Penguin.
—— (1987/1988), *Bitter Medicine*, Harmondsworth: Penguin.
—— (1988/1990), *Toxic Shock*, Harmondsworth: Penguin.
—— (1990/1991), *Burn Marks*, London: Virago.
—— (1992), *Guardian Angel*, Harmondsworth: Penguin.
—— (1994/1995), *Tunnel Vision*, Harmondsworth: Penguin.
—— (1995/1996), *V. I. for Short*, Harmondsworth: Penguin.
Poe, Edgar Allan (1967/1986), *The Fall of the House of Usher and Other Writings*, Harmondsworth: Penguin.
Sayers, Dorothy L. (1923/1989), *Whose Body?*, London: Coronet Crime.
—— (1927/1989), *Unnatural Death*, London: Coronet Crime.
—— (ed.) (1928), *Great Short Stories of Detection, Mystery and Horror*, London: Gollancz.
—— (1930/1989), *Strong Poison*, London: Coronet Crime.
—— (1935/1990), *Gaudy Night*, London: Coronet Crime.
—— (1937/1988), *Busman's Honeymoon*, London: Coronet Crime.
Scott, Manda (1996), *Hen's Teeth*, London: The Women's Press.
Stevenson, Robert Louis (1886/1979), *The Strange Case of Dr Jekyll and Mr Hyde*, Harmondsworth: Penguin.
Stout, Rex (1937/1984), *The Hand in the Glove*, London: Hogarth.
Uhnak, Dorothy (1964/1978), *Policewoman*, London: Star Books.
Wesley, Valerie Wilson (1988/1994), *When Death Comes Stealing*, London: Headline.
Wilson, Barbara, (1984/1994), *Murder in the Collective*, London: Virago.
—— (1986/1994), *Sisters of the Road*, London: Virago.
—— (1989/1994), *The Dog Collar Murders*, London: Virago.
—— (1990/1991), *Gaudí Afternoon*, London: Virago.
—— (1993), *Trouble in Transylvania*, London: Virago.
Wings, Mary (1986), *She Came Too Late*, London: The Women's Press.
—— (1988), *She Came in a Flash*, London: The Women's Press.
—— (1995), *She Came by the Book*, London: The Women's Press.
—— (1997), *She Came to the Castro*, London: The Women's Press.

CRITICAL AND HISTORICAL SOURCES

Altman, Dennis (1982), *The Homosexualization of America, the Americanization of the Homosexual*, New York: St Martin's Press.

Andersen, Hans Christian (1906/1993), *Andersen's Fairy Tales*, London: Wordsworth Children's Classics.

Barnard, Robert (1980/1990), *A Talent to Deceive: An Appreciation of Agatha Christie*, London: Fontana.

Barnes, Djuna (1936/1963), *Nightwood*, London: Faber and Faber.

Barthes, Roland (1971/1989), *Sade, Fourier, Loyola*, trans. Richard Miller, Berkeley: University of California Press.

—— (1973/1990), *The Pleasure of the Text*, trans. Richard Miller, Oxford: Blackwell.

Bataille, Georges (1962/1987), *Eroticism*, London: Marion Boyars.

Beaver, Harold (1981), 'Homosexual Signs', in *Critical Inquiry*, 8 (1981–2).

Bell, Ian A. and Graham Daldry (eds) (1990), *Watching the Detectives: Essays on Crime Fiction*, Basingstoke: Macmillan.

Binyon, T. J. (1989/1990), *'Murder Will Out': The Detective in History*, Oxford: Oxford University Press.

Bloom, Clive (ed.) (1990a), *Twentieth Century Suspense*, Basingstoke: Macmillan.

—— (1990b), *Spy Thillers: From Buchan to Le Carré*, Basingstoke: Macmillan.

Brod, Harry and Michael Kaufman (eds) (1994), *Theorizing Masculinities*, London: Sage.

Bromley, Roger (1989), 'Rewriting the Masculine Script: The Novels of Joseph Hansen', in Longhurst (1989).

Buhrke, Robin A. (1996), *A Matter of Justice: Lesbians and Gay Men in Law Enforcement*, New York: Routledge.

Burgin, Victor, James Donald and Cora Kaplan (eds) (1986), *Formations of Fantasy*, London: Routledge.

Butler, Judith (1990), *Gender Trouble: Feminism and the Subversion of Identity*, London: Routledge.

—— (1993), *Bodies That Matter: On the Discursive Limits of 'Sex'*, London: Routledge.

Byers, Thomas B. (1995), 'Terminating the Postmodern: Masculinity and Pomophobia', in *Modern Fiction Studies*, 41:1 (1995).

Califia, Pat (1988), *Macho Sluts*, Boston: Alyson Publications.

Cannadine, David (1981), 'War and Death, Grief and Mourning in Modern Britain', in Whaley (1981).

Carter, Angela (1979), *The Sadeian Woman: An Exercise in Cultural History*, London: Virago.

Castle, Terry (1993), *The Apparitional Lesbian: Female Homosexuality and Modern Culture*, New York: Columbia University Press.

Cawelti, John G. (1976), *Adventure, Mystery and Romance: Formula Stories as Art and Popular Culture*, Chicago: University of Chicago Press.

Christianson, Scott R. (1989), 'Tough Talk and Wisecracks: Language as Power in American Detective Fiction', *Journal of Popular Culture*, vol. 23: 2, Fall 1989.

___ (1990), 'A Heap of Broken Images: Hardboiled Detective Fiction and the Discourse(s) of Modernity', in Walker and Fraser (1990).

Clover, Carol (1992), *Men, Women and Chainsaws*, Princeton: Princeton University Press.

Connell, R. W. (1995), *Masculinities*, Cambridge: Polity Press.

Décuré, Nicole (1992), 'From the Closet to the Bleachers, Kate Delafield: Portrait of a Lesbian as a "Lady Cop"', *Women's Studies International Forum*, 15/2.
Dollimore, Jonathan (1991), *Sexual Dissidence: Augustine to Wilde, Freud to Foucault*, Oxford: Oxford University Press.
Duncan, Derek (1994), 'AIDS to Narration: Writing Beyond Gender', in Ledger et al. (1994).
Earnshaw, Steven (ed.) (1994), *Postmodern Surroundings*, Amsterdam: Rodopi.
Ellman, Maud (ed.) (1994), *Psychoanalytic Literary Criticism*, London: Longman.
Flanningan-Saint-Aubin, Arthur (1994), 'The Male Body and Literary Metaphors for Masculinity', in Brod and Kaufman (1994).
Fletcher, John and Andrew Benjamin (eds) (1990), *Abjection, Melancholia and Love*, London: Routledge.
Freud, Sigmund (1905/1953), 'Three essays on the Theory of Sexuality', in *The Standard Edition of the Complete Psychological Works of Sigmund Freud*, vol. VII, ed. James Strachey, London: Hogarth.
—— (1920/1955), 'Beyond the Pleasure Principle', *Standard Edition*, vol. XVIII, ed. James Strachey, London: Hogarth.
—— (1923/1961), 'The Ego and the Id', *Standard Edition*, vol. XIX, ed. James Strachey, London: Hogarth.
—— (1923/1961), 'The Economic Problem of Masochism', *Standard Edition*, vol. XIX, ed. James Strachey, London: Hogarth.
—— (1931/1961), 'Female Sexuality', *Standard Edition*, vol. XXI, ed. James Strachey, London: Hogarth.
Gamman, Lorraine (1988), 'Watching the Detectives: The Enigma of the Female Gaze', in Gamman and Marshment (1988).
——, Lorraine and Margaret Marshment (eds) (1988), *The Female Gaze: Women as Viewers of Popular Culture*, London: The Women's Press.
Garber, Margery (1992/1993), *Vested Interests: Cross-dressing and Cultural Anxiety*, London: Routledge.
Gibbs, Liz (ed.) (1994), *Daring to Dissent: Lesbian Culture from Margin to Mainstream*, London: Cassell.
Gilbert, Sandra (1987), 'Soldier's Heart: Literary Men, Literary Women and the Great War', in Higonnet et al. (1987).
Glover, David (1989), 'The Stuff that Dreams are Made Of: Masculinity, Femininity and the Thriller', in Longhurst (1989).
Grossvogel, David I. (1983), 'Agatha Christie: Containment of the Unknown', in Most and Stowe (1983).
Grosz, Elizabeth (1990a), 'The Body of Signification', in Fletcher and Benjamin (1990).
——, Elizabeth (1990b), *Jacques Lacan: A Feminist Introduction*, London: Routledge.
Gutterman, David S. (1994), 'Postmodernism and the Interrogation of Masculinity', in Brod and Kaufman (1994).
Hamer, Diane and Belinda Budge (eds) (1994), *The Good, the Bad and the Gorgeous: Popular Culture's Romance with Lesbianism*, London: Pandora.
Hart, Lynda (1994), *Fatal Women: Lesbian Sexuality and the Mark of Aggression*, London: Routledge.
—— (1998), *Between the Body and the Flesh: Performing Sadomasochism*, New York: Columbia University Press.

Haycraft, Howard (1942), *Murder for Pleasure: The Life and Times of the Detective Story*, London: Peter Davies.

Heilbrun, Carolyn G. (1991), *Hamlet's Mother and Other Women*, London: The Women's Press.

Higonnet, Margaret Randolph, Jane Jenson, Sonya Michel and Margaret Collins Weitz (eds) (1987), *Behind the Lines: Gender and the Two World Wars*, New Haven: Yale University Press.

Hilfer, Tony (1990), *The Crime Novel: A Deviant Genre*, Austin, University of Texas Press.

Hiney, Tom (1997), *Raymond Chandler: A Biography*, London: Chatto & Windus.

Holden, Inez (1943), *It Was Different at the Time*, London: John Lane.

Howard, Jean E. (1988), 'Crossdressing, the Theatre, and Gender Struggle in Early Modern England', *Shakespeare Quarterly* 39, pp. 418–40.

Humm, Maggie (1990), 'Feminist Detective Fiction', in Bloom (1990a).

—— (1991), *Border Traffic: Strategies of Contemporary Women Writers*, Manchester: Manchester University Press.

Ingman, Heather (1998), *Women's Fiction between the Wars: Mothers, Daughters and Writing*, Edinburgh: Edinburgh University Press.

Irigaray, Luce (1985), *This Sex Which Is Not One*, Ithaca: Cornell University Press.

Irons, Glenwood (ed.) (1995), *Feminism in Women's Detective Fiction*, Toronto: University of Toronto Press.

Jameson, Fredric (1970), 'On Raymond Chandler', *The Southern Review*, 1970/6.

Kaufman, Michael (1994), 'Men, Feminism, and Men's Contradictory Experiences of Power', in Brod and Kaufman (1994).

Kimmel, Michael S. (1994), 'Masculinity as Homophobia: Fear, Shame, and Silence in the Construction of Gender Identity', in Brod and Kaufman (1994).

Klein, Katherine Gregory (1988), *The Woman Detective: Gender and Genre*, Chicago: University of Illinois Press.

Knight, Stephen (1980), *Form and Ideology in Crime Fiction*, Basingstoke: Macmillan.

—— (1990), 'Radical Thrillers', in Bell and Daldry (1990).

Kristeva, Julia (1974/1984), *Revolution in Poetic Language*, New York: Columbia University Press.

—— (1974/1986), 'About Chinese Women', in Moi (1986).

—— (1979/1986), 'Women's Time', in Moi (1986).

—— (1982), *Powers of Horror: An Essay on Abjection*, New York: Columbia University Press.

Kuhn, Thomas S. (1962/1970), *The Structure of Scientific Revolutions*, second edition, Chicago: University of Chicago Press.

Lacan, Jacques (1973/1983), 'Seminar on "The Purloined Letter"', in Most and Stowe (1983).

Lauretis, Teresa de (1994), *The Practice of Love: Lesbian Sexuality and Perverse Desire*, Bloomington: Indiana University Press.

Ledger, Sally, Josephine McDonagh and Jane Spencer (eds) (1994), *Political Gender: Texts and Contexts*, Hemel Hempstead: Harvester Wheatsheaf.

Leonardi, Susan J. (1989), *Dangerous by Degrees: Women at Oxford and the Somerville College Novelists*, New Brunswick: Rutgers Unversity Press.

Light, Alison (1991), *Forever England: Femininity, Literature and Conservatism between the Wars*, London: Routledge.

Longhurst, Derek (ed.) (1989), *Gender, Genre and Narrative Pleasure*, London: Unwin Hyman.
Mac an Ghaill, Máirtín (1996), *Understanding Masculinities*, Buckingham: Open University Press.
Maltby, Richard and Ian Craven (1995), *Hollywood Cinema: An Introduction*, Oxford: Blackwell.
Mandel, Ernest (1984), *Delightful Murder: A Social History of the Crime Story*, London: Pluto.
Marriott, David (1996), 'Reading Black Masculinities', in Mac an Ghaill (1996).
Melman, Billie (1988), *Women and the Popular Imagination in the Twenties: Flappers and Nymphs*, Basingstoke: Macmillan.
Messent, Peter (1997), *Criminal Proceedings: The Contemporary American Crime Novel*, London: Pluto Press.
Meyer, Moe (ed.) (1994), *The Politics and Poetics of Camp*, London: Routledge.
Middleton, Peter (1992), *The Inward Gaze: Masculinity and Subjectivity in Modern Culture*, London: Routledge.
Modleski, Tania (1999), *Old Wives' Tales: Feminist Re-Visions of Film and Other Fictions*, London: I. B. Tauris.
Moi, Toril (ed.) (1986), *The Kristeva Reader*, Oxford: Blackwell.
Moretti, Franco (1983/1988), *Signs Taken for Wonders: Essays in the Sociology of Literary Forms*, trans. Susan Fischer, David Forgacs and David Miller, London: Verso.
Morris, Pam (1993), *Literature and Feminism*, Oxford: Blackwell.
Most, Glenn W. and William W. Stowe (eds), *The Poetics of Murder: Detective Fiction and Literary Theory*, New York: Harcourt, Brace, Jovanovich.
Munt, Sally R. (1994), *Murder by the Book? Feminism and the Crime Novel*, London: Routledge.
Nyman, Jopi (1997), *Men Alone: Masculinity, Individualism and Hard-Boiled Fiction*, Amsterdam: Rodopi.
Orwell, George (1944/1965), *The Decline of the English Murder and Other Essays*, Harmondsworth: Penguin.
Palmer, Jerry (1978), *Thrillers: Genesis and Structure of a Popular Genre*, London: Edward Arnold.
Palmer, Paulina (1993), *Contemporary Lesbian Writing: Dreams, Desires, Difference*, Buckingham: Open University Press.
—— (1997), 'The Lesbian Thriller: Transgressive Investigations', in Messent (1997).
Parkes, Colin Murray (1972/1986), *Bereavement: Studies of Grief in Adult Life*, second edition, Harmondsworth: Penguin.
Philips, Deborah and Ian Haywood (1998), *Brave New Causes: Women in British Postwar Fictions*, London: Leicester University Press.
Plain, Gill (1996), *Women's Fiction of the Second World War: Gender, Power and Resistance*, Edinburgh: Edinburgh University Press.
—— (1998), 'An Interview with Ian Rankin', *Scotlands*, 5.2, 1998.
Pope, Rebecca A. (1995), ' "Friends Is a Weak Word for It": Female Friendship and the Spectre of Lesbianism in Sara Paretsky', in Irons (1995).
Porter, Dennis (1981), *The Pursuit of Crime: Art and Ideology in Detective Fiction*, New Haven: Yale University Press.
Priestman, Martin (1991), *Detective Fiction and Literature: The Figure on the Carpet*, London: Macmillan.

Priestman, Martin (1998), *Crime Fiction: From Poe to the Present*, Plymouth: Northcote House.

Quincey, Thomas de (1854), *Miscellanies*, London: James Hogg and Sons.

Radway, Janice (1984), *Reading the Romance*, Chapel Hill: University of North Carolina Press.

Reddy, Maureen T. (1988), *Sisters in Crime: Feminism and the Crime Novel*, New York: Continuum.

Riviere, Joan (1929/1986), 'Womanliness as Masquerade' in Burgin et al. (1986).

Rowbotham, Sheila (1997/1999), *A Century of Women: The History of Women in Britain and the United States*, Harmondsworth: Penguin.

Savran, David (1998), *Taking It Like A Man: White Masculinity, Masochism, and Contemporary American Culture*, Princeton: Princeton University Press.

Schoene-Harwood, Berthold (2000), *Writing Men: Literary Masculinities from* Frankenstein *to the New Man*, Edinburgh: Edinburgh University Press.

Sedgwick, Eve Kosofsky (1985), *Between Men: English Literature and Male Homosocial Desire*, New York: Columbia University Press.

—— (1990/1994), *Epistemology of the Closet*, Harmondsworth: Penguin.

—— (1993/1994), *Tendencies*, London: Routledge.

Segal, Lynne (1990), *Slow Motion: Changing Masculinities, Changing Men*, London: Virago.

Seidler, Victor Jeleniewski (1997), *Man Enough: Embodying Masculinities*, London: Sage.

Shaw, Marion and Sabine Vanacker (1991), *Reflecting on Miss Marple*, London: Routledge.

Silverman, Kaja (1992), *Male Subjectivity at the Margins*, London: Routledge.

Sinfield, Alan (1998), *Gay and After*, London: Serpent's Tale.

Swinbourne, Alfred (1875), *Picture Logic or the Grave Made Gay*, London: Longmans, Green and Co.

Symons, Julian (1992/1994), *Bloody Murder: From the Detective Story to the Crime Novel*, third edition, London: Pan.

Taylor, Barry (1994), 'The Violence of the Event: Hannibal Lecter in the Lyotardian Sublime', in Earnshaw (1994).

Thomas, Calvin (1996), *Male Matters: Masculinity, Anxiety and the Male Body on the Line*, Urbana: University of Illinois Press.

Trotter, David (1991), 'Theory and Detective Fiction', in *Critical Quarterly*, vol. 33, no. 2 (Summer 1991), pp. 66–77.

Walker, Ronald G. and June M. Frazer (1990), *The Cunning Craft: Original Essays on Detective Fiction and Contemporary Literary Theory*, Macomb: Western Illinois University Press.

Walton, Priscilla L. and Manina Jones (1999), *Detective Agency: Women Rewriting the Hard-Boiled Tradition*, Berkeley: University of California Press.

Warner, Marina (1994a), *From the Beast to the Blonde: On Fairy Tales and Their Tellers*, London: Chatto and Windus.

—— (1994b), *Managing Monsters: Six Myths of Our Time*, London: Vintage.

—— (1998/2000), *No Go the Bogeyman: Scaring, Lulling and Making Mock*, London: Vintage.

Watson, Colin (1971/1987), *Snobbery with Violence: English Crime Stories and their Audience*, London: Methuen.

Whaley, Joachim (ed.) (1981), *Mirrors of Mortality: Studies in the Social History of Death*, London: Europa.
Whatling, Clare (1997), *Screen Dreams: Fantasising Lesbians in Film*, Manchester: Manchester University Press.
Whitford, Margaret (1991), *Luce Irigaray: Philosophy in the Feminine*, London: Routledge.
Whitlock, Gillian (1994), '"Cop It Sweet": Lesbian Crime Fiction', in Hamer and Budge (1994).
Wilson, Ann (1995), 'The Female Dick and the Crisis of Heterosexuality', in Irons (1995).
Wilson, Anna (1996), 'Death and the Mainstream: Lesbian Detective Fiction and the Killing of the Coming-out Story' in *Feminist Studies*, vol. 22, no. 2 (Summer, 1996).
Wilson, Barbara (1994), 'The Outside Edge: Lesbian Mysteries', in Gibbs (1994).
Wilson, Edmund (1945), 'Who Cares Who Killed Roger Ackroyd', in Winks (1980).
Winks, Robin (1980), *Detective Fiction: A Collection of Critical Essays*, New Jersey: Prentice Hall.
Winston, Robert P. and Nancy C. Mellerski (1992), *The Public Eye: Ideology and the Police Procedural*, New York: St Martin's Press.
Wittig, Monique (1992), *The Straight Mind*, Brighton: Harvester.
Woolf, Virginia (1938/1986), *Three Guineas*, London: Hogarth Press.
Ziegler, Harry, 'Reading Patricia Cornwell: The Pathology of Reactionary Modernism', unpublished paper.
Zimmerman, Bonnie (1989/1992), *The Safe Sea of Women: Lesbian Fiction 1969–1989*, London: Onlywomen.
Žižek, Slavoj (1991/1994), 'Two Ways to Avoid the Real of Desire', in Ellman (1994).

Index

NOTE: this index is arranged alphabetically word by word. Titles of books by main writers discussed appear under author's name. Names of fictional characters' names are within quotation marks.